Dear Arlene,

When I saw this book I thought
of you, because I know you have
a strong devotion with Mama Mary.

Love,
Beng

P.S.
I know you would share this
with Curtis too. "Grace will transformed
and heal".

365 Days with Mary 2016

Marian titles, solemnities, feasts, patronage, apparitions, miraculous icons and devotions celebrated around the world each day

Pope Francis on Mary

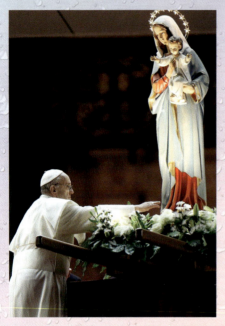

With the Holy Spirit, Mary is always present in the midst of the people. She joined the disciples in praying for the coming of the Holy Spirit (Acts 1:14) and thus made possible the missionary outburst which took place at Pentecost. She is the Mother of the Church which evangelizes, and without her we could never truly understand the spirit of the new evangelization.

Mary was able to turn a stable into a home for Jesus, with poor swaddling clothes and an abundance of love. She is the handmaid of the Father who sings his praises. She is the friend who is ever concerned that wine not be lacking in our lives. She is the woman whose heart was pierced by a sword and who understands all our pain. As mother of all, she is a sign of hope for peoples suffering the birth pangs of justice. She is the missionary who draws near to us and accompanies us throughout life, opening our hearts to faith by her maternal love. As a true mother, she walks at our side, she shares our struggles and she constantly surrounds us with God's love.

Through her many titles, often linked to her shrines, Mary shares the history of each people which has received the Gospel and she becomes a part of their historic identity. Many Christian parents ask that their children be baptized in a Marian shrine, as a sign of their faith in her motherhood which brings forth new children for God. There, in these many shrines, we can see how Mary brings together her children who with great effort come as pilgrims to see her and to be seen by her. Here they find strength from God to bear the weariness and the suffering in their lives. As she did with Juan Diego, Mary offers them maternal comfort and love, and whispers in their ear: "Let your heart not be troubled... Am I not here, who am your Mother?"

Mary is the woman of faith, who lives and advances in faith, and "her exceptional pilgrimage of faith represents a constant point of reference for the Church". Mary let herself be guided by the Holy Spirit on a journey of faith towards a destiny of service and fruitfulness.

Mary is able to recognize the traces of God's Spirit in events great and small. She constantly contemplates the mystery of God in our world, in human history and in our daily lives. We implore her maternal intercession that the Church may become a home for many peoples, a mother for all peoples, and that the way may be opened to the birth of a new world. It is the Risen Christ who tells us, with a power that fills us with confidence and unshakeable hope: "Behold, I make all things new" (Rev 21:5). With Mary we advance confidently towards the fulfillment of this promise.

Excerpt from:
EVANGELII GAUDIUM, 24 November 2013, 284-288.

Message

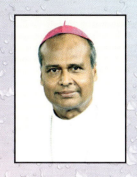

There is an old story about a workman on a scaffolding high above the nave of a cathedral who looked down and saw a woman praying before a statue of Mary. As a joke, the workman whispered, "Woman, this is Jesus." The woman ignored him. The workman whispered again, more loudly: "Woman, this is Jesus." Again, the woman ignored him. Finally, he said aloud, "Woman, don't you hear me? This is Jesus." At this point the woman looked up at the crucifix and said, "Be still now, Jesus, I'm talking to your mother."

Marian doctrine and devotion, properly understood and practised, does not lead believers away from, but rather more deeply into, the mystery of Christ. The woman in prayer who thinks that Jesus should keep still because she is talking with his mother has lost sight of the perfect harmony of wills and hearts between Mary and Jesus, which we see most clearly in the Wedding Feast at Cana where Mary commands us: "Do whatever he tells you" (John 2:5).

Mary is the mother and model of the Church, who received the divine Word in faith and offered herself to God as the "good soil" in which he can continue to accomplish his mystery of salvation. Mary is the first evangelist, showing Jesus to the world, an example to which every Christian can and should look, in understanding what faith is and how to accept and participate in salvation.

In Cardinal Newman's words, "Who can estimate the holiness and perfection of her, who was chosen to be the Mother of Christ? What must have been her gifts, who was chosen to be the only near earthly relative of the Son of God, the only one whom he was bound by nature to revere and look up to; the one appointed to train and educate him, to instruct him day by day, as he grew in wisdom and in stature?"

The glories of Mary are not only for the sake of her Son, they are for our sakes also. May our devotion to her, lead us to live like her, with her faith in receiving God's message by the angel without a doubt; her patience in enduring St. Joseph's surprise without a word; her obedience in going up to Bethlehem in the winter and bearing Our Lord in a stable; her meditative spirit in pondering what she saw and heard about Jesus; her fortitude in letting the sword go through her heart; her self-surrender in following Jesus in his ministry, passion and death. As John Paul II reminds us in his Marian encyclical Redemptoris Mater, we are called to the same heights of faith and holiness that Mary was. She enlightens us to discover the same mysteries in our own life and to respond in total faith.

May '365 Days with Mary' lead the readers to take Mary into their daily lives, becoming aware of her gentle voice throughout history to this day, assuring her guidance in our Christian journey, pointing the way to true discipleship that will ensure the coming of the kingdom: 'That all may be one'. To Jesus through Mary.

+ George Antonysamy
Archbishop of Madras-Mylapore, Chennai.

October 15, 2014

@ Salt Media, Chennai

ISBN: 978-0-692-37440-5

365 days with Mary 2016

Marian titles, solemnities, feasts, patronage,
apparitions, miraculous icons and devotions
celebrated around the world each day

Published by Salt Media, Chennai, India.

Copyright © by Miracle Hunter LLC, Chicago, IL USA

Salt Media
Old 150, New 68, Luz Church Road,
Mylapore, Chennai – 600 004
Tamil Nadu, India
Tel: 91-44-24670003

Titles of Our Lady derived from a solemnity, feast day, patronage, apparition or miraculous icon related to each day of the year, with appropriate images of Mary presented in '*365 Days with Mary 2016*' were compiled and designed by Michael O'Neill, Miracle Hunter LLC, Chicago, IL USA, and edited, co-designed and published by Salt Media - Chennai, India.

Picture on Cover: "Song of the Angels"(1881) by William Adolphe Bouguereau (1825-1905).

Sources of text:

Antiochian Orthodox Christian Archdiocese - antiochian.org
Foros de la Virgen (Spanish) - forosdelavirgen.org
International Marian Research Institue: The Mary Page - udayton.edu/mary
La Theotokos - Portal of Mariology (Italian) - latheotokos.it
Maria di Nazareth (Italian) - mariadinazareth.it
The Miracle Hunter - miraclehunter.com
Silesiani Don Bosco (Italian) - it.donbosco-torino.org
The Orthodox Church of America - oca.org
Regina Mundi - reginamundi.info
Roman Catholic Saints by James Fitzhenry- roman-catholic-saints.com
Russian Orthodox Cathedral of St John the Baptist - stjohndc.org
Where We Walked - Marian Calendar by Mary Ann Daly - wherewewalked.info

Cruz, Joan Carroll. *Miraculous Images of Our Lady: 100 Famous Catholic Portraits and Statues*
Kalvelage, Francis Mary. *Marian Shrines of France*
Kalvelage, Francis Mary, Stefano Maria Manelli and Peter Fehlner. *Marian Shrines of Italy*
Lamberty, Sister Manetta. *The Woman in Orbit*
Laurentin, René and Sbalchiero, Patrick. *Dizionario delle Apparizione della Vergine Maria.*
Santoro, Nicholas J. *Mary in Our Life, Atlas of the Names and Titles of Mary, the Mother of Jes*
and Their Place in Marian Devotion.

Sources for photos are acknowledged on each page.

For more information, please visit *365DayswithMary.com*

Author's Note

Welcome to the *365 Days with Mary* project! This has been a labor of love of mine for many years. In studying the many great Marian miracle stories - apparitions and otherwise - I was amazed to see how Our Lady is honored around the world in different times, places and cultures. I soon realized that for every day of the year there is some feast day, patronage, title or commemoration of a miraculous event being celebrated. The project came to life as *365 Days with Mary* as a way to honor Our Lady throughout the year.

The project features a daily sobriquet of Our Lady from a feast or commemoration from around the world related to that particular date. Many incomplete and erroneous lists of Marian feasts abound on the internet. For this project, each day of the year is matched to a feast or a commemoration exactly relating to it.

Some of the dates are solemnities or feasts formally established by the Church to honor Our Lady under a specific title (e.g. Our Lady Help of Christians) but have no connection to a specific event. Other dates are feasts aligned with a miraculous event as in the case of major approved apparitions like Fatima, Lourdes and Guadalupe. Some titles are celebrated by the Universal Church, others are only known to small local communities who may be celebrating the miraculous intercession of Our Lady at times of war, famine or natural disaster. Other dates included in this calendar simply commemorate the first of perhaps several miraculous events relating to an apparition or wonderworking icon. Some listings of years relating to famous images may reference the date of the creation or dedication of an icon.

For consistency, all titles of Our Lady have all been translated into English, despite some being more popularly recognized in their native language such as Our Lady of High Grace instead of Altagracia.

All entries in this project are included because they have received some form of recognition from Church authorities. (The only included exception is the alleged apparition phenomenon of Medjugorje, which at the time of publication was still under Vatican investigation.)

I hope that you are as excited about this project as I am. Flipping through the pages each day provides me with the knowledge and inspiration to honor Our Lady in a special and unique way and allows me to unite myself with the rest of the Church worldwide in a display of love for the Mother of God.

Peace and blessings,

THE
MIRACLE
HUNTER
WWW.MIRACLEHUNTER.COM

Michael O'Neill
The Miracle Hunter, Chicago

Publisher's Note

The beginnings of acknowledgement and devotion to the Mother of Jesus are present from apostolic times in the living Tradition of the early Church. A very significant fresco found in the catacombs of St. Agnes depicts Mary situated between St. Peter and St. Paul with her arms outstretched to both. Mary's prominent position between Sts. Peter and Paul illustrates the recognition by the Apostolic Church of the maternal centrality of the Savior's Mother in his young Church.

It is also clear from the number of representations of the Blessed Virgin and their locations in the catacombs that the Mother of Jesus was also recognized for her maternal intercession of protection and defense. As early as the first century to the first half of the second century, Mary's role as Spiritual Mother was recognized and her protective intercession was invoked.

The Christian witness of the first centuries of the Church also provides us with examples of direct prayer to Mary as a means of intercession to the graces and the protection of her Son. St. Ephraem (d.373), the great Eastern doctor and deacon, directly addresses the Blessed Virgin in several Marian sermons. Direct prayer to Mary is also found in a sermon of the great Eastern Father St. Gregory Nazianzen (330-389), in the writings of St. Ambrose, as well as by St. Epiphanius.

The early Church realized that direct prayer to Mary did not consist of forms of idolatry or adoration, as is sometimes mistakenly interpreted in our day, but rather as a spiritual communication of love and petition to the Mother of Jesus, who continues to care for the Mystical Body of her Son by her intercession.

Marian prayers, Marian liturgical feast days, Marian icons, Marian paintings and Marian artwork became abundant throughout the Christian world after the Council of Ephesus in 431 A.D.; an extraordinary flourishing of devotion to the Blessed Virgin both in the East and the West, the quantity and quality of which would exceed the most comprehensive study.

The Vatican Council - II strongly urged to continue to exalt Mary who "far surpasses all other creatures in heaven and on earth" (LG #54) and to pray to Mary whose intercession and protection the Church "continually experiences" (LG #62), but the Council also recommended to focus explicitly on Mary as both preeminent member of the Church as well as archetype of the Church. This is a pruning because it is often easier to honor Mary than to probe her mystery, to exalt Mary than to make our own life like hers: a total faith response to God.

The principle pruning of Mariology has been a shift away from honoring the privileges and splendors of Mary for their own sake in what has often been called an 'Isolated Mariology' to an emphasis on Mary as one with us.

"*365 Days with Mary*" is an effort to bring home this emphasis. In knowing the role of Mary in the Church and the faithful down the history, we are invited to take Mary with us each day finding inspiration and assistance in her motherly presence, to face the challenges of Christian life in the present-day milieu.

- Salt Media Team

(With excerpts from: Dr. Mark Miravalle of the Franciscan University of Steubenville, Introduction to Mary: The Heart of Marian Doctrine and Devotion, Queenship, 2006)

2015

January
Su	Mo	Tu	We	Th	Fr	Sa
				1	2	3
4	5	6	7	8	9	10
11	12	13	14	15	16	17
18	19	20	21	22	23	24
25	26	27	28	29	30	31

February
Su	Mo	Tu	We	Th	Fr	Sa
1	2	3	4	5	6	7
8	9	10	11	12	13	14
15	16	17	18	19	20	21
22	23	24	25	26	27	28

March
Su	Mo	Tu	We	Th	Fr	Sa
1	2	3	4	5	6	7
8	9	10	11	12	13	14
15	16	17	18	19	20	21
22	23	24	25	26	27	28
29	30	31				

April
Su	Mo	Tu	We	Th	Fr	Sa
			1	2	3	4
5	6	7	8	9	10	11
12	13	14	15	16	17	18
19	20	21	22	23	24	25
26	27	28	29	30		

May
Su	Mo	Tu	We	Th	Fr	Sa
					1	2
3	4	5	6	7	8	9
10	11	12	13	14	15	16
17	18	19	20	21	22	23
24	25	26	27	28	29	30
31						

June
Su	Mo	Tu	We	Th	Fr	Sa
	1	2	3	4	5	6
7	8	9	10	11	12	13
14	15	16	17	18	19	20
21	22	23	24	25	26	27
28	29	30				

July
Su	Mo	Tu	We	Th	Fr	Sa
			1	2	3	4
5	6	7	8	9	10	11
12	13	14	15	16	17	18
19	20	21	22	23	24	25
26	27	28	29	30	31	

August
Su	Mo	Tu	We	Th	Fr	Sa
						1
2	3	4	5	6	7	8
9	10	11	12	13	14	15
16	17	18	19	20	21	22
23	24	25	26	27	28	29
30	31					

September
Su	Mo	Tu	We	Th	Fr	Sa
		1	2	3	4	5
6	7	8	9	10	11	12
13	14	15	16	17	18	19
20	21	22	23	24	25	26
27	28	29	30			

October
Su	Mo	Tu	We	Th	Fr	Sa
				1	2	3
4	5	6	7	8	9	10
11	12	13	14	15	16	17
18	19	20	21	22	23	24
25	26	27	28	29	30	31

November
Su	Mo	Tu	We	Th	Fr	Sa
1	2	3	4	5	6	7
8	9	10	11	12	13	14
15	16	17	18	19	20	21
22	23	24	25	26	27	28
29	30					

December
Su	Mo	Tu	We	Th	Fr	Sa
		1	2	3	4	5
6	7	8	9	10	11	12
13	14	15	16	17	18	19
20	21	22	23	24	25	26
27	28	29	30	31		

2016

January
Su	Mo	Tu	We	Th	Fr	Sa
					1	2
3	4	5	6	7	8	9
10	11	12	13	14	15	16
17	18	19	20	21	22	23
24	25	26	27	28	29	30
31						

February
Su	Mo	Tu	We	Th	Fr	Sa
	1	2	3	4	5	6
7	8	9	10	11	12	13
14	15	16	17	18	19	20
21	22	23	24	25	26	27
28	29					

March
Su	Mo	Tu	We	Th	Fr	Sa
		1	2	3	4	5
6	7	8	9	10	11	12
13	14	15	16	17	18	19
20	21	22	23	24	25	26
27	28	29	30	31		

April
Su	Mo	Tu	We	Th	Fr	Sa
					1	2
3	4	5	6	7	8	9
10	11	12	13	14	15	16
17	18	19	20	21	22	23
24	25	26	27	28	29	30

May
Su	Mo	Tu	We	Th	Fr	Sa
1	2	3	4	5	6	7
8	9	10	11	12	13	14
15	16	17	18	19	20	21
22	23	24	25	26	27	28
29	30	31				

June
Su	Mo	Tu	We	Th	Fr	Sa
			1	2	3	4
5	6	7	8	9	10	11
12	13	14	15	16	17	18
19	20	21	22	23	24	25
26	27	28	29	30		

July
Su	Mo	Tu	We	Th	Fr	Sa
					1	2
3	4	5	6	7	8	9
10	11	12	13	14	15	16
17	18	19	20	21	22	23
24	25	26	27	28	29	30
31						

August
Su	Mo	Tu	We	Th	Fr	Sa
	1	2	3	4	5	6
7	8	9	10	11	12	13
14	15	16	17	18	19	20
21	22	23	24	25	26	27
28	29	30	31			

September
Su	Mo	Tu	We	Th	Fr	Sa
				1	2	3
4	5	6	7	8	9	10
11	12	13	14	15	16	17
18	19	20	21	22	23	24
25	26	27	28	29	30	

October
Su	Mo	Tu	We	Th	Fr	Sa
						1
2	3	4	5	6	7	8
9	10	11	12	13	14	15
16	17	18	19	20	21	22
23	24	25	26	27	28	29
30	31					

November
Su	Mo	Tu	We	Th	Fr	Sa
		1	2	3	4	5
6	7	8	9	10	11	12
13	14	15	16	17	18	19
20	21	22	23	24	25	26
27	28	29	30			

December
Su	Mo	Tu	We	Th	Fr	Sa
				1	2	3
4	5	6	7	8	9	10
11	12	13	14	15	16	17
18	19	20	21	22	23	24
25	26	27	28	29	30	31

2017

January
Su	Mo	Tu	We	Th	Fr	Sa
1	2	3	4	5	6	7
8	9	10	11	12	13	14
15	16	17	18	19	20	21
22	23	24	25	26	27	28
29	30	31				

February
Su	Mo	Tu	We	Th	Fr	Sa
			1	2	3	4
5	6	7	8	9	10	11
12	13	14	15	16	17	18
19	20	21	22	23	24	25
26	27	28				

March
Su	Mo	Tu	We	Th	Fr	Sa
			1	2	3	4
5	6	7	8	9	10	11
12	13	14	15	16	17	18
19	20	21	22	23	24	25
26	27	28	29	30	31	

April
Su	Mo	Tu	We	Th	Fr	Sa
						1
2	3	4	5	6	7	8
9	10	11	12	13	14	15
16	17	18	19	20	21	22
23	24	25	26	27	28	29
30						

May
Su	Mo	Tu	We	Th	Fr	Sa
	1	2	3	4	5	6
7	8	9	10	11	12	13
14	15	16	17	18	19	20
21	22	23	24	25	26	27
28	29	30	31			

June
Su	Mo	Tu	We	Th	Fr	Sa
				1	2	3
4	5	6	7	8	9	10
11	12	13	14	15	16	17
18	19	20	21	22	23	24
25	26	27	28	29	30	

July
Su	Mo	Tu	We	Th	Fr	Sa
						1
2	3	4	5	6	7	8
9	10	11	12	13	14	15
16	17	18	19	20	21	22
23	24	25	26	27	28	29
30	31					

August
Su	Mo	Tu	We	Th	Fr	Sa
		1	2	3	4	5
6	7	8	9	10	11	12
13	14	15	16	17	18	19
20	21	22	23	24	25	26
27	28	29	30	31		

September
Su	Mo	Tu	We	Th	Fr	Sa
					1	2
3	4	5	6	7	8	9
10	11	12	13	14	15	16
17	18	19	20	21	22	23
24	25	26	27	28	29	30

October
Su	Mo	Tu	We	Th	Fr	Sa
1	2	3	4	5	6	7
8	9	10	11	12	13	14
15	16	17	18	19	20	21
22	23	24	25	26	27	28
29	30	31				

November
Su	Mo	Tu	We	Th	Fr	Sa
			1	2	3	4
5	6	7	8	9	10	11
12	13	14	15	16	17	18
19	20	21	22	23	24	25
26	27	28	29	30		

December
Su	Mo	Tu	We	Th	Fr	Sa
					1	2
3	4	5	6	7	8	9
10	11	12	13	14	15	16
17	18	19	20	21	22	23
24	25	26	27	28	29	30
31						

Marian Calendar 2016

JANUARY

01. OUR LADY OF THE CLOUD Quito, Ecuador (1696)
02. OUR LADY OF THE PILLAR Zaragoza, Spain (40)
03. OUR LADY OF SICHEM Sichem, Israel (474)
04. OUR LADY OF THE ROSE Albano Sant'alessandro, Italy (1417)
05. OUR LADY OF THE ABUNDANCE Cursi, Italy (1641)
06. IMMACULATE CONCEPTION OF GUARDA VIEJO Guatemala (17th c.)
07. OUR LADY OF GRACE Costa Folgaria, Italy (1588)
08. OUR LADY OF PROMPT SUCCOR New Orleans, USA (1809)
09. OUR LADY OF THE LETTERS Messina, Italy (1693)
10. OUR LADY OF TEARS Rome, Italy (1546)
11. OUR LADY OF VETRANA Castellana Grotte, Italy (1691)
12. OUR LADY OF TEARS Foligno, Italy (1647)
13. OUR LADY, HELP OF CHRISTIANS Filippsdorf, Germany (1866)
14. THE DIVINE PASTORESS Santa Rosa, Venezuela (1736)
15. OUR LADY OF THE POOR Banneux, Belgium (1933)
16. OUR LADY OF VICTORY, REFUGE OF SINNERS Paris, France (1628)
17. OUR LADY OF PRAYER Pontmain, France (1871)
18. OUR LADY OF THE EXPECTATION OF ZAPOPAN Mexico (1541)
19. MOST HOLY MARY OF THE QUARRY Marsala, Italy (16th c.)
20. OUR LADY OF THE MIRACLE Rome, Italy (1842)
21. VIRGIN OF HIGH GRACE Higüey, Dominican Republic (16th c.)
22. OUR LADY OF CHARITY San Sebastián de los Reyes, Venezuela (1692)
23. OUR LADY OF PERIYANAYAGI Konankuppam, Tamil Nadu, India (17th c.)
24. ICON OF THE MOTHER OF GOD OF ELETS Russia (1060)
25. ICON OF THE MOTHER OF GOD THE "MILKGIVER" Kidron Valley, Palestine (13th c.)
26. OUR LADY OF BETHLEHEM Tumeremo, Venezuela (1788)
27. OUR LADY OF THE PILLAR Castenaso, Italia (1699)
28. OUR LADY OF THE GREEN SCAPULAR Blangy-Versailles, France (1840)
29. OUR LADY OF THE IMPOSSIBLE Serra Lima, Brazil (1755)
30. PANAGIA EVANGELISTRIA Tinos, Greece (1823)
31. OUR LADY OF HOPE Cidade da Esperança, Brazil (1966)

FEBRUARY

01. PANAGIA PARAMYTHIA Kykko, Cyprus (1997)
02. OUR LADY OF GOOD SUCCESS Quito, Ecuador (1610)
03. VIRGIN OF SUYAPA Honduras (1747)
04. OUR LADY OF THE FIRE Forlì, Italy (1428)
05. OUR LADY OF PERPETUAL HELP Port-au-Prince, Haiti (1882)
06. MOTHER OF CONSECRATED SOULS Carrizales, Venezuela (1993)
07. MOST HOLY VIRGIN MARY OF THE GATE Guastalla, Italy (1693)
08. BLESSED VIRGIN OF THE CASTLE Fiorano, Italy (13th c.)
09. VIRGIN OF ÁFRICA Ceuta, Spain (1651)
10. ICON OF THE MOTHER OF GOD OF SUMORIN Totma, Russia (1554)
11. OUR LADY OF LOURDES France (1858)
12. OUR LADY OF THE BASIN Brescia, Italy (1080)
13. OUR LADY OF MOUNT CARMEL Rute, Spain (17th c.)
14. MOTHER OF MERCY Pellevoisin, France (1876)
15. OUR LADY OF COMFORT Arezzo, Italy (1796)
16. WEEPING VIRGIN MARY Sajópálfala, Hungary (1717)
17. OUR LADY OF EXILE Florianópolis, Brazil (1673)
18. OUR LADY OF THE ROSARY Rota, Spain (16th c.)
19. VIRGIN OF CAMPANA Spain (1596)
20. OUR LADY OF THE STAIRS Massafra, Italy (1743)
21. OUR LADY OF GRACE Anderlecht, Belgium (1449)
22. OUR LADY OF THE KNOLL Castel San Pietro Terme, Italy (1550)
23. VIRGIN OF THE 40 HOURS Limache, Chile (1831)
24. THE VIRGIN GUIDE Alcaracejos, Spain (13th c.)
25. ICON OF THE MOTHER OF GOD "IVERON" North Ossetia Alania, Russia (9th c.)
26. OUR LADY OF REMEDIES Palermo, Italy (1064)
27. OUR LADY OF REMEDIES Chiclana de la Frontera, Spain (16th c.)
28. VILENSKY HODEGETRIA Vilnius, Lithuania (15th c.)

MARCH

01. VIRGIN OF LORETO Mutxamel, Spain (1513)
02. ICON OF THE MOTHER OF GOD "TIKHVIN" Mt Athos, Greece (1877)
03. QUEEN OF THE ROSARY Pompei, Italy (1884)
04. OUR LADY OF THE GUARD Marseilles, France (1214)
05. HOLY MARY OF THE CROSS Cubas, Spain (1449)
06. ICON OF THE MOTHER OF GOD "KOZELSHCHANSK" Kobeliaky, Ukraine (16th c.)
07. OUR LADY OF MONTE BERICO Vicenza, Italy (1426)
08. OUR LADY OF TEARS Campinas, Brazil (1928)
09. OUR LADY OF THE MIRACLE Motta di Livenza, Italy (1510)
10. OUR LADY OF PRADELLES France (1512)
11. MIRACULOUS MADONNA Taggia, Italy (1855)
12. OUR LADY OF FOURVIÈRE Lyon, France (1643)
13. DEVPETERUV MOTHER OF GOD Batyushkovo, Russia (1392)
14. VIRGIN OF MOUNT CARMEL Maipú, Chile (1818)
15. ICON OF THE MOTHER OF GOD "ENTHRONED" Kolomskoye, Russia (1917)
16. VLADIMIR MOTHER OF GOD Volokolamsk, Russia (1572)
17. WEEPING VIRGIN MARY Gyor, Hungary (1697)
18. OUR LADY OF MERCY Savona, Italy (1536)
19. ICON OF THE MOTHER OF GOD "THE BLESSED HEAVEN" Moscow, Russia (12th c.)
20. ICON OF THE MOTHER OF GOD "THE SURETY OF SINNERS" Odrino, Russia (1843)
21. KURSK ROOT MOTHER OF GOD New York, NY, USA (1898)
22. OUR LADY OF SORROWS Castelpetroso, Italy (1888)
23. OUR LADY OF UJARRÁS Costa Rica (16th c.)
24. OUR LADY OF THE THORN Marne, France (1400)
25. LADY OF ALL NATIONS Amsterdam, Netherlands (1945)
26. OUR LADY OF THE HAWTHORN Santa Gadea del Cid, Spain (1399)
27. THEOTOKOS OF ST. THEODORE Kostroma, Russia (1239)
28. OUR LADY OF BOCCIOLA Vacciago di Ameno, Italy (1528)
29. HOLY MARY AT THE ALTAR OF HEAVEN Rome, Italy (1636)
30. OUR LADY OF THE ROCK Alessandria della Rocca, Italy (1620)
31. OUR LADY OF THE ROSE San Vito al Tagliamento, Italy (1655)

APRIL

01. "SWEET-KISSING" ICON OF THE MOTHER OF GOD Smolensk, Russia (1103)
02. OUR LADY OF LIGHT Zeitun, Egypt (1968)
03. OUR LADY OF THE OAK Maisières, France (1803)
04. OUR LADY OF LAUSANNE Chappeles, Switzerland (1871)
05. HOLY MARY OF GIBBILMANNA Sicily, Italy (1534)
06. MOTHER THRICE ADMIRABLE Ingolstadt, Germany (1604)
07. OUR LADY OF SANCHO ABARCA Tauste, Spain (1569)
08. MADONNA OF THE FROST Basella, Italy (1356)
09. VIRGIN OF THE HAWTHORN Chauchina, Spain (1906)
10. LIFE-GIVING SPRING Zeytinburnu, Turkey (460)
11. OUR LADY OF PERPETUAL HELP Hallaar, Belgium (1502)
12. VIRGIN OF THE REVELATION Rome, Italy (1947)
13. OUR LADY OF THE CRAG Vila Velha, Brazil (1569)
14. BLESSED VIRGIN OF GRACE Salzano, Italy (1534)
15. VIRGIN OF CUAPA Nicaragua (1980)
16. ICON OF THE MOTHER OF GOD "THE UNFADING BLOOM" Moscow, Russia
17. OUR LADY OF THE MIRACLES Corbetta, Italy (1555)
18. OUR LADY OF THE OAK Roble San Bartolomeo al Mare, Italy (1671)
19. VIRGIN OF VERDÚN Minas, Uruguay (1901)
20. OUR SORROWFUL MOTHER OF THE COLLEGE Quito, Ecuador (1906)
21. OUR LADY OF THE MOST HOLY ROSARY Manaoag, Philippines (15th c.)
22. OUR LADY OF SPLENDOR Giulianova, Italy (1557)
23. OUR LADY OF THE REMEDIES Cártama, Spain (1579)
24. OUR LADY OF BUENOS AIRES Argentina (1536)
25. OUR LADY OF GOOD COUNSEL Genazzano, Italy (1467)
26. MOTHER OF GOD CROWNED Borgo Incoronta, Italy (1001)
27. OUR LADY OF MONTSERRAT Barcelona, Spain (10th c.)
28. OUR LADY OF THE CHESTNUT Bergamo, Italy (1310)
29. BLESSED VIRGIN OF GHIARA Reggio Emiliana, Italy (1596)
30. OUR LADY OF AFRICA Algiers, Algeria (1838)

MAY

01. OUR LADY OF THE COURTS Albacete, Spain (1222)
02. QUEEN OF THE ROSARY AND PEACE Itapiranga, Brazil (1994)
03. OUR LADY OF MIRACLES Jaffna Patão, Sri Lanka (1614)
04. OUR LADY OF THE BROOM Cori, Italy (1521)
05. BLESSED VIRGIN OF THE ADORATION Fivizzano, Italy (1596)
06. OUR LADY OF GRACE Piove di Sacco, Italy (1631)
07. THE MOLCHENSKAYA ICON Busynovo, Russia (17th c.)
08. OUR LADY OF LUJÁN Argentina (1630)
09. OUR LADY OF THE WOODS Imbersago, Italy (1617)
10. OUR LADY OF TRSAT Croatia (1291)
11. MADONNA OF THE ROCK Calabria, Italy (1968)
12. OUR LADY HELP OF CHRISTIANS Pra, Italy (1874)
13. OUR LADY OF THE ROSARY Fatima, Portugal (1917)
14. OUR LADY OF THE PINE Montagnaga, Italy (1729)
15. OUR LADY OF THE HARBOR Clermont-Ferrand, France (1614)
16. THE SVEN CAVES ICON OF THE MOTHER OF GOD Briansk, Russia (1288)
17. IMMACULATE CONCEPTION Marpingen, Germany (1876)
18. OUR LADY OF WESEMLIN Lucerne, Switzerland (1531)
19. VIRGIN OF PEÑA DE FRANCIA El Cabaco, Spain (1434)
20. MOTHER OF GOD Zhyrovichy, Belarus (14th c.)
21. OUR LADY OF THE ANGELS Arcola, Italy (1556)
22. OUR LADY OF MERCY Croce di Savenone, Italy (1527)
23. VIRGIN OF GRACE Aés, Spain (1575)
24. AUXILIUM CHRISTIANORUM / OUR LADY, HELP OF CHRISTIANS Germany (1861)
25. OUR LADY OF THE MEADOW Ciudad Real, Spain (1088)
26. OUR LADY OF CARAVAGGIO Italy (1432)
27. VIRGIN OF SORROWS La Codosera, Spain (1945)
28. OUR LADY OF THE BURNING FIRE Arras, France (1105)
29. OUR LADY OF GOOD DELIVERY Paris, France (14th c.)
30. OUR LADY OF THE LITTLE BRIDGE San Marino di Carpi, Italy (16th c.)
31. OUR LADY OF THE STARS Cellatica, Italy (1536)

JUNE

01. OUR LADY OF GRACE Leini, Italy (1630)
02. MADONNA OF THE TEARS Ponte Nossa, Italy (1511)
03. OUR LADY OF VLADIMIR Moscow, Russia (1395)
04. VIRGIN MARY THE PLANTER Hurlingham, Argentina (17th c.)
05. OUR LADY OF HELP Bobbio, Italy (15th c.)
06. VIRGIN OF THE ROSARY Villarreal de Huerva, Spain (13th c.)
07. OUR LADY OF THE OAK Visora di Conflenti, Italy (1578)
08. OUR LADY OF SUNDAY Saint-Bauzille-de-la-Sylve, France (1873)
09. HOLY MARY OF THE WALNUT Rieti, Italy (1505)
10. OUR LADY OF LAPA Sernancelhe, Portugal (1498)
11. OUR LADY OF MANTARA Maghdouché, Lebanon (1721)
12. OUR LADY OF MONTALTO Messina, Sicily, Italy (1294)
13. OUR LADY OF TEARS Espinhal, Portugal (13th c.)
14. OUR LADY OF THE ARBOR Lille, France (1234)
15. ICON OF THE MOTHER OF GOD Kiev-Bratsk, Russia (1654)
16. BLESSED VIRGIN OF SORROWS Campocavallo, Italy (1892)
17. MARY IN THE FOREST Dolina, Austria (1849)
18. OUR LADY OF IGOR Kiev, Ukraine (1147)
19. KAZAN ICON OF THE MOTHER OF GOD Moscow, Russia (1701)
20. OUR LADY OF CONSOLATION Turin, Italy (1104)
21. ICON OF THE MOTHER OF GOD OF YAROSLAVL Russia (1501)
22. OUR LADY OF THE CAPE Quebec, Canada (1879)
23. OUR LADY OF THE STONE Bibbiena, Italy (1347)
24. OUR LADY OF THE SHIP Chioggia, Italy (1508)
25. QUEEN OF PEACE Medjugorje, Bosnia and Herzegovina (1981)
26. THE BLESSED VIRGIN OF POWER Trompone, Italy (1562)
27. MOTHER OF GOD OF GIETRZWALD Poland (1877)
28. OUR LADY OF LONGING Matka Boza Teskniaca, Warsaw, Poland (1998)
29. OUR LADY OF LINARES Spain (1808)
30. OUR LADY OF GOOD SUCCOR Montréal, Canada (1672)

JULY

01. OUR LADY THE GUIDE Portugalete, Spain (13th c.)
02. OUR LADY OF MADHU Wanni, Sri Lanka (16th c.)
03. HODEGETRIA Mt. Athos, Greece (16th c.)
04. OUR LADY OF THE REFUGE Matamoros, Mexico (1720)
05. ECONOMISSA ICON OF THE MOST HOLY THEOTOKOS Great Lavra, Greece (8th c.)
06. HOLY MOTHER OF AKITA Japan (1973)
07. OUR LADY OF SOVIORE Italy (740)
08. OUR LADY OF THE SNOW Adro, Italy (1519)
09. OUR LADY OF ITATÍ Corrientes, Argentina (1615)
10. OUR LADY OF BOULOGNE France (13th c.)
11. OUR LADY OF MOUNT CARMEL Combarbio di Anghiari, Italy (1536)
12. KASPEROV ICON OF THE MOTHER OF GOD Kherson, Ukraine (1840)
13. OUR LADY OF GRACE Garessio Valsorda, Italy (1653)
14. MOTHER OF GOD OF CANÔLICH Andorra (1223)
15. AKHTYRSKAYA ICON OF THE MOTHER OF GOD Croydon, Australia (1739)
16. OUR LADY OF MT. CARMEL Aylesford, England (1251)
17. OUR LADY OF HUMILITY Pistoia, Italy (1490)
18. OUR LADY OF GOOD DELIVERANCE Neuilly-sur-Seine, France (14th c.)
19. OUR LADY OF THE MIRACLE Lima, Peru (1630)
20. OUR LADY OF ZOCUECA Spain (1808)
21. OUR LADY OF KAZAN Russia (1579)
22. ICON OF THE MOTHER OF GOD OF KOLOCH Russia (1143)
23. OUR LADY OF ALTINO Albino, Italy (1496)
24. MOTHER OF GOD OF RZEVSK Russia (1539)
25. MOTHER OF GOD OF THREE HANDS Mt Athos, Greece (6th c.)
26. OUR LADY OF THE BEECH TREE Castelluccio, Italy (17th c.)
27. OUR LADY OF MT CARMEL Palmoli, Italy (13th c.)
28. MARY, MOTHER OF GOD Port-au-Prince, Haiti (1985)
29. HOLY MARY OF THE MIRACLES Morbio Inferiore, Switzerland (1594)
30. ICON OF THE MOTHER OF GOD OF SVIATOGORSK Russia (1569)
31. VIRGIN OF CONSOLATION Huachana, Argentina (1820)

AUGUST

01. OUR LADY OF MERCY Barcelona, Spain (1218)
02. OUR LADY OF THE ANGELS Cartago, Costa Rica (1635)
03. HOLY MARY LADDER TO PARADISE Noto, Sicily, Italy (1498)
04. OUR LADY OF THE APPARITION Pellestrina, Italy (1716)
05. OUR LADY OF THE SNOWS Rome, Italy (352)
06. OUR LADY OF VALMALA Cuneo, Italy (1834)
07. OUR LADY OF THE ANGELS Guardavalle, Italy (13th c.)
08. HOLY MARY OF THE OAK Lucignano, Italy (1467)
09. THE WHITE LADY Messina, Italy (1282)
10. OUR LADY OF THE CRAG Bogotà, Colombia (1685)
11. VIRGIN OF THE HEAD Jaen, Spain (1227)
12. OUR LADY OF THE WOODS Montemilone, Italy (13th c.)
13. OUR LADY OF FORGETFULNESS, TRIUMPH AND MERCY Guadalajara Castilla, Spain (1831)
14. OUR LADY OF CONSOLATION Ghisalba, Italy (1453)
15. OUR LADY OF SORROWS Florence, Italy (1233)
16. OUR LADY OF GRACES Torcoroma, Colombia (1711)
17. VIRGIN OF THE THREE RIVERS Valgañón, Spain (13th c.)
18. OUR LADY OF THE LOWER Rubiana, Italy (1713)
19. OUR LADY OF VICTORY San Marco la Catola, Italy (13th c.)
20. VALAAM ICON OF THE MOTHER OF GOD Heinävesi, Finland (1878)
21. OUR LADY OF KNOCK Ireland (1879)
22. TABERNACLE OF THE MOST HIGH Ngome, South Africa (1955)
23. MARY OF SCHIAVONEA Italy (1648)
24. OUR LADY OF THE MIRACLE Tunja, Colombia (1626)
25. OUR LADY OF ROSSANO Italy (6th c.)
26. OUR LADY OF CZESTOCHOWA Poland (14th c.)
27. OUR LADY OF PRASCONDÙ Italy (1619)
28. VIRGIN OF THE KNIGHTS Villavieja de Yeltes, Spain (12th c.)
29. OUR LADY OF THE GUARD Savona, Italy (1490)
30. OUR LADY OF THE WELL Capurso, Italy (1705)
31. OUR LADY OF THE FOUNDERS Mt. Athos, Greece (1st c.)

SEPTEMBER

01. VIRGIN OF THE REMEDIES Mexico (1519)
02. OUR LADY OF THE MOUNTAIN Polsi di San Luca, Italy (1144)
03. VIRGIN OF THE MIRACLE Ruesga, Spain (14th c.)
04. OUR LADY OF VILLAVICIOSA Cordoba, Spain (14th c.)
05. OUR LADY OF PEDANCINO Cismon del Grappa, Italy (700)
06. ICON OF THE MOTHER OF GOD OF ST PETER OF MOSCOW Russia (14th c.)
07. OUR LADY OF THE HOLY CORD Valenciennes, France (1008)
08. OUR LADY OF GOOD HEALTH Velankanni, Tamil Nadu, India (16th c.)
09. HOLY MARY THE ANCIENT Panama City, Panama (16th c.)
10. OUR LADY OF KERIO Noyal-Muzillac, France (1874)
11. BLESSED VIRGIN OF MONTE BONICCA Italy (1595)
12. MEDIATRIX OF ALL GRACES Lipa, Philippines (1948)
13. OUR LADY OF THE MOUNT Bandra, Mumbai, India (1570)
14. DOLOROUS MOTHER Legau, Germany (1728)
15. OUR LADY OF THE HILL Lenola, Italy (1602)
16. OUR LADY OF THE FLAGSTONES Potosí, Colombia (1754)
17. ICON OF THE MOTHER OF GOD "THE UNBURNT BUSH" Mt. Sinai, Egypt (3rd c.)
18. OUR LADY OF HOPE Calasparra, Spain (1786)
19. OUR LADY OF LA SALETTE France (1846)
20. OUR LADY WITH THE SILVER FOOT Toul, France (1284)
21. BLESSED VIRGIN OF TRESTO Italy (1468)
22. OUR LADY OF SAFE HARBOR Lampedusa, Italy (1843)
23. OUR LADY OF VALVENERA La Rioja, Spain (9th c.)
24. OUR LADY OF WALSINGHAM England (1061)
25. OUR LADY OF THE ROSARY San Nicolás, Argentina (1983)
26. OUR LADY OF LESNA PODLASKA Poland (1683)
27. MADONNA DELLA TREVISO Treviso, Veneto, Italy (1511)
28. OUR LADY OF THE ASH Grado, Spain (17th c.)
29. OUR LADY OF TIRANO Italy (1504)
30. OUR LADY OF FORNO ALPI GRAIE Italy (1629)

OCTOBER

01. OUR LADY OF VALVERDE Italy (1711)
02. MOTHER OF GOD ROZANCOWA Krakow, Poland (1600)
03. OUR LADY OF THE FRUIT OF THE OAK Mezzana, Italy (13th c.)
04. OUR LADY OF MERCY Biancavilla, Italy (1482)
05. OUR LADY OF THE WAY Leon, Spain (1505)
06. ICON OF THE MOTHER OF GOD OF SLOVENKA Russia (1635)
07. OUR LADY OF ATOCHA Spain (8th c.)
08. OUR LADY OF GOOD REMEDY Paris, France (1197)
09. OUR LADY OF GOOD HELP Robinsonville, WI, USA (1859)
10. OUR LADY OF MERCY Gallivaggio, Italy (1492)
11. OUR LADY OF THE MILK St. Augustine, FL, USA (16th c.)
12. OUR LADY WHO APPEARED Aparecida, Brazil (1717)
13. OUR LADY OF GUADALUPE La Gomera, Canary Islands, Spain (16th c.)
14. VIRGIN OF PROTECTION Istanbul, Turkey (911)
15. VIRGIN OF THE HELPLESS Valencia, Spain (1407)
16. HOLY MARY OF THE PLAINS Santa Rosa, Argentina (1986)
17. HOLY MARY OF EL PUEBLITO Mexico (1632)
18. VIRGIN OF THE MIRACLES Almaguer, Colombia (1619)
19. "O ALL-HYMNED MOTHER" ICON Vladimir Oblast, Russia (19th c.)
20. ICON OF THE MOTHER OF GOD "TENDERNESS" OF THE PSKOV CAVES Russia (16th c.)
21. OUR LADY OF THE ROSARY Noepoli, Italy (14th c.)
22. MARY MOST HOLY Capo d'Orlando, Italy (1598)
23. VIRGIN OF AKATHISTOS Mt. Athos, Greece (1276)
24. OUR LADY OF MERCY Saint Martin d'Heuille, France (1879)
25. MOTHER OF GOD OF PHILERMOS Cetinje, Montenegro (1799)
26. ICON OF THE MOTHER OF GOD OF THE SEVEN LAKES Kazan, Russia (1615)
27. VIRGIN OF THE DOOR Otuzco, Peru (1560)
28. VIRGIN OF THE ROSARY OF EL PARAUTE Lagunillas, Venezuela (1651)
29. OUR LADY OF OROPA Piedmont, Italy (3rd c.)
30. OUR LADY OF MONDOVI Italy (16th c.)
31. OUR LADY OF THE ROSARY OF RÍO BLANCO Y PAPAYA DE JUJUY Argentina (17th c.)

NOVEMBER

01. QUEEN OF THE POOR SOULS IN PURGATORY Heede, Germany (1937)
02. OUR LADY OF THE SOULS Rome, Italy (1550)
03. OUR LADY OF MIRACLES AND VIRTUES Rennes, France (14th c.)
04. THE WEEPING VIRGIN Máriapócs, Hungary (1696)
05. OUR LADY OF THE MIRACULOUS MEDAL Monte Sião, Brazil (1939)
06. OUR LADY OF VALFLEURY France (800)
07. VIRGIN OF THE RIVER Tarazona, Spain (449)
08. OUR LADY OF HAPPY VOYAGE Bandel, West Bengal, India (1599)
09. VIRGIN OF THE ALMUDENA Madrid, Spain (15th c.)
10. OUR LADY OF THE TURNING EYES Rottweil, Germany (1643)
11. OUR LADY OF THE PORTUGUESE Diu, India (1546)
12. ICON OF THE MOTHER OF GOD OF OZERYANKA Ukraine (17th c.)
13. OUR LADY OF THE SEVEN JOYS Sion, Switzerland (1422)
14. OUR LADY OF THE GROTTO Lamego, Portugal (6th c.)
15. OUR LADY OF THE DEW Paranaguá, Brazil (17th c.)
16. OUR LADY OF THE GATE OF DAWN Vilnius, Lithuania (1363)
17. VIRGIN OF THE MIRACLE Mazarrón, Spain (1585)
18. OUR LADY OF THE ROSARY OF CHIQUINQUIRÁ Maracaibo, Venezuela (1709)
19. OUR LADY OF THE DIVINE PROVIDENCE San Juan, Puerto Rico (1920)
20. ICON OF THE MOTHER OF GOD "THE JOYFUL" Moscow, Russia (1795)
21. RECONCILER OF PEOPLE AND NATIONS Betania, Venezuela (1976)
22. ICON OF THE MOTHER OF GOD "QUICK TO HEAR" Mt. Athos, Greece (1664)
23. OUR LADY OF THE CONCEPTION Granada, Nicaragua (1721)
24. THE BLACK VIRGIN Myans, France (1248)
25. OUR LADY OF THE ROCK Fiesole, Italy (1446)
26. OUR LADY OF SOUFANIEH Damascus, Syria (1982)
27. OUR LADY OF THE MIRACULOUS MEDAL Paris, France (1830)
28. MOTHER OF THE WORD Kibeho, Rwanda (1981)
29. OUR LADY OF THE GOLDEN HEART Beauraing, Belgium (1932)
30. OUR LADY OF THE CONCEPTION San Juan de los Lagos, Mexico (1224)

DECEMBER

01. MARY COMFORTER OF THE AFFLICTED Mettenbuch, Germany (1876)
02. OUR LADY OF DIDINIA Turkey (363)
03. VIRGIN OF MONTESANTO Rome, Italy (1659)
04. ICON OF "THE ENTRY OF THE MOST HOLY THEOTOKOS INTO THE TEMPLE" Serpukhov, Russia (14th c.)
05. VIRGIN OF THE KINGS, IMMACULATE CONCEPTION La Antigua Guatemala (16th c.)
06. MAXIMOV ICON OF THE MOTHER OF GOD Vladimir, Russia (1299)
07. OUR LADY OF SORROWS Villatuelda, Spain (16th c.)
08. SANTA MARIAN KAMALEN Hagåtña, Guam (1825)
09. OUR LADY OF CAYSASAY Taal, Philippines (1603)
10. ICON OF THE MOTHER OF GOD "OF THE SIGN" Novgorod, Russia (1170)
11. OUR LADY OF WARRAQ EL-HADAR Egypt (2009)
12. OUR LADY OF GUADALUPE Mexico City, Mexico (1531)
13. QUEEN OF THE HOLY ROSARY Baños de Agua Santa, Ecuador (1570)
14. BLESSED VIRGIN OF DEFENSE Faenza, Italy (1685)
15. OUR LADY OF MONGUÍ Boyacá, Colombia (16th c.)
16. OUR LADY OF THE NEW ADVENT Denver, Colorado, USA (1991)
17. OUR LADY OF THE EARTHQUAKE Paterno, Italy (1857)
18. VIRGIN OF THE SOLITUDE Oaxaca, Mexico (1620)
19. OUR LADY OF GOOD HOPE Candolim, Goa, India (1560)
20. OUR LADY OF CRAVEGNA Italy (1492)
21. GREAT MOTHER OF AUSTRIA Mariazell, Austria (1157)
22. HOLY MARY OF GRACE San Giovanni Valdarno, Italy (1478)
23. OUR LADY OF THE GOOD NEWS Rennes, France (1720)
24. OUR LADY OF THE ROSARY Andacollo, Chile (1676)
25. COMFORTER OF THE AFFLICTED Kevelaer, Germany (1641)
26. VIRGEN DEL ROSARIO Chiquinquirá, Colombia (1562)
27. OUR LADY OF THE ROSARY Atibaia, Brazil (1817)
28. VIRGIN OF THE ASSUMPTION Elche, Spain (1370)
29. OUR LADY OF THE FLOWERS Bra, Italy (1336)
30. OUR LADY OF MIRACLES Milano, Italy (1485)
31. SANTA MARÍA LA REAL Uxue, Spain (8th c.)

January
friday
1

OUR LADY OF THE CLOUD
Quito, Ecuador (1696)

On December 30, 1696, when the Bishop of Quito, Sancho de Andrade y Figueroa, was near death, a statue of the Virgin Mary was processed through the streets in petition for his recovery. The bell of the church resounded the call for praying the Glory Be and then, according to official archdiocesan archives, initially the chaplain Don José de Ulloa y la Cadena and then everyone there witnessed the Virgin resting on a cloud between the sanctuaries of Guápulo and Quinche, with a crown on her head, a lily in her right and the Child Jesus at her left. The bishop recovered and then authorized the devotion to Our Lady of the Cloud, erecting an altar to her in Quito Cathedral.

JANUARY 2016

s	m	t	w	t	f	s
					1	2
3	4	5	6	7	8	9
10	11	12	13	14	15	16
17	18	19	20	21	22	23
24	25	26	27	28	29	30
31						

CHRISTMAS WEEK
Solemnity of Mary, Mother of God

First Reading: *Numbers 6:22-27*
Responsorial Psalm: *Ps 67:2-3.5.6.8 (2a)*
Second Reading: *Galatians 4:4-7*
Gospel Reading: *Luke 2:16-21*

Source: Venida de la Virgen del Pilar. Francisco de Goya. Wikipedia

January
saturday

2

OUR LADY OF THE PILLAR
Zaragoza, Spain (40)

According to legend, in the early days of the Church on January 2, 40 AD, the Apostle James the Greater was proclaiming the Gospel in Caesaraugusta (present day Zaragoza) by the river Ebro, when he saw Mary miraculously appearing in the flesh on a pillar calling him to return to Jerusalem. James was also instructed to build a chapel on the spot. The pillar left by the Virgin Mary is presently enshrined in the same but larger Basilica of Our Lady of the Pillar. It is believed to be the same pillar given and promised by Mary, in spite of numerous disasters that beset the church.

CHRISTMAS WEEK
Memorial of Saints Basil the Great & Gregory Nazianzen

First Reading: *1 John 2:22-28*
Responsorial Psalm: *Ps 98:1.2-3ab.3cd-4*
Gospel Reading: *John 1:19-28*

JANUARY 2016

s	m	t	w	t	f	s
					1	2
3	4	5	6	7	8	9
10	11	12	13	14	15	16
17	18	19	20	21	22	23
24	25	26	27	28	29	30
31						

January
sunday
3

OUR LADY OF SICHEM
Israel (474)

The original location of the shrine was below Mount Garizim, Israel. Later the shrine in Brabant in Louvain was constructed as a replacement. The Christians who settled there were persecuted by the Samaritans.

When the emperor gave Mount Garizim to the Christians in 474, a church was built in that place honoring the Blessed Virgin Mary. The ancient statue of Our Lady of Sichem, later became known as Our Lady of 'Montaigu', which now is the more common title, has been venerated in Belgium for centuries.

Source: Roman Catholic Saints. "Our Lady of Sichem"

JANUARY 2016

s	m	t	w	t	f	s
					1	2
3	4	5	6	7	8	9
10	11	12	13	14	15	16
17	18	19	20	21	22	23
24	25	26	27	28	29	30
31						

CHRISTMAS WEEK
Epiphany of the Lord

First Reading: *Isaiah 60:1-6*
Responsorial Psalm: *Ps 72:1-2.7-8.10-11.12-13*
Second Reading: *Ephesians 3:2-3a:5-6*
Gospel Reading: *Matthew 2:1-12*

Source: Blogspot - Parroquia Nossa Snhorada Natividade "Nossa Senhora das Rosas"

January
monday

4

OUR LADY OF THE ROSE
Albano Sant'alessandro, Italy (1417)

In the night between January 3rd and 4th, 1417, two Roman merchants, traveling from Bergamo to Brescia, were lost in a forest near the village of Albano. Lost and fearful of dying in the cold, they turned fervently to the Lord with the vow to build a chapel, if they could survive the night. Suddenly the sky opened with rays of light breaking the darkness and a beam of light showing them the way. With relieved and grateful hearts, they very quickly reached the city of Bergamo. With the basilica closed at that late hour, they found shelter in the nearby ruined tower and begin to pray in the darkness, and immediately the Immaculate Virgin and Child appeared before them.

JANUARY 2016

s	m	t	w	t	f	s
					1	2
3	4	5	6	7	8	9
10	11	12	13	14	15	16
17	18	19	20	21	22	23
24	25	26	27	28	29	30
31						

MONDAY AFTER EPIPHANY
Memorial of Saint Elizabeth Ann Seton

First Reading: *1 John 3:22-4:6*
Responsorial Psalm: *Ps 2:7bc-8,10-12a*
Gospel Reading: *Matthew 4:12-17,23-25*

January
tuesday
5

OUR LADY OF THE ABUNDANCE
Cursi, Italy (1641)

In spring 1641, the Virgin Mary appeared to a nonreligious young shepherd, Biagio Orlando Natali. The boy was afraid and tried to escape, but the Virgin called and reassured him: "I am the Queen of Heaven, and suffer for the miserable condition of men". She asked him to then build a chapel and tell the village priest because he will gather the people and lead them in procession. Biagio converted on the spot and many believers went there. The first chapel was destroyed by fire, but the rebuilt sanctuary currently hosts many pilgrims.

Source: Santuario Maria S.S. dell' Abbondanza Cursi

JANUARY 2016

s	m	t	w	t	f	s
					1	2
3	4	5	6	7	8	9
10	11	12	13	14	15	16
17	18	19	20	21	22	23
24	25	26	27	28	29	30
31						

TUESDAY AFTER EPIPHANY
Memorial of Saint John Neumann

First Reading: *1 John 4:7-10*
Responsorial Psalm: *Ps 72:1-2.3-4.7-8*
Gospel Reading: *Mark 6:34-44*

Source: Wordpress - Un Encuentro con María

IMMACULATE CONCEPTION OF GUARDA VIEJO
Guatemala City, Guatemala (17th c.)

On January 6 In Guatemala City, the fiesta of the Guarda Viejo district marks the end of the Christmas season with a Three Kings celebration. Festivities begin in the town with the feast of the Immaculate Conception. The image of the Immaculata, Also known as the Virgin of the Holy Kings, is perhaps the oldest of several statues in Guatemala City. Formerly owned by the Franciscan Third Order, it was donated to the Franciscan church in the suburban outpost of Guarda Viejo in the 1800s. This revered image was re-consecrated by Cardinal Quezada Toruño, Archbishop of Guatemala, on January 6, 2003 at a special ceremony for this occasion.

JANUARY 2016

s	m	t	w	t	f	s
					1	2
3	4	5	6	7	8	9
10	11	12	13	14	15	16
17	18	19	20	21	22	23
24	25	26	27	28	29	30
31						

WEDNESDAY AFTER EPIPHANY

First Reading: *1 John 4:11-18*
Responsorial Psalm: *Ps 72:1-2,10-11,12-13*
Gospel Reading: *Matthew 6:45-52*

January

thursday

7

OUR LADY OF GRACE
Costa Folgaria, Italy
(1588)

In January 1588, the Mother of God appeared to a monk, Peter Dosso. As she does in so many of her apparitions, she requested that he build a church in her honor in that place. The church was later constructed and for centuries, it was one of the most important Marian shrines of the Italian region of Trentino.

In 1955, Pope Pius XII, in one of the more interesting patronages ever affirmed by a Pope, proclaimed Our Lady of Grace of Costa, "the distinguished and principal patron of all skiers of Italy".

Source: Wikipedia (Italian) "Madonna delle Grazie"

JANUARY 2016

s	m	t	w	t	f	s
					1	2
3	4	5	6	7	8	9
10	11	12	13	14	15	16
17	18	19	20	21	22	23
24	25	26	27	28	29	30
31						

THURSDAY AFTER EPIPHANY

First Reading: *1 John 4:19-5:4*
Responsorial Psalm: *Ps 72:1-2,14-15,17*
Gospel Reading: *Luke 4:14-22*

Source: Blogspot - New Orleans Religion "The Ursulines: Then and Now"

January
friday
8

OUR LADY OF PROMPT SUCCOR New Orleans, Louisiana, USA (1809)

During the French Revolution of the late 18th century, a French nun, Mother St. Michel, applied with a letter to Pope Pius VII to approve her transfer to aid the Ursuline convent In New Orleans, USA. One day, she was inspired to promise to honor her and make her known under the tile of Our Lady of Prompt Succor. Once approved, she traveled to New Orleans and arranged to have a statue installed. Many miracles have been attributed to her intercession. The most famous historical events were the saving of the Ursuline convent from a disastrous fire and the victory of General Andrew Jackson's 6,000 American troops over the 15,000 British soldiers on the plains of Chalmette.

JANUARY 2016

s	m	t	w	t	f	s
					1	2
3	4	5	6	7	8	9
10	11	12	13	14	15	16
17	18	19	20	21	22	23
24	25	26	27	28	29	30
31						

FRIDAY AFTER EPIPHANY

First Reading: *1 John 5:5-13*
Responsorial Psalm: *Ps 147:12-13,14-15, 19-20*
Gospel Reading: *Luke 5:12-16*

January

saturday

9

OUR LADY OF THE LETTERS
Messina, Italy (1693)

Earthquakes shook most of Sicily in 1693. The town of Messina was saved through the intercession of the Virgin Mary . On January 9 of that year, the Virgin Mary appeared to a girl who was very ill named Paola Alfonsina at the time when the rumblings were just beginning. In this vision she saw the window of her room open suddenly to a beautiful woman dressed in white with a blue mantle, smiling and saying, "Fear not". The Madonna came again with the message that the inhabitants should keep hope and wait in the cathedral in front of the altar of the Madonna della Lettera. The Italian coast was besieged by a tsunami and earthquake, but Messina incurred minimal damage and flooding, being spared the devastation of other areas. Afterwards, the Madonna comforted Paola and others over the next few days.

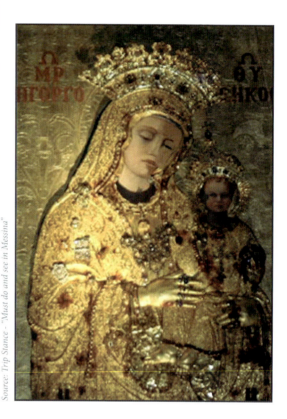

Source: Trip Stance - "Must do and see in Messina"

JANUARY 2016

s	m	t	w	t	f	s
					1	2
3	4	5	6	7	8	9
10	11	12	13	14	15	16
17	18	19	20	21	22	23
24	25	26	27	28	29	30
31						

SATURDAY AFTER EPIPHANY

First Reading: *1 John 5:14-21*
Responsorial Psalm: *Ps 149:1-2,3-4,5-6a&9b*
Gospel Reading: *Luke 3:22-30*

Source: Congregação Oblatos de Maria Virgen – "Presença"

OUR LADY OF TEARS
Rome, Italy (1546)

In 1546, in a street fight near the shrine of the Madonna del Portico d'Ottavia near the Roman Ghetto, one man begged another to spare his life for love of the Virgin Mary, then stabbed him in the back when he hugged him in forgiveness. The image wept three days. The 15th-century fresco was then moved into the nearby church of San Salvatore de Cacabariis. In 1612 church reconstruction began, and in 1616 the image was reinstalled and the church rededicated to the Weeping Madonna. The image of Mother and Child was crowned on May 20, 1643.

BAPTISM OF THE LORD

First Reading: *Isaiah 55:1-11*
Responsorial Psalm: *Ps 12:2-3.4bcd.5-6(3)*
Second Reading: *1 John 5:1-9*
Gospel Reading: *Mark 1:7-11*

JANUARY 2016

s	m	t	w	t	f	s
					1	2
3	4	5	6	7	8	9
10	11	12	13	14	15	16
17	18	19	20	21	22	23
24	25	26	27	28	29	30
31						

January
monday

11

OUR LADY OF VETRANA
Castellana Grotte, Italy (1691)

In Castellana, a small town located on the side of a basin in the south-east of Murge, there was a small chapel with a miraculous fresco of the Mother of God credited with freeing the region of the plague in the seventeenth century. Since then she has been called "the Ventrana".

Since the end of the plague, the shrine has become a destination for the faithful and pilgrims who continually come to venerate the sacred image. The miracles of the Virgin Vetrana obtained from her Divine Son are numerous throughout the ages.

Source: Flickr - Magno Alessandro: "Madonna della Vetrana, Castellana Grotte"

JANUARY 2016

s	m	t	w	t	f	s
					1	2
3	4	5	6	7	8	9
10	11	12	13	14	15	16
17	18	19	20	21	22	23
24	25	26	27	28	29	30
31						

1ST WEEK IN ORDINARY TIME

First Reading: *1 Samuel 1:1-8*
Responsorial Psalm: *Ps 116:12-13, 14-17, 18-19*
Gospel Reading: *Mark 1:14-20*

Source: Gazzetta di Foligno Online - Foligno, "Città della Madonna"

OUR LADY OF THE TEARS
Foligno, Italy (1646)

In 1646, in a dispute between two individuals occurring in the street under an image of the Madonna with Child, one man pleaded that his life be spared in the name of the Virgin Mary depicted there, but the other replied in a completely different way, mortally wounding him, at which point the Madonna began to cry. The devotion spread far and wide. A wooden statue, kept in the current sanctuary in the church of St. Augustine, after the original Shrine of Our Lady of Tears was destroyed during the disastrous bombing of the allies in 1944 on the city. From the 17th century to today her feast is celebrated on the Sunday before the feast of St. Anthony Abbot in the month of January.

1ST WEEK IN ORDINARY TIME

First Reading: *1 Samuel 1:9-20*
Responsorial Psalm: *1 Samuel 2:1, 4-5, 6-7, 8ABCD*
Gospel Reading: *Mark 1:21-28*

JANUARY 2016

s	m	t	w	t	f	s
					1	2
3	4	5	6	7	8	9
10	11	12	13	14	15	16
17	18	19	20	21	22	23
24	25	26	27	28	29	30
31						

January
wednesday
13

OUR LADY, HELP OF CHRISTIANS
Filippsdorf, Germany (1866)

Filippsdorf is a pilgrimage site in the north of Bohemia. In this town there lived a weaver by the name of Magdalena Kade (1835 - 1903) who was in 1866 very ill. On January 13th at 4 a.m. the Blessed Virgin Mary appeared to her and promised her healing. The next day she was miraculously cured and lived a healthy life for many years. Her house was given the title of 'Gnadenhaus' (house of Grace) due to the visit of the Virgin Mary and became visited by so many pilgrims that a 'Gnadenkapelle' (chapel of grace) was built which was later replaced by a monumental church under the title of Maria, Helferin der Christen (Mary, Help of Christians) which was later made a Minor Basilica.

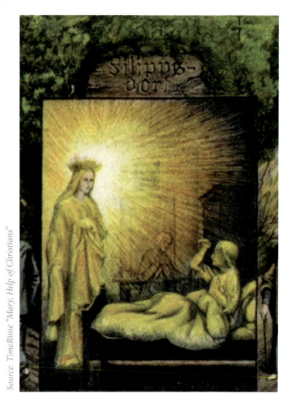

Source: TimeRine "Mary, Help of Christians"

JANUARY 2016

s	m	t	w	t	f	s
					1	2
3	4	5	6	7	8	9
10	11	12	13	14	15	16
17	18	19	20	21	22	23
24	25	26	27	28	29	30
31						

1ST WEEK IN ORDINARY TIME

First Reading: *1 Samuel 3:1-10, 19-20*
Responsorial Psalm: *Ps 40:2 AND 5, 7-8A, 8B-9, 10*
Gospel Reading: *Mark 1:29-39*

Source: Wikipedia (Spanish) - "Divina Pastora de las Almas"

January
thursday
14

THE DIVINE PASTORESS
Santa Rosa, Venezuela (1736)

Around 1736, the pastor of Santa Rosa Catholic Church in central Venezuela, ordered a statue of the Immaculate Conception, but instead received a Holy Shepherdess statue ordered by a nearby church. He immediately tried to forward the statue along to its proper destination, but it suddenly became so heavy that it was immovable. And so Santa Rosa kept the Divina Pastora, who became the patron saint of the state of Lara. On January 14, 1855, the statue was carried in procession during a cholera epidemic, which ended that day. Now every January 14, statues of the Holy Shepherdess, Child Jesus and sheep are carried in a large procession to the cathedral.

JANUARY 2016

s	m	t	w	t	f	s
					1	2
3	4	5	6	7	8	9
10	11	12	13	14	15	16
17	18	19	20	21	22	23
24	25	26	27	28	29	30
31						

1ST WEEK IN ORDINARY TIME

First Reading: *1 Samuel 4:1-11*
Responsorial Psalm: *Ps 44:10-11, 14-15, 24-25*
Gospel Reading: *Mark 1:40-45*

January
friday
15

OUR LADY OF THE POOR
Banneux, Belgium
(1933)

In a garden behind the Beco family's cottage, the Blessed Mother is said to have appeared to Mariette Beco (age 11) eight times. Calling herself the "Virgin of the Poor," Mary promised to intercede for the poor, the sick and the suffering. In her final apparition she declared "I am the Mother of the Saviour, the Mother of God. Pray very much". Then she imposed her hands on Mariette's head and blessed her with the sign of the cross. She said, "Adieu - till we meet in God." After 14 years of investigation, the apparitions were officially approved by the Church in 1949. In 1985, Pope John Paul II went to Banneux and had an audience with Mariette at the sacristy.

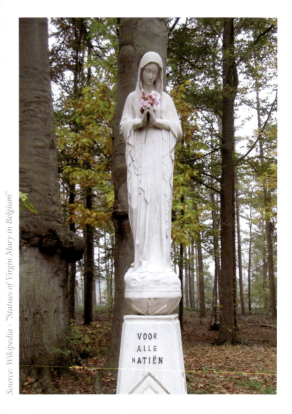

Source: Wikipedia - "Statues of Virgin Mary in Belgium"

JANUARY 2016

s	m	t	w	t	f	s
					1	2
3	4	5	6	7	8	9
10	11	12	13	14	15	16
17	18	19	20	21	22	23
24	25	26	27	28	29	30
31						

1ST WEEK IN ORDINARY TIME

First Reading: *1 Samuel 8:4-7, 10-22A*
Responsorial Psalm: *Ps 89:16-17, 18-19*
Gospel Reading: *Mark 2:1-12*

Source: Paróquia Nossa Senhora das Vitórias

January
saturday
16

OUR LADY OF VICTORY, REFUGE OF SINNERS
Paris, France (1628)

In 1628 in thanksgiving for his successes in capturing the city of La Rochelle, King Louis XIII funded the construction of a new Augustinian monastery in Paris. In it was a chapel dedicated to Our Lady of Victory containing a statue of the Virgin with crown and scepter, carved from the miraculous oak of Montaigue.

Half a century later, the church's name was expanded when a chapel was added under the title Refuge of Sinnersin 1674. January 16, became the sanctuary's patronal feast of Our Lady, Refuge of Sinners. Pope Pius IX gave the instruction for the crowning of the chapel In 1853.

1ST WEEK IN ORDINARY TIME

First Reading: *1 Samuel 9:1-4, 17-19; 10:1*
Responsorial Psalm: *Ps 21:2-3, 4-5, 6-7*
Gospel Reading: *Mark 2:13-17*

JANUARY 2016

s	m	t	w	t	f	s
					1	2
3	4	5	6	7	8	9
10	11	12	13	14	15	16
17	18	19	20	21	22	23
24	25	26	27	28	29	30
31						

January

sunday

17

OUR LADY OF PRAYER
Pontmain, France (1871)

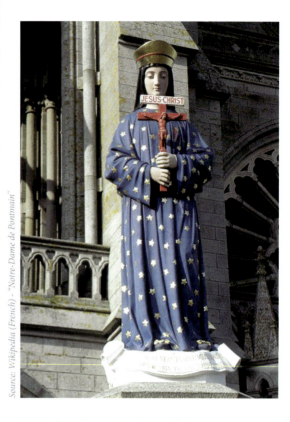

During the devastation of the Franco-Prussian War, Mary appeared on a farm to students at the nearby convent school. Mary's message was written on a banner that unfurled from her feet: "But pray my children. God will hear you in a short time. My Son allows Himself to be moved by compassion." Our Lady wore a blue robe embroidered with numerous golden stars. On her head she had a black veil and a gold crown and on her feet blue shoes with gold ribbons. The apparition was motionless at first for the initial two hours. After the Rosary began to be prayed, a small red cross appeared over heart and a blue oval frame with four candles appeared around her while the stars in her robe seemed to increase. The Bishop of Laval, recognized the authenticity of the apparition in 1872.

JANUARY 2016

s	m	t	w	t	f	s
					1	2
3	4	5	6	7	8	9
10	11	12	13	14	15	16
17	18	19	20	21	22	23
24	25	26	27	28	29	30
31						

2ND SUNDAY IN ORDINARY TIME

First Reading: *Isaiah 62:1-5*
Responsorial Psalm: *Ps 96:1-2, 2-3, 7-8, 9-10*
Second Reading: *1 Corinthians 12:4-11*
Gospel Reading: *John 2:1-11*

Source: Roman Catholic Saints - "Our Lady of Zapopan"

OUR LADY OF THE EXPECTATION OF ZAPOPAN
Mexico (1541)

The Virgin of Zapopan is venerated as the Patron of Jalisco state and the city of Guadalajara, and is likewise recognized throughout all Mexico. Franciscan Fray Antonio de Segovia, who had baptized thousands of Indians in the years following the miraculous Guadalupan events, in 1541 gave the statue to the new mission of Nuestra Señora de la Concepción de Zapopan near present-day Guadalajara. After she interceded for the region with the plague of 1653, popular piety increased. Wearing the sky-blue sash of a nineteenth-century general with a scepter and staff, she is known as La Generala. On January 18, 1921, Archbishop Francisco Orozco y Jiménez crowned her Queen of Jalisco. Her feast day is October 12.

JANUARY 2016

s	m	t	w	t	f	s
					1	2
3	4	5	6	7	8	9
10	11	12	13	14	15	16
17	18	19	20	21	22	23
24	25	26	27	28	29	30
31						

2ND WEEK IN ORDINARY TIME

First Reading: *1 Samuel 15:16-23*
Responsorial Psalm: *Ps 50:8-9, 16BC-17, 21 AND 23*
Gospel Reading: *Mark 2:18-22*

January
tuesday
19

MOST HOLY MARY OF THE QUARRY
Marsala, Italy
(16th c.)

On January 19 Marsala commemorates the anniversary of the finding of the statue of St. Mary of the Quarry in the early 1500s, after four years of digging under Father Leonardo Savina, who was given an insight in a dream that an ancient image was buried in a grotto. When the statue finally was discovered a number of miraculous healings quickly occurred. The Madonna became patron of the city, and the grotto turned into a popular place of worship and prayer. When a bomb destroyed the church May 11, 1943, the statue remained intact.

Source: Marsala Turismo - "Chiesa dell'Addolorata a Marsala"

JANUARY 2016

s	m	t	w	t	f	s
					1	2
3	4	5	6	7	8	9
10	11	12	13	14	15	16
17	18	19	20	21	22	23
24	25	26	27	28	29	30
31						

2ND WEEK IN ORDINARY TIME

First Reading: *1 Samuel 16:1-13*
Responsorial Psalm: *Ps 89:20, 21-22, 27-28*
Gospel Reading: *Mark 2:23-28*

Source: Catholic Tradition - "From Ratisbonne to Reflections"

January
wednesday
20

OUR LADY OF THE MIRACLE
Rome, Italy (1842)

Marie Alphonse Ratisbonne, an anti-Catholic Jew, befriended a baron during his travels in Rome and began wearing the Miraculous Medal as a simple challenge. On January 20, 1842 while waiting for the baron in the church Sant Andrea delle Fratte, Ratisbonne encountered a vision of Our Lady and soon after converted to Catholicism, later becoming a priest and establishing a religious community devoted to the conversion of the Jews.

The following month, the Vatican held a canonical investigation after many depositions, it concluded that his sudden conversion was entirely miraculous; an act of God wrought through the powerful intercession of the Virgin.

2ND WEEK IN ORDINARY TIME

First Reading: *1 Samuel 17:32-33, 37, 40-51*
Responsorial Psalm: *Ps 144:1B, 2, 9-10*
Gospel Reading: *Mark 3:1-6*

JANUARY 2016

s	m	t	w	t	f	s
					1	2
3	4	5	6	7	8	9
10	11	12	13	14	15	16
17	18	19	20	21	22	23
24	25	26	27	28	29	30
31						

January
thursday
21

VIRGIN OF HIGH GRACE
Higuey, Dominican Republic (16th c.)

In the early 1500s, Spanish gentlemen Alonso and Antonio de Trexo built haciendas near the new town of Salvaleón de Higüey, on the island of Hispaniola, some 100 miles from Santo Domingo. They brought with them a 13" x 18" painting on linen, called the Virgin of Highgrace after a beloved standing statue from their homeland of Altagracia in Extremadura. The brothers gifted this painting to the church of the town, where its reputation for miracles attracted the attention of the Archbishop, who had it carried to Santo Domingo in a sealed trunk. But it disappeared en route, reappearing at the same time in Higüey church, where it has stayed. Travelers passing through the port of Higüey would stop to ask Our Lady of High Grace to protect them.

Source: Wikipedia (Spanish) - "Basílica de Higüey"

JANUARY 2016

s	m	t	w	t	f	s
					1	2
3	4	5	6	7	8	9
10	11	12	13	14	15	16
17	18	19	20	21	22	23
24	25	26	27	28	29	30
31						

2ND WEEK IN ORDINARY TIME
Memorial of Saint Agnes, Virgin and Martyr

First Reading: *1 Samuel 18:6-9; 19:1-7*
Responsorial Psalm: *Ps 56:2-3, 9-10A, 10B-11, 12-13*
Gospel Reading: *Mark 3:7-12*

Source: CAIDV Aragua - "Ahora Le Toco A San Sebastián"

January
friday
22

OUR LADY OF CHARITY
San Sebastián de los Reyes, Venezuela (1692)

Military leader Luis Jiménez de Rojas brought an image of Our Lady of Charity from Spain for the chapel at his hacienda El Chaparral, now the town of San Juan de los Morros in the state of Guarico. In 1691, the hacienda burned down.

The picture of Our Lady was found in the ruins, intact, with its lamp still burning. This generated a surge of popular devotion, and on January 22, 1692, the Bishop of Caracas installed the image in the village church of San Sebastian de los Reyes and authorized the construction of a sanctuary completed in 1725. On every January 22nd, a morning procession takes place through the streets of the town.

2ND WEEK IN ORDINARY TIME
Day of Prayer for the Legal Protection of Unborn Children

First Reading: *1 Samuel 24:3-21*
Responsorial Psalm: *Ps 57:2, 3-4, 6 AND 11*
Gospel Reading: *Mark 3:13-19*

JANUARY 2016

s	m	t	w	t	f	s
					1	2
3	4	5	6	7	8	9
10	11	12	13	14	15	16
17	18	19	20	21	22	23
24	25	26	27	28	29	30
31						

January
saturday
23

OUR LADY OF PERIANAYAGI
Konankuppam, India
(17th c.)

Source: Foros de La Virgen - "Nuestra Señora de Grondici, India"

During the 17th century, Fr. Beschi, a Jesuit missionary popularly known as "Veeramamunivar", brought two statues of Mother Mary to Elakurichi. Passing through the forest, he fell asleep under a tree. Children who were grazing their cattle playfully hid one of the statues behind a bush. Later the Virgin appeared in a dream to a childless man called Kachirayar from Konankuppam and told him to build a chapel where he finds a statue of her. If he did this, she said, he would be blessed with a child. Kachirayar searched and found the statue. He built a chapel on the spot. The miracle happened as he had dreamt: his wife gave birth to a child.

JANUARY 2016

s	m	t	w	t	f	s
					1	2
3	4	5	6	7	8	9
10	11	12	13	14	15	16
17	18	19	20	21	22	23
24	25	26	27	28	29	30
31						

2ND WEEK IN ORDINARY TIME

First Reading: *2 Samuel 1:1-4, 11-12, 19, 23-27*
Responsorial Psalm: *Ps 80:2-3, 5-7*
Gospel Reading: *Mark 3:20-21*

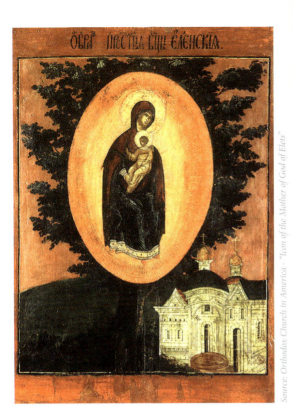

Source: Orthodox Church in America – "Icon of the Mother of God of Elets"

ICON OF THE MOTHER OF GOD OF ELETS
Russia (1060)

The Elets Icon of the Mother of God appeared in the year 1060. It received its name because it appeared in a cathedral church dedicated to the Smolensk Icon of the Mother of God in the city of Elets, Orlov province. January 11 (on the old Orthodox calendar and January 24th on the new) was established as the feast day of this icon.

3RD SUNDAY IN ORDINARY TIME

First Reading: *Nehemiah 8:2-4A, 5-6, 8-10*
Responsorial Psalm: *Ps 19:8, 9, 10, 15*
Second Reading: *1 Corinthians 12:12-30*
Gospel Reading: *Luke 1:1-4; 4:14-21*

JANUARY 2016

s	m	t	w	t	f	s
					1	2
3	4	5	6	7	8	9
10	11	12	13	14	15	16
17	18	19	20	21	22	23
24	25	26	27	28	29	30
31						

January
monday
25

ICON OF THE MOTHER OF GOD THE "MILKGIVER"
Kidron Valley, Palestine (13th c.)

The "Milk-Giver" Icon of the Mother of God was originally located at the Lavra of St Sava near Jerusalem. Before his death, he foretold that a royal pilgrim having the same name as himself would visit the Lavra. St Sava told the brethren to give the wonderworking icon to that pilgrim as a blessing.

In the thirteenth century, St Sava of Serbia visited the Lavra. As he approached the reliquary of the founder, the brethren asked the visitor his name, and he told them he was Archbishop Sava of Serbia. Obeying the instructions of their founder, the monks gave St Sava the "Milk-Giver" Icon.

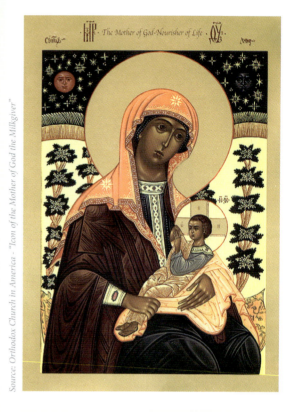

JANUARY 2016

s	m	t	w	t	f	s
					1	2
3	4	5	6	7	8	9
10	11	12	13	14	15	16
17	18	19	20	21	22	23
24	25	26	27	28	29	30
31						

3RD WEEK IN ORDINARY TIME
Feast of the Conversion of Saint Paul, Apostle

First Reading: *Acts 22:3-16 or Acts 9:1-22*
Responsorial Psalm: *Ps 117:1BC, 2*
Gospel Reading: *Mark 16:15-18*

Source: Facebook "Madre Amada Ntra. Sra. de Belén."

January
tuesday
26

OUR LADY OF BETHLEHEM
Tumeremo, Venezuela (1788)

Despite the governor's orders, on January 26, 1788, Catalan Capuchin friars set up a mission in Venezuela on the eastern border. The settlement was dedicated to Our Lady of Bethlehem as its patron. Around 1880, a statue was installed by the friars of the Virgin and Child in the church of Our Lady of Bethlehem.

Now, a newer statue is processed through the streets during the annual fiesta on January 26, while the original remains above the central altar of the parish church. The week-long festivities, lasting over a week, culminate in a solemn mass, procession, and consecration to the Virgin on the anniversary date of the founding of the mission.

JANUARY 2016

s	m	t	w	t	f	s
					1	2
3	4	5	6	7	8	9
10	11	12	13	14	15	16
17	18	19	20	21	22	23
24	25	26	27	28	29	30
31						

3RD WEEK IN ORDINARY TIME
Timothy & Titus, Bishops - Memorial

First Reading: *2 Timothy 1:1-8*
Responsorial Psalm: *Ps 96:1-2a,2b-3.7-8a.10*
Gospel Reading: *Mark 3:31-35*

January
wednesday
27

OUR LADY OF THE PILLAR
Castenaso, Italy
(1699)

A painting in 1672 of Our Lady of the Pillar, the famous miracle of the Black Virgin appearing to the apostle St. James in Saragossa, Spain was placed in small town of Castenaso's chapel. On January 27, 1699, Maria Maddalena Azzaroni quickly passed by the chapel on her way to her aunt's house to ask for some oil. She normally would stop to say a brief prayer there - but not this time. She heard a voice saying "Maria Maddalena, have you given up your devotions to the Madonna?" and went back. The Virgin Mary stepped out of the painting with arms outstretched and asked for the girl's faithful devotion. The Church approved this prodigious event four years later and a sanctuary was constructed. Maddalena entered a convent sometime later.

Source: Foros de La Virgen - "Nuestra Señora del Pilar de Castenaso, Italia"

JANUARY 2016

s	m	t	w	t	f	s
					1	2
3	4	5	6	7	8	9
10	11	12	13	14	15	16
17	18	19	20	21	22	23
24	25	26	27	28	29	30
31						

3RD WEEK IN ORDINARY TIME

First Reading: *2 Samuel 7:4-17*
Responsorial Psalm: *Ps 89:4-5, 27-28, 29-30*
Gospel Reading: *Mark 4:1-20*

Source: Blogspot-Infallible Catholic "The Blessed Virgin Mary - The New Ark of the Covenant"

OUR LADY OF THE GREEN SCAPULAR
Blangy-Versailles, France (1840)

Nine years after St. Catherine Laboure, the Blessed Virgin Mary appeared to Sister Justina Bisqueyburu in the same convent, holding the Immaculate Heart illuminated in her hands and gave her the Green Scapular. On two subsequent occasions, this vision of the Green Scapular was repeated and she realized that she must tell everything to her spiritual director. Scapulars began to be manufactured and distributed by the Sisters in Paris, then across France when formal approval was received from Pope Pius IX in 1870. The square of cloth tied with green laces has an image of the Virgin holding her Immaculate Heart in her right hand just as she appeared to Sister Justyna.

JANUARY 2016

s	m	t	w	t	f	s
					1	2
3	4	5	6	7	8	9
10	11	12	13	14	15	16
17	18	19	20	21	22	23
24	25	26	27	28	29	30
31						

3RD WEEK IN ORDINARY TIME
Saint Thomas Aquinas - Memorial

First Reading: *2 Samuel 7:18-19, 24-29*
Responsorial Psalm: *Ps 132:1-2, 3-5, 11, 12, 13-14*
Gospel Reading: *MK 4:21-25*

January
friday
29

OUR LADY OF THE IMPOSSIBLE
Serra Lima, Brazil (1758)

In the eighteenth century, around 1758, Colonel Antonio Ferreira de Lima, along with Abreu Ferreira and his wife, brought from Portugal an image of Nossa Senhora dos Impossíveis (Our Lady of the Impossible) and made donated land to build a shrine in honor of Our Lady of the Impossible.

Currently, the shrine holds the honorary title of 13th Basilica of Brazil and is considered one of the seven wonders of the state of Rio Grande do Norte and one of the largest places of pilgrimage in Northeast Brazil.

Source: Igreja Catolica "Orações a Nossa Senhora"

JANUARY 2016

s	m	t	w	t	f	s
					1	2
3	4	5	6	7	8	9
10	11	12	13	14	15	16
17	18	19	20	21	22	23
24	25	26	27	28	29	30
31						

3RD WEEK IN ORDINARY TIME

First Reading: *2 Samuel 1:1-4A, 5-10A, 13-17*
Responsorial Psalm: *Ps 51:3-4, 5-6A, 6BCD-7, 10-11*
Gospel Reading: *Mark 4:26-34*

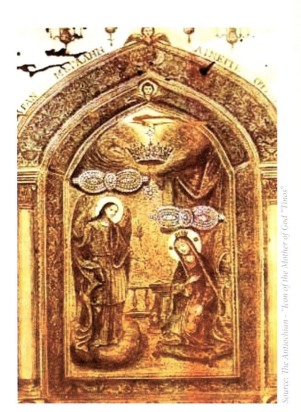

Source: The Antiochian - "Icon of the Mother of God "Tinos"

PANAGIA EVANGELISTRIA
Tinos, Greece (1823)

Pelagia, a nun, experienced apparitions in 1822 of Our Lady telling her where to search for an icon to be the place of a future shrine to be erected there in her name on the island of Tinos. At the instruction of the priest who heard Pelagia's story, the townspeople on January 30, 1823 finally uncovered an ancient icon of the Annunciation. The church of Megalokhari (Great Joys) was built to house the miraculous icon and provide a place for the many pilgrims who arrive to celebrate the icon's discovery even during the harsh winter weather of the Aegean. Community leaders after the Eucharist carry the holy icon on a gold and silver pedestal to the sound of bells throughout the city, which is decorated for a festival.

3RD WEEK IN ORDINARY TIME

First Reading: *2 Samuel 12:1-7A, 10-17*
Responsorial Psalm: *Ps 51:12-13, 14-15, 16-17*
Gospel Reading: *Mark 4:35-41*

JANUARY 2016

s	m	t	w	t	f	s
					1	2
3	4	5	6	7	8	9
10	11	12	13	14	15	16
17	18	19	20	21	22	23
24	25	26	27	28	29	30
31						

January
sunday

31

OUR LADY OF HOPE
Cidade da Esperança, Brazil (1966)

The image of Our Lady of Hope was brought by explorer Pedro Álvares Cabral when he discovered Brazil in his travels to the Indies. in 1500, the first Masses were said on Brazilian soil near a large cross and image of the Mother of Hope. A replica statue was placed in the Brasilia Cathedral as well as in 11 other parishes claiming her as patron at the time of founding of Cidade da Esperança. Begun on January 31, 1966, Cidade da Esperança was the nation's first public housing development, and was emulated by those in other states. A church dedicated to Our Lady of Hope was constructed and celebrates its patronal feast on the date of the inauguration of the community.

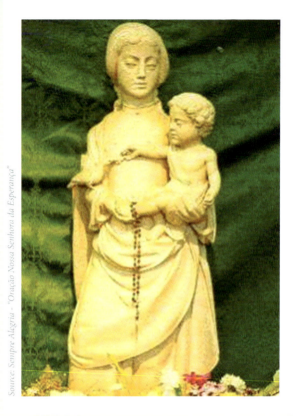

Source: Sempre Alegria - "Oração Nossa Senhora da Esperança"

JANUARY 2016

s	m	t	w	t	f	s
					1	2
3	4	5	6	7	8	9
10	11	12	13	14	15	16
17	18	19	20	21	22	23
24	25	26	27	28	29	30
31						

4TH SUNDAY IN ORDINARY TIME

First Reading: *Jeremiah 1:4-5, 17-19*
Responsorial Psalm: *Ps 71:1-2, 3-4, 5-6, 15-17*
Second Reading: *1 Corinthians 12:31—13:13*
Gospel Reading: *Luke 4:21-30*

Source: Diakonima "The value and the power of prayer Salutations"

PANAGIA PARAMYTHIA
Kykko, Cyprus (1997)

Both figures - Virgin and Child - were seen to be weeping by a novice monk on the icon of Panagia Paramythia, the All-Holy Consoler, in Kykko monastery, Cyprus on February 1, 1997. Tears flowing down their faces were observed for a month by many people, both monks and the faithful. A 14th century copy of the one in Vatopedi Monastery on Mt. Athos, the icon was originally in the Monastery of the Virgin of Helicon three miles north, abandoned around 1800 and now in ruins. The icon is located near the Kykkiotissa, the famed wonderworking icon of Kykko Monastery, believed in pious tradition to have been painted by St. Luke. The tears were interpreted by both the Abbot and Archbishop to be a call from God to repentance.

4TH WEEK IN ORDINARY TIME

First Reading: *2 Samuel 15:13-14, 30; 16:5-13*
Responsorial Psalm: *Ps 3:2-3, 4-5, 6-7*
Gospel Reading: *Mark 5:1-20*

FEBRUARY 2016

s	m	t	w	t	f	s
	1	2	3	4	5	6
7	8	9	10	11	12	13
14	15	16	17	18	19	20
21	22	23	24	25	26	27
28	29					

February
tuesday

2

OUR LADY OF GOOD SUCCESS
Quito, Ecuador
(1610)

Spanish-born Conceptionist sister Ven. Mariana de Jésus Torres was praying and saw a vision of the Blessed Mother who made prophecies regarding the worldwide crisis in the Church and society that would begin in the 19th century and extend throughout the 20th century. Truly religious souls would be reduced to a small number and many vocations would perish. Great impurity would reign and people would be without any care for spiritual matters.

Our Lady commanded that a statue be made to her likeness under the title of Good Success. The statue was begun by a sculptor and completed by angels according to legend. The statue was blessed on February 2, 1611.

Source: Wikipedia "Our Lady of Good Success"

FEBRUARY 2016

s	m	t	w	t	f	s
	1	2	3	4	5	6
7	8	9	10	11	12	13
14	15	16	17	18	19	20
21	22	23	24	25	26	27
28	29					

4ᵀᴴ WEEK IN ORDINARY TIME
Feast of the Presentation of the Lord

First Reading: *Malachi 3: 1-4*
Responsorial Psalm: *Ps 24: 7.8.9.10*
Second Reading: *Hebrews 2: 14-18*
Gospel Reading: *Luke 2: 22-40*

Source: *Seminario FIDES "Novena a nuestra Señora de Suyapa"*

3

VIRGIN OF SUYAPA
Honduras (1747)

The tiny image of Our Lady of the Conception of Suyapa was found by a humble young peasant in 1747. Two young field workers were half way home in the dark when they realized that they should spend the night and tried to rest on the hard ground. Finding an uncomfortable object on his back, he picked it up and threw it far away. Strangely enough, he tried to sleep again and felt the object again and instead he put it away in his knapsack. At day break he discovered that the mysterious object was a small image of Our Lady carved in cedar wood.

In 1925, Pius XI declared Our Lady of Suyapa patroness of the Republic of Honduras, and February 3 was chosen as her feast day with proper Mass and office. The first shrine was blessed in 1780.

4TH WEEK IN ORDINARY TIME

First Reading: *2 Samuel 24:2, 9-17*
Responsorial Psalm: *Ps 32:1-2, 5, 6, 7*
Gospel Reading: *Mark 6:1-6*

FEBRUARY 2016

s	m	t	w	t	f	s
	1	2	3	4	5	6
7	8	9	10	11	12	13
14	15	16	17	18	19	20
21	22	23	24	25	26	27
28	29					

February

thursday

4

OUR LADY OF THE FIRE
Forlì, Italy (1428)

A fire broke out in a school in Forlì during the night of February 3 - 4, 1428, and burned for a few days. A favorite image of the school children, an wooden icon of the Virgin and Child was found to be unburnt amidst the ashes. The miraculous image was placed in the cathedral the next Sunday by order of the governor and the papal legate. A side aisle chapel in the cathedral was built in 1636 from marble and dedicated to Our Lady of Fire. This image became famous throughout the region with reproductions found on doorways as a protection against fire.

The Madonna of Fire is the patron of Forlì, where her festa lasts from February 4 to the nearest Sunday. In celebration the city is covered with fiery yellow acacias, and sweet bread with raisins is a popular treat sold throughout the city.

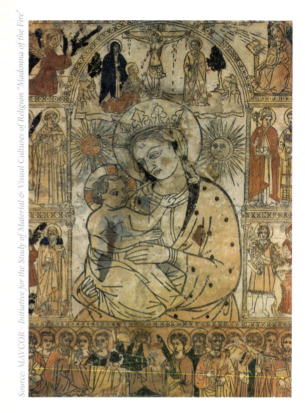

FEBRUARY 2016

s	m	t	w	t	f	s
	1	2	3	4	5	6
7	8	9	10	11	12	13
14	15	16	17	18	19	20
21	22	23	24	25	26	27
28	29					

4TH WEEK IN ORDINARY TIME

First Reading: *1 Kings 2:1-4, 10-12*
Responsorial Psalm: *1 Chronicles 29:10, 11AB, 11D-12A*
Gospel Reading: *Mark 6:7-13*

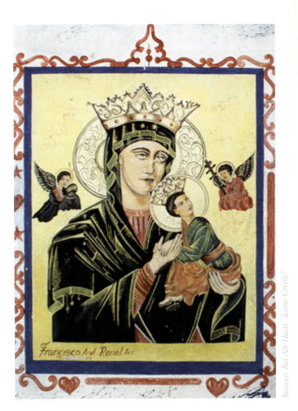

Source: Bel Air Haiti "Icone Creole"

Francisco And Revel fter

February
friday

5

OUR LADY OF PERPETUAL HELP
Port-au-Prince, Haiti (1882)

A replica of the famous icon of Rome was installed in St. Francis' Church in Port-au-Prince and processed to a hill above the city suffering from a smallpox epidemic. February 5, 1882, the date of the procession, was the end of the epidemic. In 2007, the 125th anniversary of her miraculous intervention was celebrated on February 5. The National Shrine of Our Lady of Perpetual Help was the church in Bel Air as designated by the Haitian Catholic Bishops' Conference, but was destroyed in a 2010 earthquake. On December 8, 2010, the bishops of Haiti renewed the country's consecration to her. Our Lady of Perpetual Help became the official Patroness of Haiti in 1942 and her feast day is celebrated on June 27.

4ᵀᴴ WEEK IN ORDINARY TIME

First Reading: *Sirach 47:2-11*
Responsorial Psalm: *Ps 18:31, 47 AND 50, 51*
Gospel Reading: *Mark 6:14-29*

FEBRUARY 2016

s	m	t	w	t	f	s
	1	2	3	4	5	6
7	8	9	10	11	12	13
14	15	16	17	18	19	20
21	22	23	24	25	26	27
28	29					

February
saturday

6

MOTHER OF CONSECRATED SOULS
Carrizales, Venezuela (1993)

Three nuns of the Servants of Jesus Convent, along with a praying family in attendance, claimed to see for several hours on February 6, 1993 from the evening until morning a vision of the Virgin Mary illuminated in blue light on a banana tree. Following the vision, there were two instances of colors sent from heaven as a sign: the next day, silver frost covered the garden and a colorful substance coated convent interior. On February 19 the Virgin appeared again under the title of "Mother of the Consecrated Souls" and again the frost-like substance appeared on the property. A subsequent investigation did not establish the events as supernatural, but the Bishop of Los Teques authorized public devotion at the chapel in 1998.

Source: Obituarios de Venezuela "Virgen María madre de las almas consagradas"

FEBRUARY 2016

s	m	t	w	t	f	s
	1	2	3	4	5	6
7	8	9	10	11	12	13
14	15	16	17	18	19	20
21	22	23	24	25	26	27
28	29					

4TH WEEK IN ORDINARY TIME

First Reading: *1 Kings 3:4-13*
Responsorial Psalm: *Ps 119:9, 10, 11, 12, 13, 14*
Gospel Reading: *Mark 6:30-34*

Source: Salesians Don Bosco • "MADONNA DELLA APORIA IN GUASTALLA"

February
sunday
7

MOST HOLY VIRGIN MARY OF THE GATE
Guastalla, Italy (1693)

In 1646, on the walls surrounding the city of Guastalla, an artist painted near the barracks of the guards of the entrance into the city, an image known as the Madonna della Porta with the infant Jesus in her arms with St. Francis of Assisi and St. Charles Borromeo at her side. Eventually the walls were torn down with only the section with the old fresco remaining.

On February 7, 1693, Giambattista Zagni of Solapur, became seriously ill and faithfully beseeched Our Lady with a candle. Suddenly he was healed and news traveled quickly and soon other favors and graces followed. A regular canonical process recognized these facts and the image was later canonically crowned by decree of Pope Pius X.

5TH SUNDAY IN ORDINARY TIME

First Reading: *Isaiah 6:1-2A, 3-8*
Responsorial Psalm: *Ps 138:1-2, 2-3, 4-5, 7-8*
Second Reading: *1 Corinthians 15:1-11*
Gospel Reading: *Luke 5:1-11*

FEBRUARY 2016

s	m	t	w	t	f	s
	1	2	3	4	5	6
7	8	9	10	11	12	13
14	15	16	17	18	19	20
21	22	23	24	25	26	27
28	29					

February
monday

8

BLESSED VIRGIN OF THE CASTLE
Fiorano, Italy
(13th c.)

In the 1400s, an image of the Madonna and Child was painted above the entrance of Fiorano Castle. The fortress was destroyed in 1510, but the painting of the Blessed Virgin remained intact, and a town arose in the ruins.

On February 8, 1558, when Spanish troops set fire to the town, the flames, on reaching the image of Mary, divided so as not to harm it. So began the great devotion of the people of Fiorano for their Madonna, reinforced later by their liberation from the plague of 1630, which led to the building of the beautiful Sanctuary to the Virgin in thanksgiving. The Virgin of the Castle is celebrated on September 8, feast of the Nativity of the Virgin.

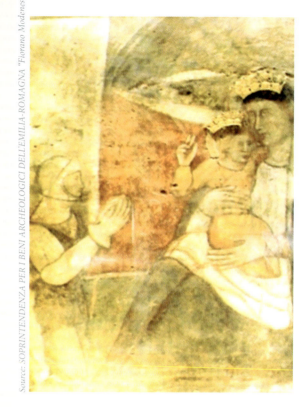

FEBRUARY 2016

s	m	t	w	t	f	s
	1	2	3	4	5	6
7	8	9	10	11	12	13
14	15	16	17	18	19	20
21	22	23	24	25	26	27
28	29					

5TH WEEK IN ORDINARY TIME

First Reading: *1 Kings 8:1-7, 9-13*
Responsorial Psalm: *Ps 132:6-7, 8-10*
Gospel Reading: *Mark 6:53-56*

Source: El Centinela de Ceuta "VIRGEN DE AFRICA, PATRONA DE CEUTA"

February
tuesday

9

VIRGIN OF ÁFRICA
Ceuta, Spain (1651)

The pietà statue of the Virgin of Africa, patron of the Spanish city of Ceuta in north Africa, is the subject of a legend that after Emperor Justinian gave it to governor Procopius, it was hidden underground during the Muslim period (c. 711-1415) and then found illuminated on a hill. More likely, Henry the Navigator sent it to Ceuta after conquering the city for Portugal. On February 9, 1651, a plague ended when the statue was processed. In accordance with a vow, officials process annually on this date to the Iglesia de África for a thanksgiving mass and floral offering. The main feast day of the Virgin of Africa is August 5. The statue was canonically crowned on November 10, 1946. The Virgin of Africa was declared patron of Ceuta on November 24, 1949, and proclaimed Mayor on March 5, 1954.

5TH WEEK IN ORDINARY TIME

First Reading: *1 Kings 8:22-23, 27-30*
Responsorial Psalm: *Ps 84:3, 4, 5 AND 10, 11*
Gospel Reading: *Mark 7:1-13*

FEBRUARY 2016

s	m	t	w	t	f	s
	1	2	3	4	5	6
7	8	9	10	11	12	13
14	15	16	17	18	19	20
21	22	23	24	25	26	27
28	29					

February
wednesday
10

ICON OF THE MOTHER OF GOD OF SUMORIN
Totma, Russia (1554)

Source: Russian Orthodox Cathedral of St. John the Baptist, Washington, D.C. "The Totma-Sumorin Icon"

The Sumorin Totma Icon of the Mother of God became renowned for numerous healings at the Spaso-Sumorin monastery of the city of Totma. In the year 1554 St. Theodosius received the grant for building a church.

The icon thereafter received the name Sumorin Totma (Sumorin is the family name of St. Theodosius, and Totma is a city). After the death of the monk, the wonderworking icon was put in a case in front of the crypt of the saint at the Ascension church of the monastery.

St Theodosius has appeared to many of the sick, holding this icon in his hands.

FEBRUARY 2016

s	m	t	w	t	f	s
	1	2	3	4	5	6
7	8	9	10	11	12	13
14	15	16	17	18	19	20
21	22	23	24	25	26	27
28	29					

ASH WEDNESDAY

First Reading: *Joel 2:12-18*
Responsorial Psalm: *Ps 51:3-4, 5-6AB, 12-13, 14 AND 17*
Second Reading: *2 Corinthians 5:20—6:2*
Gospel Reading: *Matthew 6:1-6, 16-18*

Source: Wikipedia "Sanctuary of Our Lady of Lourdes"

thursday

11

OUR LADY OF LOURDES
France (1858)

On February 11, 1858, Bernadette Soubirous, 14, went to gather firewood with her younger sister and a friend. On that day and over the next five months, she saw the lady she called simply That One.

On February 25, the visionary dug into some ground near the grotto at the behest of Our Lady, revealing a spring which later became known for its healing power. On March 25, Our Lady said in the uneducated girl's dialect: "I am the Immaculate Conception." St. Bernadette became a Sister of Charity of Nevers, where her incorrupt body is now enshrined.

The Catholic Church celebrates February 11 as her feast day, though in Lourdes, the biggest pilgrimage is the Assumption, August 15.

THURSDAY AFTER ASH WEDNESDAY

First Reading: *Deuteronomy 30:15-20*
Responsorial Psalm: *Ps 1:1-2, 3, 4 AND 6*
Gospel Reading: *Luke 9:22-25*

FEBRUARY 2016

s	m	t	w	t	f	s
	1	2	3	4	5	6
7	8	9	10	11	12	13
14	15	16	17	18	19	20
21	22	23	24	25	26	27
28	29					

February

friday

12

OUR LADY OF THE BASIN
Brescia, Italy
(1080)

Inspired by his great love of Mary, St. Constantius decided to erect a church in her honor. While looking at materials with some carpenters, Costanzo saw a white dove reappear, calmly, repeatedly taking in its beak a chip of wood in the air and transporting it to the Mount. He curiously followed it, and came into the town of Conche, where he realized that the dove had arranged the chips so as to trace the perimeter of a building. Looking up, Costanzo saw a Lady with the Child in her arms, lifted up on the perimeter marked by the dove.

Therefore he built the church in that place as proof of his conversion and his love for the Virgin.

Source: Salesians Don Bosco - "La Madonna di San Costanzo in Conche (Bs)"

FEBRUARY 2016

s	m	t	w	t	f	s
	1	2	3	4	5	6
7	8	9	10	11	12	13
14	15	16	17	18	19	20
21	22	23	24	25	26	27
28	29					

FRIDAY AFTER AFTER ASH WEDNESDAY

First Reading: *Isaiah 58:1-9A*
Responsorial Psalm: *Ps 51:3-4, 5-6AB, 18-19*
Gospel Reading: *Matthew 9:14-15*

Source: Blogspot - Virgen del Carmen Patrona de Rute

February
saturday

13

OUR LADY OF MOUNT CARMEL
Rute, Spain (17th c.)

On February 13, 1924, Our Lady of Mt. Carmel was proclaimed patron of the town of Rute in southern Spain as authorized by Pope Pius XI. This statue is dated to the late 1600s, the time of the carving of head and hands. The patron of Rute is celebrated three times per year. The anniversary fiesta lasts three days, culminating on February 13 with mass, presentation of gifts made for the Virgin from the Chief of the Brotherhood and the Fiesta Queen, and a scapular-kissing ceremony in honor of Our Lady of Mt. Carmel. July 16 is the focus of another three-day celebration as her liturgical feast day. On the last Sunday of June, the statue goes in *traslado* (procession) through the streets of the town to Santa Catalina Mártir, the main parish church.

SATURDAY AFTER AFTER ASH WEDNESDAY

First Reading: *Isaiah 58:9B-14*
Responsorial Psalm: *Ps 86:1-2, 3-4, 5-6*
Gospel Reading: *Luke 5:27-32*

FEBRUARY 2016

s	m	t	w	t	f	s
	1	2	3	4	5	6
7	8	9	10	11	12	13
14	15	16	17	18	19	20
21	22	23	24	25	26	27
28	29					

February
sunday
14

MOTHER OF MERCY
Pellevoisin, France
(1876)

In 1876, a young woman, Estelle Faguette, lay dying from tuberculosis. But on the 13th of February, when all were expecting her death, Our Lady appeared near the sickbed. This occurred on three successive nights, and then, as Our Lady had promised, the sick woman was instantly cured. During the visits, Our Lady of Pellevoisin frequently spoke to Estelle saying: "I am all-merciful and have great influence over my Son. What distresses me most is the lack of respect for my Son. Make known my glory." She was granted another vision of Our Lady, robed in white and wearing on her breast a white scapular with the image of the Sacred Heart of Jesus. Again and again Mary pointed to the great need for penance and a return to God.

Source: Wikipedia "Our Lay[f] of Pellevoisin"

FEBRUARY 2016

s	m	t	w	t	f	s
	1	2	3	4	5	6
7	8	9	10	11	12	13
14	15	16	17	18	19	20
21	22	23	24	25	26	27
28	29					

1ST SUNDAY OF LENT

First Reading: *Deuteronomy 26:4-10*
Responsorial Psalm: *Ps 91:1-2, 10-11, 12-13, 14-15*
Second Reading: *Romans 10:8-13*
Gospel Reading: *Luke 4:1-13*

February
monday

15

OUR LADY OF COMFORT
Arezzo, Italy (1796)

On June 3, 1781 a terrible earthquake devastated the regions surrounding Arezzo, causing hundreds of casualties and great fear for the city. On February 15, 1796, another earthquake threatened the city. At dusk three craftsmen prayed penitentially and lit a lamp before a popular image of the Virgin blackened by the smoke of a stove. The Madonna of Provenzano image suddenly changed to white and bright. The word spread that Our Lady wanted to comfort all inhabitants of Arezzo and free them from the scourge of earthquakes. When the news spread, the bishop, accompanied by other priests solemnly carried it to the cathedral and established the canonical process to determine the truth of the events.

1ST WEEK OF LENT

First Reading: *Leviticus 19:1-2, 11-18*
Responsorial Psalm: *Ps 50: 1&8.16-17.20-21*
Gospel Reading: *Matthew 25:31-46*

FEBRUARY 2016

s	m	t	w	t	f	s
	1	2	3	4	5	6
7	8	9	10	11	12	13
14	15	16	17	18	19	20
21	22	23	24	25	26	27
28	29					

February

tuesday

16

WEEPING VIRGIN MARY
Sajópálfala, Hungary
(1717)

Sajópálfala, a town in northeastern Hungary, was destroyed and deserted during the occupation by the Turkish at the end of the 15th century. The area was then resettled and shortly thereafter a painting of the Madonna and Child perspired and wept bloody tears in the town's church, from January 6 to February 16, 1717. The picture was then taken to Eger by the investigating bishop. It stayed in the Franciscan church, becoming the central element of an annual pilgrimage to Our Lady of Sorrows on her feast. The object of devotion was lost for a period until the original weeping image was located in 1969 in a church in the diocese of Pécs, where a friar had protected it. In 1973, the Weeping Virgin returned to the Church of the Visitation after 256 years.

Source: Church's website: http://sajopalfala-gorkat.borsodweb.hu

FEBRUARY 2016

s	m	t	w	t	f	s
	1	2	3	4	5	6
7	8	9	10	11	12	13
14	15	16	17	18	19	20
21	22	23	24	25	26	27
28	29					

1ST WEEK OF LENT

First Reading: *Isaiah 55:10-11*
Responsorial Psalm: *Ps 34:4-5, 6-7, 16-17, 18-19*
Gospel Reading: *Matthew 6:7-15*

Source: baixaki "Sagrada Família - Catedral Nossa Senhora do Desterro - Jundiaí- São Paulo

OUR LADY OF EXILE
Florianópolis, Brazil (1673)

Explorer Francisco Dias Velho of São Paulo founded the town of Nossa Senhora do Desterro on Santa Catarina Island in southern Brazil on February 17, 1673 according to local acccounts. Amongst the occupants of the area were his family, two Jesuits, a few other Brazilians, and hundreds of Indian workers. Florianópolis, the present-day city, grew from this founding settlement. Its chapel transformed into the Cathedral, named for the city's patron, Our Lady of Exile. On this date, she is still venerated annually there. A sculpture in the Cathedral depicting the Holy Family on their way to Egypt was carved of lindenwood by the Demetz workshop in the Italian Tyrol, The statue was blessed May 30, 1902.

1ST WEEK OF LENT

First Reading: *Jonah 3:1-10*
Responsorial Psalm: *Ps 51:3-4, 12-13, 18-19*
Gospel Reading: *Luke 11:29-32*

FEBRUARY 2016

s	m	t	w	t	f	s
	1	2	3	4	5	6
7	8	9	10	11	12	13
14	15	16	17	18	19	20
21	22	23	24	25	26	27
28	29					

February
thursday
18

OUR LADY OF THE ROSARY
Rota, Spain (1807)

Rota, a small Atlantic coastal city in southern Spain, honors Our Lady of the Rosaryas its patron saint. Her statue, dating from the 16th century, can be found in the parish church of Nuestra Señora de la O in a blue-tiled chapel there.

On February 18, 1807, the statue was carried in procession with the statue of Christ of the Chapel to pray for the end of a dangerous drought at the behest of the town council. Rains came and saved the crops that very day. Designed to be dressed, the statue is a *candelero* image with finely carved and painted head, hands, and child, mounted on a plain support. On the Feast of Our Lady of the Rosary, October 7, 2003, the statue was canonically crowned.

Source: Blogspot - La Pasión en Rota "Nuestra Patrona"

FEBRUARY 2016

s	m	t	w	t	f	s
	1	2	3	4	5	6
7	8	9	10	11	12	13
14	15	16	17	18	19	20
21	22	23	24	25	26	27
28	29					

1ST WEEK OF LENT

First Reading: *EST C:12, 14-16, 23-25*
Responsorial Psalm: *Ps 138:1-2AB, 2CDE-3, 7C-8*
Gospel Reading: *Matthew 7:7-12*

February
friday

19

VIRGIN OF CAMPANA
Spain (1596)

Source: Cofradía de San Cristóbal de Valencia "Febrero"

Tradition has it that after rebuilding the parish on the remains of an old chapel from 1507, workmen were carrying out excavations in 1596.

The workers ended their workday, but forgot their tools and, in coming back for them, there was a collapse in the excavations. Miraculously the image of the Virgin was found intact. Many miracles followed.

Today these events are remembered by townspeople who venerate their patron on February 16 - 19 with processions, flowers, bells, and a 21 gun salute.

The Virgin of Campana was proclaimed Patroness of Campana and crowned canonically on April 25, 1915.

1ST WEEK OF LENT

First Reading: *Ezekiel 18:21-28*
Responsorial Psalm: *Ps 130:1-2, 3-4, 5-7A, 7BC-8*
Gospel Reading: *Matthew 5:20-26*

FEBRUARY 2016

s	m	t	w	t	f	s
	1	2	3	4	5	6
7	8	9	10	11	12	13
14	15	16	17	18	19	20
21	22	23	24	25	26	27
28	29					

February

saturday

20

OUR LADY OF THE STAIRS
Massafra, Italy
(1743)

In the Valley of Roses, hunters found a wild deer kneeling before an image of the Madonna and Child, apparently from the crypt of Santa Maria Prisca, which collapsed in the earthquake of 324. Near a great tufa staircase on the gorge wall, a chapel was built to house the Madonna of the Deer, known since the 900s as the Madonna of the Stair. The present sanctuary was opened to the faithful in 1737. A few years later, residents of Massafra credited the Madonna of the Stair with saving them from an earthquake that devastated the region on February 20, 1743, and in 1776 the Pope designated her the city's patron. The city holds festivities in her honor on February 20 and the first Sunday in May.

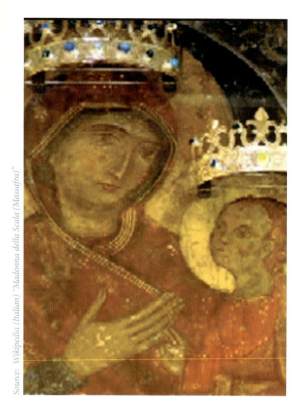

Source: Wikipedia (Italian) "Madonna della Scala (Massafra)"

FEBRUARY 2016

s	m	t	w	t	f	s
	1	2	3	4	5	6
7	8	9	10	11	12	13
14	15	16	17	18	19	20
21	22	23	24	25	26	27
28	29					

1ST WEEK OF LENT

First Reading: *Deuteronomy 26:16-19*
Responsorial Psalm: *Ps 119:1-2, 4-5, 7-8*
Gospel Reading: *Matthew 5:43-48*

IMAGE
DE
NOTRE DAME DE GRACE
VIERGE MIRACULEUSE
VÉNÉRÉE
DANS L'ÉGLISE DE BERZÉE.

Source: Peregrinations: Journal of Medieval Art and Architecture

February
sunday
21

OUR LADY
OF GRACE
Anderlecht, Belgium
(1449)

Two trees - a linden tree and two hawthorn trees - were planted on a hilltop in the Scheut area near Brussels in 1443. An old farmer attached a small wooden statue of the Virgin and Child to one of these trees. On the night before Pentecost in the year 1449, a glow was observed emanating from this place, and so began the pilgrimage to Our Lady of Grace. On February 21, 1450, the chapel's corner stone was laid by the Count of Charolais. In 1531 a church of Gothic style was dedicated to the Mother of Grace in 1531. Despite the French Revolution, the statuette survived and now rests in Notre Dame de Grâce in the Collegiate Church of Sts. Peter and Guy in Anderlecht. It is processed on the Saturday closest to September 12, the feast day of St. Guy.

2ND SUNDAY OF LENT

First Reading: *Genesis 15:5-12, 17-18*
Responsorial Psalm: *Ps 27:1, 7-8, 8-9, 13-14*
Second Reading: *Philippians 3:17—4:1*
Gospel Reading: *Luke 9:28B-36*

FEBRUARY 2016

s	m	t	w	t	f	s
	1	2	3	4	5	6
7	8	9	10	11	12	13
14	15	16	17	18	19	20
21	22	23	24	25	26	27
28	29					

February
monday
22

OUR LADY OF THE KNOLL
Castel San Pietro Terme, Italy (1550)

On February 22, 1550, Madonna appeared before Antonia Bedini, a blind elderly woman begging for bread. In her vision she said "Go home, and you'll find what you need in the cupboard, for as long as you live." Antonia listened and went home, and sure enough there was plenty of bread in her cupboard for her to eat until she died nine months later. The attention of the town turned to miracle and many other miracles were claimed. In 1551, construction begun in the Poggio district on the sanctuary. The famed icon of the Madonna was placed on its main altar, seated between Sts. Francis and Jerome, in a red robe, blue mantle and greenish veil, with a naked Christ Child bouncing on her knee.

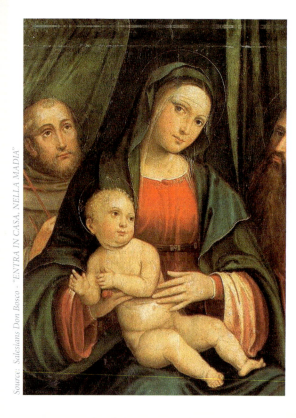

Source: Salesians Don Bosco - "ENTRA IN CASA, NELLA MADIA"

FEBRUARY 2016

s	m	t	w	t	f	s
	1	2	3	4	5	6
7	8	9	10	11	12	13
14	15	16	17	18	19	20
21	22	23	24	25	26	27
28	29					

2ND WEEK OF LENT
Feast of the Chair of Saint Peter, Apostle

First Reading: *1 Peter 5:1-4*
Responsorial Psalm: *Ps 23:1-3A, 4, 5, 6*
Gospel Reading: *Matthew 16:13-19*

Source: JBlogspot - Chile Iglesias Catolicas - "IGLESIA SANTA CRUZ DE LIMACHE"

THE IMMACULATA OF THE 40 HOURS
Limache, Chile (1831)

The story goes that in 1831, fishermen found a chest floating in the sea; inside was a beautiful statue of the Virgin in a white robe and dark blue mantle. Devotion remained private for many years, but eventually grew to the point that the statue was moved to the parish Church of Santa Cruz. The Immaculata of Limache became known as the Virgin of the 40 Hours after saving some sailors from a 40-hour storm, or because the statue was found after a 40-hour storm. Now, a nine-day novena precedes the fiesta in February, which of course is summertime in Chile. On Sunday, the image processes through the city, passing the penitentiary, whose inmates shout a greeting.

2ND WEEK OF LENT

First Reading: *Isaiah 1:10, 16-20*
Responsorial Psalm: *Ps 50:8-9, 16BC-17, 21 AND 23*
Gospel Reading: *Matthew 23:1-12*

FEBRUARY 2016

s	m	t	w	t	f	s
	1	2	3	4	5	6
7	8	9	10	11	12	13
14	15	16	17	18	19	20
21	22	23	24	25	26	27
28	29					

February
wednesday
24

THE VIRGIN GUIDE
Alcaracejos, Spain
(13th c.)

Virgin of Guidance is the shared patron of four Sierra Morena towns: Fuente la Lancha, Villanueva del Duque, Hinojosa del Duque, and Alcaracejos. According to legend, a herder located the small statue of the Virgin in the hollow of a oak tree whose acorns bore a similar image on their caps. Another tradition recounts that the herder discovered it in the basin of a fountain. When he tried to bring it home, the image had disappeared. He found it again there on the next day, and the story repeated: the man sought again to bring it home, but it inexplicably returned. The present bronze image there is a 1939 replica as the original statue was lost during the Civil War;. There is a procession on February 24 of every year, from Villanueva to Alcaracejos, where it will stay until Easter.

Source: Blogspot – Parroquia San Mateo Villanueva

FEBRUARY 2016

s	m	t	w	t	f	s
		1	2	3	4	5	6
7	8	9	10	11	12	13
14	15	16	17	18	19	20
21	22	23	24	25	26	27
28	29

2ND WEEK OF LENT

First Reading: *Isaiah 1:10, 16-20*
Responsorial Psalm: *Ps 50:8-9, 16BC-17, 21 AND 23*
Gospel Reading: *Matthew 23:1-12*

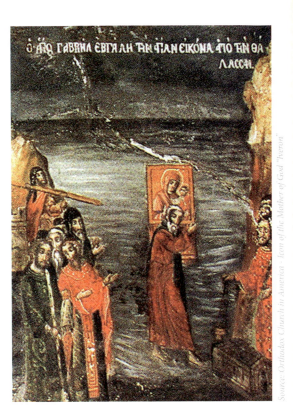

Source: Orthodox Church in America • Icon of the Mother of God "Iveron"

thursday

25

ICON OF THE MOTHER OF GOD "IVERON" North Ossetia Alania, Russia (9th c.)

During the reign of Emperor Theophilus (829-842) the soldiers pillaged the Byzantine empire, searching for and destroying hidden images in an iconoclastic fury.

Near Nicaea a pious widow was concealing an icon of the Virgin Mary that became pierced by the spear of a soldier. Blood flowed from the wound on the face of the Mother of God. The widow after prayer cast it to sea.

Time passed and the monks of the Iveron beheld the floating icon in a pillar of light. An apparition of Mary to the monks inspired them to lead a Georgian monk Gabriel to the sea where he walked on the water to obtain the icon.

2ND WEEK OF LENT

First Reading: *Isaiah 1:10, 16-20*
Responsorial Psalm: *Ps 50:8-9, 16BC-17, 21 AND 23*
Gospel Reading: *Matthew 23:1-12*

FEBRUARY 2016

s	m	t	w	t	f	s
	1	2	3	4	5	6
7	8	9	10	11	12	13
14	15	16	17	18	19	20
21	22	23	24	25	26	27
28	29					

February

friday

26

OUR LADY OF REMEDIES
Palermo, Italy
(1064)

The Arab-ruled Palermo was approached by militia of the Norman brothers Robert Guiscard and Roger I in 1064. When tarantulas entered their campsite. In a vision, the Madonna recommended to Roger that he build a fire. The plague of spiders ceased, but the Normans had to give up the attack at that time. In 1072, the Normans finally took Palermo and Roger built a church there dedicated to Madonna dei Rimedi. A Carmelite monastery was built in 1610, and a new church was dedicated to her in 1625 and was rebuilt in 1948. Cardinal Ernesto Ruffini donated a statue of the Madonna from the archbishop's courtyard on February 26, 1950. The statue of the Madonna of Remedies was canonically crowned on July 16, 1951. Her feast day is celebrated on September 8.

Source: Blogspot - palermo dm torni "Palermo e dintorni ma anche..."

FEBRUARY 2016

s	m	t	w	t	f	s
	1	2	3	4	5	6
7	8	9	10	11	12	13
14	15	16	17	18	19	20
21	22	23	24	25	26	27
28	29					

2ND WEEK OF LENT

First Reading: *Genesis 37:3-4, 12-13A, 17B-28A*
Responsorial Psalm: *Ps 105:16-17, 18-19, 20-21*
Gospel Reading: *Matthew 21:33-43, 45-46*

Source: Cruz de Guía Chiclana – "Virgen de los Remedios, Madre de los chiclaneros"

saturday

27

OUR LADY OF REMEDIES
Chiclana de la Frontera, Spain (16th c.)

A miraculous light brought a shepherd to a small statuette of the Virgin Mary in 16th century Spain. Dedicated to Our Lady of Remedies, a shrine was built at that place. When a terrible drought ravaged the region. In 1738, the city councilmen on February 13 ordered a novena and procession for nine days with Our Lady of Remedies moving from the monastery to the church. When the processions ended on February 24, there was a downpour of rain that continued until the 27th. Nuestra Señora de los Remedios was declared patron of Chiclana de la Frontera that very day. On June 12, 1916, Pope Benedict XV confirmed her patronage of the town. Chiclana honors her annually on her patronal feast of September 8.

2ND WEEK OF LENT

First Reading: *Micah 7:14-15, 18-20*
Responsorial Psalm: *Ps 103:1-2, 3-4, 9-10, 11-12*
Gospel Reading: *Luke 15:1-3, 11-32*

FEBRUARY 2016

s	m	t	w	t	f	s
	1	2	3	4	5	6
7	8	9	10	11	12	13
14	15	16	17	18	19	20
21	22	23	24	25	26	27
28	29					

February
sunday

28

VILENSKY HODEGETRIA
Vilnius, Lithuania
(15th c.)

According to Orthodox tradition, St. Luke the Evangelist wrote (painted) this icon, later owned by the royalty of Byzantium. It is an icon of the style of *Hodegetria* (way-pointing) with the Mother gesturing toward her Son. When the last Byzantine fortress in Greece was overtaken by the Ottomans, the losing emperor in 1460 took the icon of the Virgin with him to Rome. It was brought to Moscow in 1472 and later sent to Vilnius with his granddaughter. During World War I, the Vilnius Hodegetria, painted on linden and cypress boards, was lost to history when the Russian Orthodox Church needed to shuttle out their sacred objects from the places of war. The transfer is celebrated on February 28 at The Holy Spirit Monastery in Vilnius where a copy is preserved.

Source: Lithuanian eparchy · www.orthodoxy.lt

FEBRUARY 2016

s	m	t	w	t	f	s
	1	2	3	4	5	6
7	8	9	10	11	12	13
14	15	16	17	18	19	20
21	22	23	24	25	26	27
28	29					

3RD SUNDAY OF LENT

First Reading: *Exodus 3:1-8A, 13-15*
Responsorial Psalm: *Ps 103: 1-2, 3-4, 6-7, 8, 11*
Second Reading: *1 Corinthians 10:1-6, 10-12*
Gospel Reading: *Luke 13:1-9*

Source: Wikipedia (Spanish) – Virgin de Loreto

VIRGIN OF LORETO
Mutxamel, Spain
(1513)

When the region around Mutxamel encountered a severe drought in 1545, the townspeople carried their image of the Virgin in procession three miles south in Santa Faz to the monastery shrine of St. Veronica. On the return trip, Father Lloréns Boix suddenly found the image too heavy to carry. Near the town of San Juan, he lifted the protective veil to examine the image, noticing Virgin's left eye crying a tear. The rains came soon afterwards. The fiesta of La Llágrima, the Tear, is celebrated annually in Mutxamel on March 1. The patronal fiesta of the town occurs on September 9 in honor of the Virgin of Loreto, including a reenactment of "Moors and Christians". During the Spanish Civil War, the icon was swept away to Switzerland for safekeeping in 1936.

3RD WEEK OF LENT

First Reading: *Daniel 3:25, 34-43*
Responsorial Psalm: *Ps 25:4-5AB, 6 AND 7BC, 8-9*
Gospel Reading: *Matthew 18:21-35*

MARCH 2016

s	m	t	w	t	f	s
		1	2	3	4	5
6	7	8	9	10	11	12
13	14	15	16	17	18	19
20	21	22	23	24	25	26
27	28	29	30	31		

March
wednesday

2

ICON OF THE MOTHER OF GOD "TIKHVIN" Mt Athos, Greece (1877)

On March 2, 1877 (February 17 on the old calendar) seven monks remained in the church after prayers. They were astonished to see tears flowing from the right eye of the icon, and collecting on the frame. Then a single large tear came from the left eye.

The monks wiped the tears from the icon's face, then left the church and locked the doors behind them. Three hours later, they returned for Vespers and saw traces of tears on the icon, and a single tear in the left eye. Again they wiped the tears from the icon, but they did not reappear.

The monks established an annual commemoration for March 2 (Feb 17 old calendar).

Source: Icon painters Vjatcheslav and Tatjana Mikhailenko - Gallery

MARCH 2016

s	m	t	w	t	f	s
		1	2	3	4	5
6	7	8	9	10	11	12
13	14	15	16	17	18	19
20	21	22	23	24	25	26
27	28	29	30	31		

3RD WEEK OF LENT

First Reading: *Deuteronomy 4:1, 5-9*
Responsorial Psalm: *Ps 147:12-13, 15-16, 19-20*
Gospel Reading: *Matthew 5:17-19*

Source: The Catholic Tour "The Shrines of Southern Italy"

March
thursday

3

QUEEN OF THE ROSARY
Pompei, Italy
(1884)

Blessed Bartolo Longo founded the Shrine of Our Lady of the Rosary and enshrined a miraculous image there that he had commissioned an artist to restore. Many healings have ensued including one involving Fortuna Agrelli who was suffering from three incurable diseases. The Virgin appeared as the Queen of the Rosary on March 3, 1884 to her after she and her parents had prayed for her healing. The Feast day of the Queen of the Rosary of Pompeii is celebrated on May 8th.

The present structure of The Shrine of Our Lady of the Rosary was begun at the request of Pope Pius XI. John Paul II first visited the shrine in 1979 and a year later on Oct. 26, 1980 beatified the founder of the shrine, Bartolo Longo.

3RD WEEK OF LENT

First Reading: *Jeremiah 7:23-28*
Responsorial Psalm: *Ps 95:1-2, 6-7, 8-9*
Gospel Reading: *Luke 11:14-23*

MARCH 2016

s	m	t	w	t	f	s
		1	2	3	4	5
6	7	8	9	10	11	12
13	14	15	16	17	18	19
20	21	22	23	24	25	26
27	28	29	30	31		

March
friday

4

OUR LADY OF THE GUARD
Marseilles, France (1214)

Source: Site officiel de la Basilique Notre-dame de la Garde marseille galeries photos

In 1214 - year of the battle of Bouvines and of the birth of Saint Louis – a priest of Marseilles whose first name was Pierre erected a small sanctuary dedicated to the Virgin Mary upon the rocky triangle forming the top of a 161 meter-high hill facing the town of Marseille, which was very small at the time.

As the hill was called «La Garde», the sanctuary quite naturally took the name "Our Lady of La Garde" So at its origin the chapel had neither apparition nor miracle; it was simply born of a priest's devotion.

On August 14, 2014 the town celebrated the 150th anniversary of the consecration of the Basilica of Our Lady of the Guard.

MARCH 2016

s	m	t	w	t	f	s
		1	2	3	4	5
6	7	8	9	10	11	12
13	14	15	16	17	18	19
20	21	22	23	24	25	26
27	28	29	30	31		

3RD WEEK OF LENT

First Reading: *Hosea 14:2-10*
Responsorial Psalm: *Ps 81:6C-8A, 8BC-9, 10-11AB, 14 AND*
Gospel Reading: *Mark 12:28-34*

Source: Hermandad de Santa María de la Cruz y de la Santa Juana

March
saturday

5

HOLY MARY OF THE CROSS
Cubas, Spain (1449)

Starting on March 3rd, 19th,1449, twelve year old Inés Martínez, saw the Virgin Mary in six visions. While she was tending to pigs, the girl saw the Mother of God dressed in gold. To mark the location of the shrine she requested, Mary took a small cross and planted it. For many years this anniversary was celebrated with a procession from the town to the rural sanctuary, later becoming a Franciscan convent where the nuns would expose the cross. Sadly eight sisters were martyred and the shrine burned during the Civil War. Rebuilding began in 1988 and on March 5, 1994, the Bishop of Getafe dedicated the new church with convent and declared it a Diocesan shrine. In recent years, the pilgrimage has been resumed in March.

MARCH 2016

s	m	t	w	t	f	s
		1	2	3	4	5
6	7	8	9	10	11	12
13	14	15	16	17	18	19
20	21	22	23	24	25	26
27	28	29	30	31		

3RD WEEK OF LENT

First Reading: *Hosea 6:1-6*
Responsorial Psalm: *Ps 51:3-4, 18-19, 20-21AB*
Gospel Reading: *Luke 18:9-14*

March

sunday

6

ICON OF THE MOTHER OF GOD "KOZELSHCHANSK" Kobeliaky, Ukraine (16TH C.)

This Italian Marian icon was brought to Russia in the 18th century by an Italian attendant to Empress Elizabeth. The lady and her icon later went to the Ukraine after she married an army clerk. The icon's feast on March 6 (February 21 old Orthodox calendar) commemorates the healing in 1881 of Maria, daughter of Count Vladimir Kapnist, who then owned the icon. After time spent cleaning the icon and in prayer, Maria's mysterious crippling illness disappeared. With a growing reknown for miracles, the icon was moved to a chapel built for it in Kozelschyna, later enlarged to a church with a convent. After some time in hiding, the icon returned in 1993 to the Nativity of the Mother of God church in Kozelschyna.

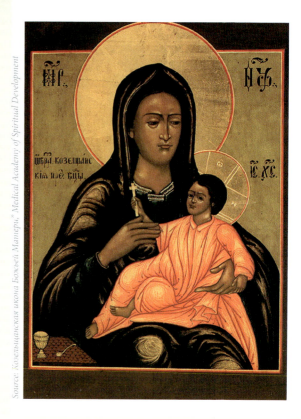

MARCH 2016

s	m	t	w	t	f	s
		1	2	3	4	5
6	7	8	9	10	11	12
13	14	15	16	17	18	19
20	21	22	23	24	25	26
27	28	29	30	31		

4TH SUNDAY OF LENT

First Reading: *Josiah 5:9A, 10-12*
Responsorial Psalm: *Ps 34:2-3, 4-5, 6-7*
Second Reading: *2 Corinthians 5:17-21*
Gospel Reading: *Luke 15:1-3, 11-32*

Source: Delcampe Auctions - Santino: Madonna di Monte Berico - Vicenza. Anno: 1954

OUR LADY OF MONTE BERICO
Vicenza, Italy (1426)

On March 7, 1426, the Blessed Virgin appeared in Monte Berico, to an elderly 70 year old woman, Vincenza Pasini in the fields. She said, "I ask you to build a church here in my honor. If they do, the plague will stop, otherwise the destruction will continue." But neither the bishop nor the priests believed her and the plague continued. The Virgin appeared again on August 1 and after a healing spring was found in that place according to her promise, on August 25, 1428 the bishop climbed Mount Berico to start the construction of the church. The plague ceased, and the Bishop recognized the apparitions as authentic. After a century, the source was exhausted, but in 1955, during excavations for the new convent, a spring of water was found.

MARCH 2016

s	m	t	w	t	f	s
		1	2	3	4	5
6	7	8	9	10	11	12
13	14	15	16	17	18	19
20	21	22	23	24	25	26
27	28	29	30	31		

4ᵀᴴ WEEK OF LENT

First Reading: *Josiah 5:9A, 10-12*
Responsorial Psalm: *Ps 34:2-3, 4-5, 6-7*
Gospel Reading: *2 Corinthians 5:17-21*

March

tuesday

8

OUR LADY OF TEARS
Campinas, Brazil
(1928)

Amália Aguirre helped found the Missionaries of Jesus Crucified in 1928, taking the name Sister Amália of the Scourged Jesus. She received mystical gifts of the stigmata and visions of Jesus who gave her three prayers to the Sorrowful Heart of Mary. Four months later, in another vision, Mary appeared in a violet robe, blue mantle, and a white veil and handed Amalia an illuminated "rosary of tears" to be said with the three prayers. She later saw Mary on April 8, 1930, with a medal of Our Dear Lady of Tears.

Francisco de Campos Barreto, Bishop of Campinas, the Institute's founder, issued an Imprimatur in 1934 to the Rosary of Tears and promoted the medal, recounting the many miracles in Brazil and Europe.

MARCH 2016

s	m	t	w	t	f	s
		1	2	3	4	5
6	7	8	9	10	11	12
13	14	15	16	17	18	19
20	21	22	23	24	25	26
27	28	29	30	31		

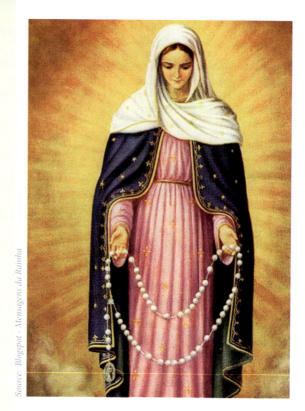

Source: Blogspot - Mensagens da Rainha

4TH WEEK OF LENT

First Reading: *Ezekiel 47:1-9, 12*
Responsorial Psalm: *Ps 46:2-3, 5-6, 8-9*
Gospel Reading: *John 5:1-16*

Source: UNITALSI Sottosezione di Trieste – Galleria Fotografica

March
wednesday

9

OUR LADY OF THE MIRACLE
Motta di Livenza, Italy (1510)

Seventy-nine year old Giovanni Cigana went to get a friend's help with plowing his field on March 9, 1510. When he stopped to pray at a small shrine along the way, he encountered a beautiful girl in white seated on wheat. When it dawned on him that he was speaking to the Mother of God, he fell to his knees. She rose up and asked that he, his family, and the people of Treviso fast for three Saturdays in repentance to obtain Christ's pardon for their sins, and that a church be built on the site. Cigana went home and told the story and predicted a solar miracle as Our Lady promised. That evening, the sun appeared blood red. Within a few days, the people of the area had built a wooden church. The sanctuary celebrates her feast on March 9th.

4TH WEEK OF LENT

First Reading: *Isaiah 49:8-15*
Responsorial Psalm: *Ps 145:8-9, 13cd-14, 17-18*
Gospel Reading: *John 5:17-30*

MARCH 2016

s	m	t	w	t	f	s
		1	2	3	4	5
6	7	8	9	10	11	12
13	14	15	16	17	18	19
20	21	22	23	24	25	26
27	28	29	30	31		

March

thursday

10

OUR LADY OF PRADELLES
France (1538)

In 1512, a statue was found in the soil of a field by the hospital, later the location of the chapel bell tower. Devotion to Our Lady of Pradelles began at that point but the event that brought her fame occurred March 10, 1588, during the wars of religion. Huguenot troops, having ravaged the region for some time, came to attack Pradelles, but they were defeated and the town survived. The Virgin Mary's intercession is credited with the protection of the inhabitants in this victory. In 1793, the statue was burned by revolutionaries who threw it onto a fire. Although it was half-burnt when pulled out, it was later restored with local pine and in 1802 returned to the chapel. The image was crowned solemnly on July 18, 1869. On the feast of the Assumption, August 15, the annual pilgrimage takes place.

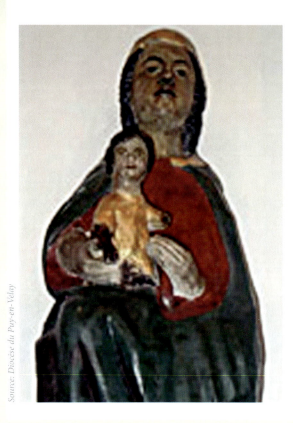

Source: Diocèse du Puy-en-Velay

MARCH 2016

s	m	t	w	t	f	s
		1	2	3	4	5
6	7	8	9	10	11	12
13	14	15	16	17	18	19
20	21	22	23	24	25	26
27	28	29	30	31		

4TH WEEK OF LENT

First Reading: *Exodus 32:7-14*
Responsorial Psalm: *Ps 106:19-20, 21-22, 23*
Gospel Reading: *John 5:31-47*

Source: Wikipedia (Italian) - Taggia

March
friday
11

MIRACULOUS MADONNA
Taggia, Italy (1855)

The first movement of the eyes occurred March 11, 1855 near the end of a week of prayer for the proclamation of the dogma of the Immaculate Conception. The miracle continued for some days, witnessed by many.

The pastor, Don Stefano Semeria, informed the bishop, who went to Taggia and began a canonical proceeding that gathered some 120 testimonials. On June 1, 1856 the statue of the Miraculous Madonna was solemnly crowned and a decree promulgated recognizing the miracles. The coronation anniversary is celebrated on the first Sunday in June. Taggia celebrates the patronal feast of the Miraculous Madonna annually on March 11.

4TH WEEK OF LENT

First Reading: *Wisdom 2:1A, 12-22*
Responsorial Psalm: *Ps 34:17-18, 19-20, 21 AND 23*
Gospel Reading: *John 7:1-2, 10, 25-30*

MARCH 2016

s	m	t	w	t	f	s
		1	2	3	4	5
6	7	8	9	10	11	12
13	14	15	16	17	18	19
20	21	22	23	24	25	26
27	28	29	30	31		

March

saturday

12

OUR LADY OF FOURVIÈRE
Lyon, France (1643)

Around 1180, a chapel was constructed and dedicated to St. Thomas à Becket, recently martyred there, and to Our Lady. On April 29, 1552, Huguenots destroyed the chapel there on Fourvière hill above Lyon and its Black Virgin statue. Both were soon replaced afterwards by the Catholics of Lyon.

On March 12, 1643, city officials made a vow to the Virgin to erect two statues in her honor her with candles and gold during an outbreak of black plague. On the feast of the Nativity of the Virgin Mary,September 8, a pilgrimage was established to honor her. After the epidemic ended in Lyon that year, pilgrims began streaming to Fourvière. The September 8 pilgrimage and offering still takes place to this day.

Source: Ver La Tradition - "Hommage à la Vierge noire"

MARCH 2016

s	m	t	w	t	f	s
		1	2	3	4	5
6	7	8	9	10	11	12
13	14	15	16	17	18	19
20	21	22	23	24	25	26
27	28	29	30	31		

4TH WEEK OF LENT

First Reading: *Jeremiah 11:18-20*
Responsorial Psalm: *Ps 7:2-3, 9BC-10, 11-12*
Gospel Reading: *John 7:40-53*

Source: Diocesan Site www.ikudroshram.ru

DEVPETERUV MOTHER OF GOD
Batyushkovo, Russia (1392)

The Devpeteruv Mother of God is an icon of Tenderness style, showing Mother and Child cheek to cheek. According to pious tradition, the icon appeared miraculously on March 13, 1392 (February 29 in the old calendar). The written record does not say much about its early history or the origin of its name. The earliest written account of the Devpeteruv Mother of God icon places the 12" image in the stone church of St. Nicholas built in 1666 in Batyushkovo, a village 35 miles from Moscow.

The icon and bejeweled sheath were stolen in the 1930s, when attackers killed the watchman. After the image was found nearby in the mud without its jewels, the priest returned the icon to its place of honor in the church.

5TH SUNDAY OF LENT

First Reading: *Isaiah 43:16-21*
Responsorial Psalm: *Ps 126:1-2, 2-3, 4-5, 6*
Second Reading: *Philippians 3:8-14*
Gospel Reading: *John 8:1-11*

MARCH 2016

s	m	t	w	t	f	s
		1	2	3	4	5
6	7	8	9	10	11	12
13	14	15	16	17	18	19
20	21	22	23	24	25	26
27	28	29	30	31		

March
monday
14

VIRGIN OF MOUNT CARMEL
Maipú, Chile (1818)

Our Lady of Mt. Carmel was proclaimed "Patrona Generalísima de las Armas de Chile," protector of the liberation army by General O'Higgins on February 11, 1817. But a year later, residents and clergy joined the revolutionaries in requesting help from the Virgin on March 14, 1818, when Spanish forces pushed the Chilenos back to Santiago vowing to build a shrine to Our Lady of Mt. Carmel should they win. At the battle of Maipú on April 5, their prayers were quickly answered.

The first stone of the Chapel of Victory was laid that November and the chapel was blessed in 1892. During his apostolic visit to Chile, Pope John Paul II crowned the statue of Our Lady of Maipú on April 3, 1987.

Source: Wikipedia (Spanish) - Virgen del Carmen de Chile

MARCH 2016

s	m	t	w	t	f	s
		1	2	3	4	5
6	7	8	9	10	11	12
13	14	15	16	17	18	19
20	21	22	23	24	25	26
27	28	29	30	31		

5TH WEEK OF LENT

First Reading: *Daniel 13:1-9, 15-17, 19-30, 33-62*
Responsorial Psalm: *Ps 23:1-3A, 3B-4, 5, 6*
Gospel Reading: *John 8:12-20*

March
tuesday
15

ICON OF THE MOTHER OF GOD "ENTHRONED" Kolomskoye, Russia (1917)

Source: Orthodox Church in America – Icon of the Mother of God "Enthroned"

The "Enthroned" (or "Reigning") Icon of the Mother of God appeared on March 15, 1917 (March 2 on the old Orthodox calendar), the day of Tsar Nicholas's abdication, in the village of Kolomskoye near Moscow.

In February 1917, an elderly woman named Eudokia saw the Mother of God in a dream telling her to go to Kolomskoye to find a large blackened icon in a church. After the vision was repeated three times, she went there to search for the icon. In the basement of the church covered in dust the icon of Panachranta (seated) type was revealed and news of the icon's discovery spread throughout Russia, and there were several healing miracles.

5TH WEEK OF LENT

First Reading: *Numbers 21:4-9*
Responsorial Psalm: *Ps 102:2-3, 16-18, 19-21*
Gospel Reading: *John 8:21-30*

MARCH 2016

s	m	t	w	t	f	s
		1	2	3	4	5
6	7	8	9	10	11	12
13	14	15	16	17	18	19
20	21	22	23	24	25	26
27	28	29	30	31		

March
wednesday
16

VLADIMIR MOTHER OF GOD
Volokolamsk, Russia
(1572)

The Volokolamsk Icon of the Mother of God is a copy of the Vladimir Icon of the Moscow Dormition cathedral. The icon was transferred from Zvenigorod to the Dormition monastery of St Joseph of Volokolamsk in 1572 on March 16 (March 2 old calendar). It is identifiable by the images in the margins of St. Cyprian and St. Gerontius.

The name of Cyprian is associated with the first arrival of the ancient Vladimir Icon from Constantinople to Moscow in the year 1395, and Gerontius in 1480 the Vladimir Icon came finally to Moscow. The Volokolamsk Icon was dedicated atop the gate in the church at the south gates of the monastery of St Joseph of Volokolamsk in the year 1588.

MARCH 2016

s	m	t	w	t	f	s
			1	2	3	4	5
6	7	8	9	10	11	12
13	14	15	16	17	18	19
20	21	22	23	24	25	26
27	28	29	30	31		

5TH WEEK OF LENT

First Reading: *Daniel 3:14-20, 91-92, 95*
Responsorial Psalm: *Daniel 3:52, 53, 54, 55, 56*
Gospel Reading: *John 8:31-42*

Source: Catholic Architecture and History of Toledo, Ohio "The Irish Madonna of St. Stephen's"

March
thursday
17

WEEPING VIRGIN MARY
Gyor, Hungary (1697)

Walter Lynch, Catholic bishop of Clonfert, Ireland, took the painting of the Comforter of the Afflicted with him into exile after Cromwell's takeover in 1649. In Vienna he had met the bishop of Gyor, Hungary, who had invited him there. Bishop Lynch served in Gyor until his death in 1663, when he was buried in the Cathedral and the painting was installed there. On March 17, 1697, the Irish picture of the Virgin began weeping at early mass in Gyor Cathedral, where for three hours thousands of people watched her tears fall on to the sleeping child below her praying hands. The tears were wiped but started up again and the icon was removed from its frame. A law passed that year in Dublin banning Catholic bishops from Ireland was the reason for tears according to some.

MARCH 2016

s	m	t	w	t	f	s
		1	2	3	4	5
6	7	8	9	10	11	12
13	14	15	16	17	18	19
20	21	22	23	24	25	26
27	28	29	30	31		

5TH WEEK OF LENT

First Reading: *Genesis 17:3-9*
Responsorial Psalm: *Ps 105:4-5, 6-7, 8-9*
Gospel Reading: *John 8:51-59*

March

friday

18

OUR LADY OF MERCY
Savona, Italy (1536)

On the morning of March 18, farmer Antonio Botta was on his way to work in his vineyard in San Bernardo. He saw a brilliant light with a figure of a woman who said that she was the Virgin Mary and urged him to atonement and prayer. Some weeks later, she appeared sitting on a rock in a stream, and encouraged him to pray.

Botta told the people just what he had seen and heard and was at once believed. A large church was erected on the site and many pilgrims visited the "Mother of Mercy."

On March 18, 1660, Mons. Gregoire Ardizzone, declared Our Lady of Mercy "patroness and protectress of the city".

On March 18, there is a procession organized in her honor.

Source: Wikipedia (Italian) - Santuario di Nostra Signora della Misericordia (Savona)

MARCH 2016

s	m	t	w	t	f	s
		1	2	3	4	5
6	7	8	9	10	11	12
13	14	15	16	17	18	19
20	21	22	23	24	25	26
27	28	29	30	31		

5TH WEEK OF LENT

First Reading: *Jeremiah 20:10-13*
Responsorial Psalm: *Ps 18:2-3A, 3BC-4, 5-6, 7*
Gospel Reading: *John 10:31-42*

Source: Icon Kuznetsov - http://www.iconkuznetsov.ru

March
saturday

19

ICON OF THE MOTHER OF GOD "THE BLESSED HEAVEN"
Moscow, Russia (12th c.)

The "Blessed Heaven" Icon of the Mother of God is in the Moscow Archangel Orthodox cathedral in the Kremlin. Previously, this icon was at Smolensk and brought to Moscow by Sophia, daughter of the Lithuanian prince Vitovt, when she became the wife of Prince Basil of Moscow (1389-1425).

On the icon, the Mother of God is depicted in full stature, with a scepter in Her right hand. On her left arm is the Divine Infant, and both of them are crowned. Certain people call also this icon of the Mother of God "What Shall we call Thee?"

This icon is also commemorated on the Sunday of All Saints.

5TH WEEK OF LENT
Solemnity of Saint Joseph, husband of the Blessed Virgin Mary

First Reading: *2 Samuel 7:4-5A, 12-14A, 16*
Responsorial Psalm: *Ps 89:2-3, 4-5, 27 AND 29*
Second Reading: *Romans 4: 13.16-18,22*
Gospel Reading: *Matthew 1: 16,18-21,24a*

MARCH 2016

s	m	t	w	t	f	s
		1	2	3	4	5
6	7	8	9	10	11	12
13	14	15	16	17	18	19
20	21	22	23	24	25	26
27	28	29	30	31		

March
sunday
20

ICON OF THE MOTHER OF GOD "THE SURETY OF SINNERS"
Odrino, Russia (1843)

The Icon of the Mother of God "Surety of Sinners" is known by this name because of the inscription on the icon. The author and origination date of the icon is unknown.

In 1843 it was revealed to many of the people in dreams that the icon was endowed with miraculous power. They solemnly brought the icon into the church. Believers began to flock to it to pray for the healing of their sorrows and sicknesses. The first to receive healing was a crippled child, whose mother prayed fervently before the icon in 1844. The icon also gained renown during a cholera epidemic, when many people fell ill, and were restored to health after praying before the icon.

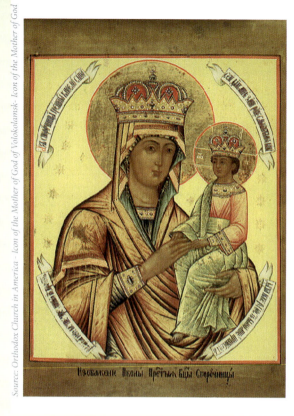

MARCH 2016

s	m	t	w	t	f	s
		1	2	3	4	5
6	7	8	9	10	11	12
13	14	15	16	17	18	19
20	21	22	23	24	25	26
27	28	29	30	31		

PALM SUNDAY OF THE LORD'S PASSION

First Reading: *Isaiah 50:4-7*
Responsorial Psalm: *Ps 22:8-9, 17-18, 19-20, 23-24*
Second Reading: *Philippians 2:6-11*
Gospel Reading: *Luke 22:14—23:56*

Source: Kursk Root Hermitage – "The Wonderworking Kursk Root Icon of Our Lady of the Sign"

March
monday

21

KURSK ROOT MOTHER OF GOD
New York, NY, USA
(1898)

The Kursk Root Mother of God icon had resided for hundreds of years in Kursk. When an anarchist's bomb exploded under the icon on March 21, 1898, the precious image was unharmed despite the cast-iron baldachin and marble pedestal, the church windows, and the cupola all being destroyed.

On September 8, 1295, some men had come to hunt in the forests there. One of them noticed the icon at the root of a tree, and when he lifted it up, he released a spring of water. A chapel for the image was built near the spot, where the number of pilgrims and miracles grew. The icon has been translated to many locations and finally to New York, where since 1957 it has resided in the Church of the Mother of God of the Sign.

MARCH 2016

s	m	t	w	t	f	s
		1	2	3	4	5
6	7	8	9	10	11	12
13	14	15	16	17	18	19
20	21	22	23	24	25	26
27	28	29	30	31		

HOLY WEEK

First Reading: *Isaiah 42:1-7*
Responsorial Psalm: *Ps 27:1, 2, 3, 13-14*
Gospel Reading: *John 12:1-11*

March
tuesday
22

OUR LADY OF SORROWS
Castelpetroso, Italy (1888)

On March 22, 1888, two women, Fabiana Cecchino (35) and Serafina Giovanna Valentino (33) were sent to look for some sheep that had strayed on a neighboring hill and had a vision of Mary first as the Pieta and later as Our Lady of Sorrows in a cave at Castelpetroso, Italy. They returned home in tears and reported the vision to the disbelieving townspeople.

A spring appeared at the apparition site in May 1888. This water has been used by the faithful in the same manner as that of Lourdes, and many favors are piously believed to have been received.

Mgr. Macarone-Palmieri, Bishop of the diocese of Bojano, skeptical at first, witnessed an apparition three times during his investigation.

Source: Santuario Maria Santissima Addolorata Castelpetroso

MARCH 2016

s	m	t	w	t	f	s
		1	2	3	4	5
6	7	8	9	10	11	12
13	14	15	16	17	18	19
20	21	22	23	24	25	26
27	28	29	30	31		

HOLY WEEK

First Reading: *Isaiah 49:1-6*
Responsorial Psalm: *Ps 71:1-2, 3-4A, 5AB-6AB, 15 AND 17*
Gospel Reading: *John 13:21-33, 36-38*

Source: Revista Pasos de Fe - "Costa Rica, Paraíso, Cartago. Festividad de Ntra Srn de Ujarraz"

March
wednesday

23

OUR LADY OF UJARRÁS
Costa Rica (16th c.)

In the 16th century, a native was fishing in the Pacuare River when he saw a wooden box that he picked up without opening it and brought it to his people.

When he reached Ujarrás on his way to Cartago, he could not lift the box even with the help of others. They opened the box to discover a beautiful statue of the Virgin Mary. He told the monks at the Franciscan monastery what was happening. She was then given the full name of Our Lady of the Immaculate Conception of Ujarrás.

From this place spread the devotion to the Our Lady of Ujarrás to several parts of the country, including the ancient capital of Cartago.

HOLY WEEK

First Reading: *Isaiah 50:4-9A*
Responsorial Psalm: *Ps 69:8-10, 21-22, 31 AND 33-34*
Gospel Reading: *Matthew 26:14-25*

MARCH 2016

s	m	t	w	t	f	s
		1	2	3	4	5
6	7	8	9	10	11	12
13	14	15	16	17	18	19
20	21	22	23	24	25	26
27	28	29	30	31		

March

thursday

24

OUR LADY OF THE THORN
Marne, France (1400)

On the eve of the Annunciation on March 24, 1400, a supernatural light drew some shepherds to a thorn bush, where they discovered a statue of the Virgin and Child made of stone. Construction of a church began In 1406 but it was not completed until 1527, the Gothic structure is set above the fields of Champagne. Pope Pius X named it a Basilica Minor in 1914. The statue is also of the Gothic type, but with its fully clothed Child would indicate an earlier date.

The image may belong to a preceding shrine at the site, believed to have been a stopping point for pilgrims since the late 12th century. The feast of Our Lady of the Thorn is celebrated on May 8 with rosary and Mass, and a diocesan pilgrimage on the following Sunday.

Source: Panoramio - Sébastien L. "Photo of Notre Dame de l'Epine."

MARCH 2016

s	m	t	w	t	f	s
		1	2	3	4	5
6	7	8	9	10	11	12
13	14	15	16	17	18	19
20	21	22	23	24	25	26
27	28	29	30	31		

HOLY THURSDAY

First Reading: *Exodus 12:1-8, 11-14*
Responsorial Psalm: *Ps 116:12-13, 15-16bc, 17-18*
Second Reading: *1 Corinthians 11:23-26*
Gospel Reading: *John 13:1-15*

Source: Messengers of Our Lady of All Nations - Gallery

March

friday

25

LADY OF ALL NATIONS
Amsterdam, Netherlands (1945)

In a series of 56 apparitions lasting 14 years, many prophecies were given to Ida Peederman by the Lady of All Nations, along with a prayer and an image of the Blessed Mother standing on a globe with a cross behind her.

Two weeks after Pope Pius XII proclaimed the dogma of the Assumption, Ida was given the title of "Lady or Mother of All Nations", and details of Mary as "Co-Redemptrix, Mediatrix, and Advocate." She was told that this would be the "last and greatest Marian dogma."

After some controversy, the appearances were declared supernatural by the local ordinary in 2002.

GOOD FRIDAY OF THE LORD'S PASSION

First Reading: *Isaiah 52:13—53:12*
Responsorial Psalm: *Ps 31:2, 6, 12-13, 15-16, 17, 25*
Second Reading: *Hebrews 4:14-16; 5:7-9*
Gospel Reading: *John 18:1—19:42*

MARCH 2016

s	m	t	w	t	f	s
		1	2	3	4	5
6	7	8	9	10	11	12
13	14	15	16	17	18	19
20	21	22	23	24	25	26
27	28	29	30	31		

March

saturday

26

OUR LADY OF THE HAWTHORN
Santa Gadea del Cid, Spain (1399)

In Santa Gadea del Cid in the province of Burgos, Spain, where on March 25, 1399, two shepherd boys, Pedro and Juan, found an oak tree with a beehive. They returned the next evening, Wednesday of Holy Week, to gather wax and honey and saw a vision of the Blessed Virgin Mary. According to testimony on parchment and signed by a notary in Santa Gadea, the boys saw a group of ghostly people around a huge thornbush. On top of the hawnthorn was a lady brighter than the sun, so brilliant that they could not look at her without being blinded.

Source: Wikipedia (Spanish) - Virgen del Espino

MARCH 2016

s	m	t	w	t	f	s
		1	2	3	4	5
6	7	8	9	10	11	12
13	14	15	16	17	18	19
20	21	22	23	24	25	26
27	28	29	30	31		

HOLY SATURDAY

First Reading: *Genesis 1:1—2:2*
Responsorial Psalm: *Ps 104:1-2, 5-6, 10, 12, 13-14, 24, 35*
Second Reading: *Genesis 22:1-18*
Gospel Reading: *Luke 24:1-12*

Source: Cosaque ami de Dieu "Fête le 16 août : Icône de la Mère de Dieu de Saint Théodore"

THEOTOKOS OF ST. THEODORE
Kostroma, Russia (1239)

Another icon purportedly from St. Luke, the origins of the name are not surely known. One theory is that in 1239 the people of Kostroma saw the icon being carried through the streets by a mysterious soldier resembling St. Theodore. On August 16, 1239, a prince found it hanging on an evergreen tree. Another story relates that around 1260, when Tatars threatened Kostroma, Russian militia rode out with the icon before them, and St. Theodore dashed between the armies. The icon rests in Kostroma Cathedral. On March 27, 1613, the wonderworking icon was used by Xenia Shestova, to bless her son Mikhail Romanov, newly chosen Tsar. In Moscow, the Romanov dynasty acknowledged the "Feodorovskaya" as their spiritual patron.

THE RESURRECTION OF THE LORD
The Mass of Easter Day

First Reading: *Acts 10:34A, 37-43*
Responsorial Psalm: *Ps 118:1-2, 16-17, 22-23*
Second Reading: *Colossians3:1-4*
Gospel Reading: *John 20:1-9*

MARCH 2016

s	m	t	w	t	f	s
		1	2	3	4	5
6	7	8	9	10	11	12
13	14	15	16	17	18	19
20	21	22	23	24	25	26
27	28	29	30	31		

March
monday
28

OUR LADY OF BOCCIOLA
Vacciago di Ameno, Italy (1528)

The Shrine of Bocciola in Ameno finds its origin on Monday, May 28, 1543, when "the Blessed Virgin Mary appeared to a girl who kept the beasts". Giulia Manfredi of Vacciago, dumb from birth, suddenly saw in a blaze in the branches of a blackthorn the Madonna and Child. Our Lady asked them to increase their devotion and in return would be her special protection. As proof of the truth of the promise and the appearance, Giulia Manfredi began to speak. When she told the neighbors what had happened and what had been commanded, suddenly the church bells began to ring without being touched by anyone. The church has been elevated by Pope Gregory XVI in 1844 with the official title of "Sanctuary".

Source: La Theotokos - Portale di mariologica - Enciclopedia "VACCIAGO DI AMENO (ITALIA)"

MARCH 2016

s	m	t	w	t	f	s
		1	2	3	4	5
6	7	8	9	10	11	12
13	14	15	16	17	18	19
20	21	22	23	24	25	26
27	28	29	30	31		

EASTER WEEK

First Reading: *Acts 2:14, 22-33*
Responsorial Psalm: *Ps 16:1-2A AND 5, 7-8, 9-10, 11*
Gospel Reading: *Matthew 28:8-15*

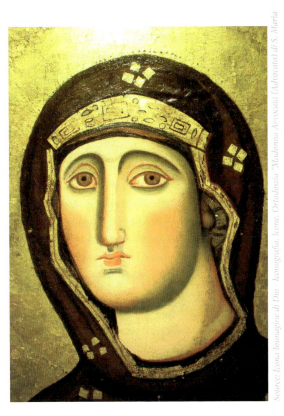

Source: Icona Immagine di Dio - Iconografia, Icone Ortodossa "Madonna Avvocata (Advocata) di S. Maria

March

tuesday

29

HOLY MARY AT THE ALTAR OF HEAVEN
Rome, Italy (1636)

Located on one of Rome's seven hills, the Capitoline or Campidoglio, the Church of Santa Maria in Ara Coeli (Altar of Heaven) is the Church of Santa Maria in Ara Coeli (Altar of Heaven), where the temple of Juno once stood. According to legend, the sibyl there told Caesar Augustus, "Here is the altar of God's son," foretelling the coming of Christianity. In the 13th century, Franciscan friars built a church honoring a tradition that Mary, holding the divine Child, appeared to Augustus there. On the high altar is an icon from the Chalkoprateia Church in Constantinople. The image was processed through the streets of Rome During the plague of 1348. On March 29, 1636, the Madonna d'Aracoeli was solemnly crowned. In 1948, the Roman people before the icon were consecrated to the Immaculate Heart of Mary.

MARCH 2016

s	m	t	w	t	f	s
		1	2	3	4	5
6	7	8	9	10	11	12
13	14	15	16	17	18	19
20	21	22	23	24	25	26
27	28	29	30	31		

EASTER WEEK

First Reading: *Acts 2:36-41*
Responsorial Psalm: *Ps 33:4-5, 18-19, 20 AND 22*
Gospel Reading: *John 20:11-18*

March
wednesday
30

OUR LADY OF THE ROCK
Alessandria della Rocca, Italy (1620)

In 1620, Alessandria, a blind young woman had her sight restored during an apparition of the Madonna. Mary requested that a church be constructed for the veneration of a statue that would be found hidden in the rocks of a hill. Convinced by the miracle of Alessandria's sight, the townspeople excavated in the spot she was told and found a beautiful white Parisian marble statue. A church was built to house the statue, and the first Hermits of St. Anthony Abbot promoted its cult. A new sanctuary was built in 1820 by the Hermits who brought the image back on March 30, 1873. At the close of the Marian Eucharistic Congress in 1939, the sacred image was officially crowned.

Source: Alessandria della Rocca "Festa della Madonna città di PARMA"a

MARCH 2016

s	m	t	w	t	f	s
		1	2	3	4	5
6	7	8	9	10	11	12
13	14	15	16	17	18	19
20	21	22	23	24	25	26
27	28	29	30	31		

EASTER WEEK

First Reading: *Acts 3:1-10*
Responsorial Psalm: *Ps 105:1-2, 3-4, 6-7, 8-9*
Gospel Reading: *Luke 24:13-35*

Source: Silesiani Don Bosco - "Santuario Madonna di Rosa - San Vito al Tagliamento (PN)"

March

thursday

31

OUR LADY OF THE ROSE
San Vito al Tagliamento, Italy (1655)

On February 2, 1655, Giacomo Giacomuzzi di Rosa and his family was in church. Mariute, his eight year old daughter, stayed with her aunts, suffering from epilepsy. Suddenly her eyes fixed on the image of the Virgin on the wall, and the girl's face lit up as if in ecstasy. Her aunts later bombarded her with questions. Mariute reported the words of the apparition. Many did not believe her father but a Franciscan, Father Vitale Vitali, investigated and concluded that the Virgin had appeared and spoken to the girl. On the evening of March 31, 1655, the image was taken to San Nicolò by two oxen followed by everyone with banners and torches. They were accompanied by three angels lighting the sky.

EASTER WEEK

First Reading: *Acts 3:11-26*
Responsorial Psalm: *Ps 8:2AB AND 5, 6-7, 8-9*
Gospel Reading: *Luke 24:35-48*

MARCH 2016

s	m	t	w	t	f	s
		1	2	3	4	5
6	7	8	9	10	11	12
13	14	15	16	17	18	19
20	21	22	23	24	25	26
27	28	29	30	31		

April

friday

1

"SWEET-KISSING" ICON OF THE MOTHER OF GOD
Smolensk, Russia (1103)

The Smolensk "Tenderness" Icon of the Mother of God manifested itself in the year 1103 at Smolensk. There is another Smolensk "Tenderness" Icon from the vicinity of Okopa (south of Smolensk). This icon was in the encampment of the Russian armies of the military commander Shein, restraining the Polish besiegers from destroying Smolensk for twenty months (1611-1613).

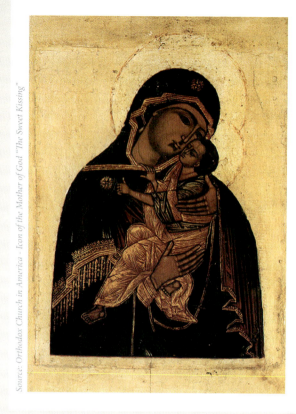

Source: Orthodox Church in America – Icon of the Mother of God "The Sweet Kissing"

APRIL 2016

s	m	t	w	t	*f*	s
					1	2
3	4	5	6	7	8	9
10	11	12	13	14	15	16
17	18	19	20	21	22	23
24	25	26	27	28	29	30

EASTER WEEK

First Reading: *Acts 4:1-12*
Responsorial Psalm: *Ps 118:1-2 AND 4, 22-24, 25-27A*
Gospel Reading: *John 21:1-14*

Source: Zeitun-eg.org

April
saturday

2

OUR LADY OF LIGHT
Zeitun, Egypt
(1968)

Our Lady was reported to appear for a span of three years in Zeitoun, Egypt hovering above Saint Mark's Coptic Church, accompanied by white doves and glowing orbs. The city shut off all power to prove it was a hoax but the apparitions continued.

These apparitions attracted large crowds by night, sometimes up to 250,000 people. Over the years, millions of Christians, Jews, Moslems, and unbelievers gathered to view the sight and the live images were broadcast on television.

On May 5, 1968, Coptic Orthodox Pope Kyrillos VI approved the apparition. The apparitions were witnessed by an envoy of Rome on April 28 who sent a report to Pope Paul VI.

EASTER WEEK

First Reading: *Acts 4:13-21*
Responsorial Psalm: *Ps 118:1 AND 14-15AB, 16-18, 19-21*
Gospel Reading: *Mark 16:9-15*

APRIL 2016

s	m	t	w	t	f	s
					1	2
3	4	5	6	7	8	9
10	11	12	13	14	15	16
17	18	19	20	21	22	23
24	25	26	27	28	29	30

April

sunday

3

OUR LADY OF THE OAK
Maisières, France (1803)

On the morning of April 3rd, 1803, in the Valley of the Loue near Ornans, about 20 kilometers from Besançon, 23 year old Cecile Mille, saw "a beautiful, tall lady dressed in white, accompanied by four little girls also wearing white clothes, each carrying a lit candle. This beautiful lady continued walking all the way to the 'Oak of Our Lady'".

On August 15, 1803, Cecile and a few others saw two "lights" that were coming out of the Oak of Our Lady near the lower branches. A closer inspection led to the discovery of a 19 centimeter clay statue of the Virgin with Child.

Source: Geo Caching - "Notre-Dame du Chêne"

APRIL 2016

s	m	t	w	t	f	s
					1	2
3	4	5	6	7	8	9
10	11	12	13	14	15	16
17	18	19	20	21	22	23
24	25	26	27	28	29	30

2ND SUNDAY OF EASTER
Divine Mercy Sunday

First Reading: *Acts 5:12-16*
Responsorial Psalm: *Ps 118:2-4, 13-15, 22-24*
Second Reading: *Revelation 1:9-11A, 12-13, 17-19*
Gospel Reading: *John 20:19-31*

Source: Salesians Don Bosco - RIVISTA MARIA AUSILIATRICE

April
monday

4

OUR LADY OF LAUSANNE
Chappeles, Switzerland (1871)

Mary appeared twice to twenty-one year old Marie-Francoise Decotterd. The seer was seriously ill from birth and continuously suffered. On April 4, 1871, the Heavenly Mother appeared for the first time and urged her to devote her life of sacrifice and expiation in the service of Jesus Christ and the salvation of souls in the world. The second time she appeared on May 9, 1872, wearing a white dress with a crucifix on her chest, and heralded the end of her sufferings and her passage into the heavenly world with the promise of "an infinite reward and eternal happiness".

2ND WEEK OF EASTER
Solemnity of the Annunciation of the Lord

First Reading: *Isaiah 7:10-14; 8:10*
Responsorial Psalm: *Ps 40:7-8A, 8B-9, 10, 11*
Second Reading: *Hebrews 10:4-10*
Gospel Reading: *Luke 1:26-38*

APRIL 2016

s	m	t	w	t	f	s
					1	2
3	4	5	6	7	8	9
10	11	12	13	14	15	16
17	18	19	20	21	22	23
24	25	26	27	28	29	30

April
tuesday
5

HOLY MARY OF GIBBILMANNA
Sicily, Italy (1534)

On Easter Sunday, April 5, 1534 a boat carrying the statue took refuge from a storm near the village of Castello di Roccella. Legend has it that Mary appeared to a Capuchin friar who lived in Gibilmanna, telling him to fetch the statue from the ox-drawn wagon and build a shrine. Like in many stories about miraculous statues of the Virgin Mary, at a certain point the statue became so heavy that the oxen refused to move any further. This became an indication that this spot was to be selected for a shrine to be erected for Mary.

Source: Blogspot - Arte Sacra "SSA RAINHA OUR QUEEN"

APRIL 2016

s	m	t	w	t	*f*	s
					1	2
3	4	5	6	7	8	9
10	11	12	13	14	15	16
17	18	19	20	21	22	23
24	25	26	27	28	29	30

2ND WEEK OF EASTER

First Reading: *Acts 4:32-37*
Responsorial Psalm: *Ps 93:1AB, 1CD-2, 5*
Gospel Reading: *John 3:7B-15*

Source: Wikipedia - Mater Ter Admirabilis

6

MOTHER THRICE ADMIRABLE
Ingolstadt, Germany (1604)

In Ingolstadt, Germany on April 6, 1604, the devotional society Jesuit College of the Catholic University Colloquium Marianum at the Jesuit College of the Catholic University was chanting the Litany of Loreto, at the foot of a replica of the ancient Roman icon Salus Populi Romani (Health of the Roman People). Fr. Jakob Rem, the creator of the group, experienced an apparition of the Mother of God, who told him that *Mater Admirabilis* was her favorite title from the Litany. When the singing reached that invocation, she disappeared, and Father Rem asked the cantor to repeat it twice more. The practice of the Colloquium repeating it three times in the Litany became standard when the reason for the original repetition was revealed and the icon was called Mother Thrice Admirable.

APRIL 2016

s	m	t	w	t	f	s
					1	2
3	4	5	6	7	8	9
10	11	12	13	14	15	16
17	18	19	20	21	22	23
24	25	26	27	28	29	30

2ND WEEK OF EASTER

First Reading: *Acts 5:17-26*
Responsorial Psalm: *Ps 34:2-3, 4-5, 6-7, 8-9*
Gospel Reading: *John 3:16-21*

April
thursday
7

OUR LADY OF SANCHO ABARCA
Tauste, Spain (1569)

From the fourteenth century the church Mudejar Santa Maria, located on a hill at the top of the village, overlooking the mouth of the Ebro River in Arba celebrates from April 20th to 24th feasts held in honor of the Virgin of Sancho Abarca, whose feast day is the 21st. The day commemorates the appearance of the holy image of Our Lady of Sancho Abarca on April 7th, 1569. One hundred years later, the statue was canonically crowned.

In 2007, the church building was renovated and altarpiece of the Coronation of Mary was restored.

APRIL 2016

s	m	t	w	t	f	s
					1	2
3	4	5	6	7	8	9
10	11	12	13	14	15	16
17	18	19	20	21	22	23
24	25	26	27	28	29	30

2ND WEEK OF EASTER
Memorial of Saint John Baptist De La Salle

First Reading: *Acts 5:27-33*
Responsorial Psalm: *Ps 34:2 AND 9, 17-18, 19-20*
Gospel Reading: *John 3:31-36*

Source: Urgnano Turistica

April
friday
8

MADONNA OF THE FROST
Basella, Italy (1356)

The Virgin appeared to Marina Cassone, a teenage peasant. During the night between April 7th and 8th there had been a heavy frost that devastated the countryside. In the morning the girl ran to the field to see the damage and began to mourn. At that moment a lady with a tender hand promised her that the crops would survive if after nine days she would come back to the same place and receive her instructions. Nine days later Our Lady commended her for returning and told her of an ancient church buried below her feet with an alter marked by three stones. The townspeople came when they heard word of this and excavated the ruins. The Bishop of Bergamo on May 1, 1356 placed the first stone of the new shrine to the Virgin.

APRIL 2016

s	m	t	w	t	f	s
					1	2
3	4	5	6	7	8	9
10	11	12	13	14	15	16
17	18	19	20	21	22	23
24	25	26	27	28	29	30

2ND WEEK OF EASTER

First Reading: *Acts 5:34-42*
Responsorial Psalm: *Ps 27:1, 4, 13-14*
Gospel Reading: *John 6:1-15*

April

saturday

9

VIRGIN OF THE HAWTHORN
Chauchina, Spain (1906)

Rosario Granados Martín age sixty-five was known in the Spanish farming town of Chauchina for her virtue and for her leg severely wounded by cancer. One day on April 9, 1906, the widow limped in the morning to a thorn bush where she cared for her wounds and their dressing. A sorrowful woman with a black rosary came up to her, and offered her a cure from her affliction if she would accompany her to the cemetery far away. Much to the surprise of witnesses in the town, the old woman walked with east down the path after Our Lady. Rosario fell asleep when the two women knelt to say the rosary. When she woke up, the black-clad woman was gone but so were her sores. After she recounted the experience to the people of the town, a chapel was built and statue canonically crowned.

APRIL 2016

s	m	t	w	t	f	s
					1	2
3	4	5	6	7	8	9
10	11	12	13	14	15	16
17	18	19	20	21	22	23
24	25	26	27	28	29	30

2ND WEEK OF EASTER

First Reading: *Acts 6:1-7*
Responsorial Psalm: *Ps 33:1-2, 4-5, 18-19*
Gospel Reading: *John 6:16-21*

Source: Icon Reader – A Reader's Guide to Orthodox Icons

April
sunday
10

LIFE-GIVING SPRING
Zeytinburnu, Turkey (460)

A tradition around 1320 holds that this sacred spring outside Constantinople was dedicated to the Mother of God in the early Christian period. Nestled among plane and cypress trees near the city's Golden Gate, it was overgrown, slimy, and forgotten by April 4, 450, when a soldier named Leo Marcullus stopped there to help a lost and thirsty blind man. Leo heard a voice say to take the water and give it to the thirsty man and take the slime and put it on the man's eyes. The voice also asked that he build a temple there. Leo found the spring, restored sight to the blind man with its mud, and after becoming Emperor in 457, built a church at the spot. In commemoration of its dedication in 460, the Mother of God as Life-Giving Spring on the Friday after Easter.

APRIL 2016

s	m	t	w	t	f	s
					1	2
3	4	5	6	7	8	9
10	11	12	13	14	15	16
17	18	19	20	21	22	23
24	25	26	27	28	29	30

3RD SUNDAY OF EASTER

First Reading: *Acts 5:27-32, 40B-41*
Responsorial Psalm: *Ps 30:2, 4, 5-6, 11-12, 13*
Second Reading: *Revelation 5:11-14*
Gospel Reading: *John 21:1-19*

April
monday
11

OUR LADY OF PERPETUAL HELP
Hallaar, Belgium (1502)

Due to inclement weather, Holy Cross Parish in Hallaar canceled its annual procession because of bad weather on the date of April 11, 1502. But the next day, after looking in confusion at the white robes of the Virgin Mary's statue splattered with mud, the priest and sexton discovered muddy tracks coming in and out of the church. The news spread that Our Lady made the procession alone, attracting pilgrims and guaranteeing that the statue would be accompanied in the procession from that date on. The three-day celebration of Our Dear Lady of Perpetual Help, perhaps named for the famed Roman icon, occurs on the first weekend in April, with the procession on Sunday.

Source: Flickr – ArcheoNet Vlaanderen "Onze-Lieve-Vrouw ten Hemel Opgenomen, Overmere"

APRIL 2016

s	m	t	w	t	f	s
					1	2
3	4	5	6	7	8	9
10	11	12	13	14	15	16
17	18	19	20	21	22	23
24	25	26	27	28	29	30

3RD WEEK OF EASTER
Memorial of Saint Stanislaus, Bishop and Martyr

First Reading: *Act 6:8-15*
Responsorial Psalm: *Ps 119:23-24, 26-27, 29-30*
Gospel Reading: *John 6:22-29*

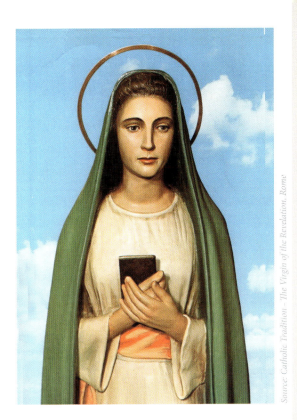

Source: Catholic Tradition – The Virgin of the Revelation, Rome

April
tuesday
12

VIRGIN OF THE REVELATION
Rome, Italy (1947)

Bruno Cornacchiola was a poor anti-Catholic tram conductor who began to plot an assassination of the Pope. On April 12, he and his children encountered the Virgin for 80 minutes in a grotto at Tre Fontane.

Bruno reported that the "beautiful woman" which his children first saw had a motherly but sad expression. She wore a green mantle over a white dress with a rose-colored sash around her waist. In her hands she held an ash-gray book close to her breast, while at her feet he could see a crucifix which had been smashed, on top of a black cloth.

Although quickly approved for faith expression in 1947, there has been no definitive judgment about the supernatural character of the events.

APRIL 2016

s	m	t	w	t	f	s
					1	2
3	4	5	6	7	8	9
10	11	12	13	14	15	16
17	18	19	20	21	22	23
24	25	26	27	28	29	30

3RD WEEK OF EASTER

First Reading: *Acts 7:51—8:1A*
Responsorial Psalm: *Ps 31:3CD-4, 6 & 7B & 8A, 17 & 21AB*
Gospel Reading: *John 6:30-35*

April
wednesday
13

OUR LADY OF THE CRAG
Vila Velha, Brazil (1569)

Perched on a giant rock across the bay from the state capital, Vitória, the monastery of Our Lady of the Crag got its start in 1558, when Franciscan missionary Pedro Palácios arrived, bringing from Portugal a painting of Nossa Senhora das Alegrias, Our Lady of Joys—the first oil painting in Brazil. In 1569, the statue of Our Lady of the Crag arrived from Lisbon. The shrine is named after a famous Black Virgin of Peña de Francia from Salamanca. Over the years, the Brazilian sanctuary, too, became a magnet for pilgrims. Its Hall of Miracles displays many ex-votos left in thanks. In 1570, the Festa da Penha began, starting on Easter and culminating eight days later, a celebration that now attracts some 600,000 participants.

Source: Blogspot - Iupestana2 "Festa de Nossa Senhora da Penha - RJ"

APRIL 2016

s	m	t	w	t	f	s
					1	2
3	4	5	6	7	8	9
10	11	12	13	14	15	16
17	18	19	20	21	22	23
24	25	26	27	28	29	30

3RD WEEK OF EASTER

First Reading: *Acts 8:1B-8*
Responsorial Psalm: *Ps 66:1-3A, 4-5, 6-7A*
Gospel Reading: *John 6:35-40*

April
thursday
14

BLESSED VIRGIN OF GRACE
Salzano, Italy (1534)

On April 14,1534 a miracle occured at Robegano: Constantina, a crippled girl, was healed while praying in front of a fourteenth century icon, then on display in a chapel near the church. On the following September 13th, the construction of a new parish sanctuary began that would house the sacred image. The project was completed on March 24, 1603 and later in 1611 Robegano became an autonomous parish. It was consecrated on September 12, 1707 by Joseph Mary Bottari, Bishop of Pola.

On the side walls are two paintings by the Viennese architect Ludwig Mayer from 1896-7 that depict the miracle of Constantina, in prayer before the image of Our Lady, and walking without the use of crutches.

APRIL 2016

s	m	t	w	t	f	s
					1	2
3	4	5	6	7	8	9
10	11	12	13	14	15	16
17	18	19	20	21	22	23
24	25	26	27	28	29	30

3RD WEEK OF EASTER

3RD WEEK OF EASTER

First Reading: *Acts 8:26-40*
Responsorial Psalm: *Ps 66:8-9, 16-17, 20*
Gospel Reading: *John 6:44-51*

April
friday
15

VIRGIN OF CUAPA
Nicaragua (1980)

Sacristan Bernardo Martinez entered the chapel to see a supernatural light coming from a statue of the Blessed Virgin. On another day, the Virgin appeared clothed in white, asking for a return to prayer and admonishing the people of Nicaragua to change.

After the initial four apparitions, the Virgin subsequently appeared in later years with messages of the destruction of atheistic communism. She also requested the propagation of the devotion to the shoulder wounds of Christ.

Bishop Pablo Antonio Vega, Prelate Bishop of Juigalpa, approved the visions as supernatural in 1982.

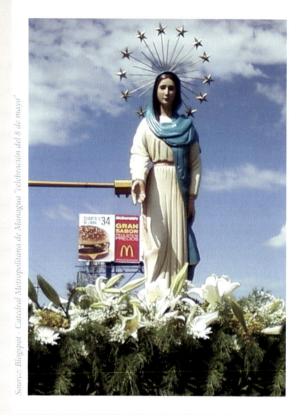

APRIL 2016

s	m	t	w	t	*f*	s
					1	2
3	4	5	6	7	8	9
10	11	12	13	14	15	16
17	18	19	20	21	22	23
24	25	26	27	28	29	30

3RD WEEK OF EASTER

First Reading: *Acts 9:1-20*
Responsorial Psalm: *Ps 117:1BC, 2*
Gospel Reading: *John 6:52-59*

Source: Mir Ikon – http://jutrikon.org

April
saturday

16

ICON OF THE MOTHER OF GOD "THE UNFADING BLOOM"
Moscow, Russia

In Moscow, Russia the icon of the the Mother of God of "the Unfading Bloom", holds her Divine Son in her right arm, and is a bouquet of white lilies - symbolizing her purity - in her left hand. These flowers traditionally and symbolically speak of the unfading flower of virginity and spotlessness of the All-Pure Virgin, whom the hymns of the Church recall: "Thou art the Root of virginity and the Unfading Blossom of purity." Miraculous copies of this icon are also found at Moscow, Voronezh, and other places in Russia.

3RD WEEK OF EASTER

First Reading:	*Acts 9:31-42*
Responsorial Psalm:	*Ps 116:12-13, 14-15, 16-17*
Gospel Reading:	*John 6:60-69*

APRIL 2016

s	m	t	w	t	f	s
					1	2
3	4	5	6	7	8	9
10	11	12	13	14	15	16
17	18	19	20	21	22	23
24	25	26	27	28	29	30

April
sunday
17

OUR LADY OF THE MIRACLES
Corbetta, Italy (1555)

On the facade of San Nicolas de Corbetta was painted a beautiful picture of the Madonna, seated on her throne with the Child.

Legend says that on April 17, 1555 the Child Jesus left the table and went to the plaza to play ball with three children.

The Madonna, surprised by the escape of the Child, also ran down to the square to bring him back, as a good mother would.

From that time the church became a place of pilgrimage and many miracles were documented. Thus Pope Paul IV called her "Our Lady of Miracles". The sudden healing of a deaf mute child sent surprise and excitement throughout the region.

Source: Storia Dei Sardi "LOMBARDIA: SANTUARIO ARCIVESCOVILE DI BEATA VERGINE DEI"

APRIL 2016

s	m	t	w	t	f	s
					1	2
3	4	5	6	7	8	9
10	11	12	13	14	15	16
17	18	19	20	21	22	23
24	25	26	27	28	29	30

4th SUNDAY OF EASTER

First Reading: *Acts 13:14, 43-52*
Responsorial Psalm: *Ps 100:1-2, 3, 5*
Second Reading: *Rev 7:9, 14B-17*
Gospel Reading: *John 10:27-30*

April
monday

18

OUR LADY OF THE OAK
Roble San Bartolomeo al Mare, Italy (1671)

Source: Marie di Nazareth "Apparizione di San Bartolomeo al Mare (IM)

On the night of April 3, 1671, after working all day in the field, Giacinto di Rollo, 50, called to his wife saying his arm was hurt. His left arm had no feeling and no medical attention helped him. On April 18, putting his arm in a sling, he took his donkey to graze. A woman dressed in turquoise shining like the sun told him to trust her for help. Then she told him to go to the Madonna della Rovere to fulfill the vow he had made. It became known to him that this woman was Mary.

The solemn coronation of the statue took place on September 8, 1921 in the cemetery, where he had established a majestic altar.

4th WEEK OF EASTER

First Reading: *Acts 11:1-18*
Responsorial Psalm: *Ps 42:2-3; 43:3, 4*
Gospel Reading: *John 10:1-10*

APRIL 2016

s	m	t	w	t	f	s
					1	2
3	4	5	6	7	8	9
10	11	12	13	14	15	16
17	18	19	20	21	22	23
24	25	26	27	28	29	30

April

VIRGIN OF VERDÚN
Minas, Uruguay
(1901)

The 10' statue of the Virgin of the Verdun, illuminated nightly, overlooks the town of Minas in southeastern Uruguay. Dedicated April 19, 1910, the shrine attracts thousands of visitors annually, particularly on this date, which the Catholic diocese chose for the annual pilgrimage and celebration at the sanctuary because it was the date in 1825 on which the famous 33 patriots crossed the Río de la Plata to liberate Uruguay from Brazil.

The statue is a traditional Immaculate Conception image: standing, childless, head uncovered, in a white robe and blue mantle, a crescent moon at her feet.

Source: Wordpress - Growth and Good Works "places: cerro verdun, minas"

APRIL 2016

s	m	t	w	t	*f*	s
					1	2
3	4	5	6	7	8	9
10	11	12	13	14	15	16
17	18	19	20	21	22	23
24	25	26	27	28	29	30

4ᵗʰ WEEK OF EASTER

First Reading: *Acts 11:19-26*
Responsorial Psalm: *Ps 87:1B-3, 4-5, 6-7*
Gospel Reading: *John 10:22-30*

Source: St Joseph Catholic Church "SORROWFUL MOTHER CHAPLET"

OUR SORROWFUL MOTHER OF THE COLLEGE
Quito, Ecuador (1906)

In the refectory of the Jesuit College of St. Gabriel on the night of April 20, 1906, an oleograph of the Virgin of Sorrows hanging on the wall began to open and shut its eyes in front of 35 boarding students and two monks. The prodigious image was transferred to the school chapel, where the prodigy recurred six times. Skeptics and believers alike testified to the occurance. After a canonical investigation which consulted physicists, chemists, physicians and theologians, Church authorities declared that it was worthy of belief.

The image was canonically crowned on April 22, 1956, during the 50th anniversary celebration.

APRIL 2016

s	m	t	w	t	f	s
					1	2
3	4	5	6	7	8	9
10	11	12	13	14	15	16
17	18	19	20	21	22	23
24	25	26	27	28	29	30

4TH Week of Easter

First Reading: *Acts 12:24—13:5A*
Responsorial Psalm: *Ps 67:2-3, 5, 6 AND 8*
Gospel Reading: *John 12:44-50*

April
thursday
21

OUR LADY OF THE MOST HOLY ROSARY
Manaoag, Philippines (15th c.)

In the 17th century, news got around that a Pangasinan man coming home from his farm had experienced a vision of the Virgin. That night, an illuminated figure appeared on a hill, that of a mother with her infant standing in a tree. She requested of him by name, "Son, I want a church here in my honor. My children shall receive many favors in this place."

The local parish priest was of course skeptical of the account, but soon pilgrims began flocking and miracles occurring.

A groundswell of support of the faithful for the devotion resulted in a bamboo chapel at the apparition site, containing a Spanish ivory statue brought by a Dominican missionary in 1605. That spot was then named Manaoag, from "mantatawag," the call.

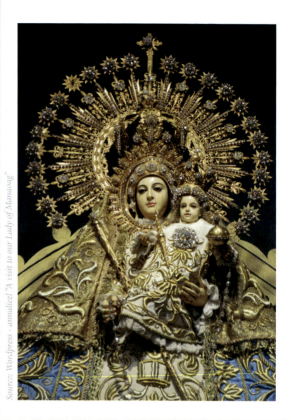

Source: Wordpress - annalizel "A visit to our Lady of Manaoag"

APRIL 2016

s	m	t	w	t	*f*	s
					1	2
3	4	5	6	7	8	9
10	11	12	13	14	15	16
17	18	19	20	21	22	23
24	25	26	27	28	29	30

4th WEEK OF EASTER

First Reading: *Acts 13:13-25*
Responsorial Psalm: *Ps 89:2-3, 21-22, 25 AND 27*
Gospel Reading: *John 13:16-20*

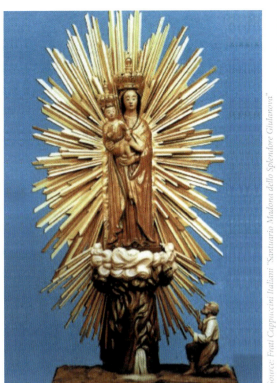

Source: Frati Cappuccini Italiani "Santuario Madona dello Splendore Giulianova"

April
friday
22

OUR LADY OF SPLENDOR
Giulianova, Italy (1557)

One day around noon, a pious farmer named Bertolino stopped gathering firewood to rest under an olive tree on a little hill outside the walls of Giulianova. He was about to get up when he saw a light in the branches, and in its center the Virgin Mary, who told him to hurry to Giulianova, and spread the story of the vision. She told him to ask the clergy for a procession to honor her and to build a sanctuary. When one of the governor's men struck him and fell mute and paralyzed, the governor believed, and called the clergy and people to go in procession to the site. They all saw the Virgin, and under the tree, a spring had welled up. News of the apparition coincided with the end of a plague that had devastated the whole region.

APRIL 2016

s	m	t	w	t	f	s
					1	2
3	4	5	6	7	8	9
10	11	12	13	14	15	16
17	18	19	20	21	22	23
24	25	26	27	28	29	30

4ᵗʰ WEEK OF EASTER

First Reading: *Acts 13:26-33*
Responsorial Psalm: *Ps 2:6-7, 8-9, 10-11AB*
Gospel Reading: *John 14:1-6*

April
saturday

23

OUR LADY OF THE REMEDIES
Cártama, Spain
(1579)

A shepherd found what he thought was a little doll and decided to take it to his daughter as gift, but every time he brought it home, it disappeared and returned to where he found it. When he recognized it as an image of the Virgin Mary, he built a chapel there.

The name of the Remedies dates to 1579 as a result of her intercession in the plague suffered by the region.

On April 23, 1579, it was decided by the inhabitants to take the image of their patron in procession for stopping the plague. The Municipal Council and diocesan bishop decided to celebrate thereafter in thanksgiving every April 23.

Source: Valle del Guadalhorce "Santuarios Cartam aErmitadelos Remedios"

APRIL 2016

s	m	t	w	t	f	s
					1	2
3	4	5	6	7	8	9
10	11	12	13	14	15	16
17	18	19	20	21	22	23
24	25	26	27	28	29	30

4th WEEK OF EASTER

First Reading: *Acts 13:44-52*
Responsorial Psalm: *Ps 98:1, 2-3AB, 3CD-4*
Gospel Reading: *John 14:7-14*

Source: Wikipedia (Spanish) "Nuestra Señora del Buen Aire"

OUR LADY OF BUENOS AIRES
Argentina (1536)

The port city of Buenos Aires was founded and named in 1536 by Pedro de Mendoza, a Spanish explorer who brought a statue of Santa María del Buen Ayre. Mariners had long held a devotion to Our Lady of Good Air as patron of seafaring and as a result her title was altered in Argentina and some other places to Nuestra Señora de los Buenos Aires, Our Lady of Good Winds.

For the 500th anniversary celebration of the arrival of the statue to Sardinia on April 24, 1870, the Bishop of Eritrea canonically crowned the Madonna of Bonaria as the representative of Pope Pius IX. This ceremonies of this date have inspired devotees of Our Lady of Good Air to continue to celebrate April 24 in her honor.

5TH SUNDAY OF EASTER

First Reading: *Acts 14:21-27*
Responsorial Psalm: *Ps 145:8-9, 10-11, 12-13*
Second Reading: *Revelation 21:1-5A*
Gospel Reading: *John 13:31-33A, 34-35*

APRIL 2016

s	m	t	w	t	f	s
					1	2
3	4	5	6	7	8	9
10	11	12	13	14	15	16
17	18	19	20	21	22	23
24	25	26	27	28	29	30

April

monday

25

OUR LADY OF GOOD COUNSEL
Genazzano, Italy (1467)

On April 25, 1467 on the feast of St. Mark at about 4 pm in Genezzano, a most pleasant melody began to resound from heaven. The townspeople started to look for the source of the music when, above the roofs and towers of the churches, a small illuminated white cloud descended to the church of the Mother of Good Counsel. Within seconds the chapel was full of people who, astonished, came to admire the heavenly phenomenon. The little cloud was dissipated, revealing a beautiful painting of Our Lady and her Divine Son.

The image was crowned as "Our Lady of Good Counsel" in 1682 in the Vatican Basilica. Pope Leo XIII gave special meaning by adding it to the Litany of the Virgin Mary. Her feast is April 26th.

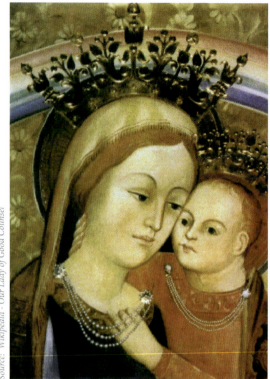

Source: Wikipedia - Our Lady of Good Counsel

APRIL 2016

s	m	t	w	t	f	s
					1	2
3	4	5	6	7	8	9
10	11	12	13	14	15	16
17	18	19	20	21	22	23
24	25	26	27	28	29	30

5TH WEEK OF EASTER
Feast of Saint Mark, Evangelist

First Reading: *1 Peter 5:5B-14*
Responsorial Psalm: *Ps 89: 2-3.6-7.16-17*
Gospel Reading: *Mark 16: 15-20*

Source: Oltre Foci Press "Rubata La Corona della Madonna dell'Incoronata di Foggia"

April
tuesday
26

MOTHER OF GOD CROWNED
Borgo Incoronta, Italy (1001)

On April 26th (the last Saturday of April) of 1001 the Virgin appeared on an oak tree in the forest of Cervaro to two people: the Count of Ariano Irpino, who was hunting and a shepherd named Strazzacappa. The Virgin appeared as the Mother of God and asked them to build a church on the place of the promised joys and blessings. The Virgin was accompanied by two angels who held onto her head a triple crown. The count was hunting on the site in the evening when a great glow rose from a tree and saw that Mary said:

"Do not fear, my son, because I am the Mother of God will find a statue of this tree will become a pledge of blessing to many. You'll place it in the church that you care to build here in my honor."

APRIL 2016

s	m	t	w	t	f	s
					1	2
3	4	5	6	7	8	9
10	11	12	13	14	15	16
17	18	19	20	21	22	23
24	25	26	27	28	29	30

5TH WEEK OF EASTER

First Reading: *Acts 14:19-28*
Responsorial Psalm: *Ps 145:10-11, 12-13AB, 21*
Gospel Reading: *John 14:27-31A*

April
wednesday
27

OUR LADY OF MONTSERRAT
Barcelona, Spain (10th c.)

According to legend, the first image of the Virgin of Montserrat shepherd children found in the year 880 . After seeing a light in the mountains, the children found the image of the Virgin in a cave. Upon hearing the news, the Bishop of Manresa attempted to move the image to the city, but the transfer was impossible because the statue was too heavy. The bishop took it as the desire of the Virgin of stay in place where she had been found and ordered the construction of a chapel.

It is said that the black color of the face of the Virgin and Child is due to exposure to candles.

Source: Rosicrucian Order - rosicrucian.org

APRIL 2016

s	m	t	w	t	f	s
					1	2
3	4	5	6	7	8	9
10	11	12	13	14	15	16
17	18	19	20	21	22	23
24	25	26	27	28	29	30

5TH WEEK OF EASTER

First Reading: *Acts 15:1-6*
Responsorial Psalm: *Ps 122:1-2, 3-4AB, 4CD-5*
Gospel Reading: *John 15:1-8*

Source: Silesians Don Bosco "LA MADONNA DELLA CASTAGNA"

April
thursday
28

OUR LADY OF THE CHESTNUT
Bergamo, Italy (1310)

On April 28, 1310 in a forest on the outskirts of Bergamo, Our Lady appeared to a humble peasant, and entrusted him with the task of building a church on that the site in her honor. The priest owner of the land heard the news, excitedly gathered the elders of Breno, of Ossanego, of Fontana, and gave his farm in order to build a church in honor of Our Lady.

The full approval of the diocesan bishop was obtained and he began work immediately with the erection of an altar and, later, even the church.

5TH WEEK OF EASTER

First Reading: *Acts 15:7-21*
Responsorial Psalm: *Ps 96:1-2A, 2B-3, 10*
Gospel Reading: *John 15:9-11*

APRIL 2016

s	m	t	w	t	f	s
					1	2
3	4	5	6	7	8	9
10	11	12	13	14	15	16
17	18	19	20	21	22	23
24	25	26	27	28	29	30

April
friday
29

BLESSED VIRGIN OF GHIARA
Reggio Emiliana, Italy (1596)

On April 29, 1596, a young seventeen year old named Marchino, dumb from birth, obtained the ability to speak, praying before the image. The miraculous event caused a remarkable rising of the faithful. They also began pilgrimages of the brotherhoods.

Pope Clement VIII, who approved the miracle in a letter of July 29, 1596 the Sacred Congregation of Rites, also authorized pilgrimages.

A few days later, there were several miracles obtained through the intercession of the Blessed Virgin of Ghiara consisting in regaining speech and hearing

Source: Silesians Don Bosco "Madonna della Ghiara"

APRIL 2016

s	m	t	w	t	f	s
					1	2
3	4	5	6	7	8	9
10	11	12	13	14	15	16
17	18	19	20	21	22	23
24	25	26	27	28	29	30

5TH WEEK OF EASTER
Mem. of St Catherine of Siena, Virgin & Doctor of the Church

First Reading: *ACTS 15:22-31*
Responsorial Psalm: *Ps 57:8-9, 10 AND 12*
Gospel Reading: *John 15:12-17*

Source: Blogspot - Escapcommague "AVE MARIA "POUR NOUS ET POUR LES MUSULMANS"

April
saturday

30

OUR LADY OF AFRICA
Algiers, Algeria (1838)

After centuries of Islamic rule, the French conquered Algiers and the Catholic Church established a diocese there for the first time in 1838. The new bishop of Algiers visited Lyons, France in 1840 where he received a bronze statue of the Virgin with outstretched hands -- a dark-complexioned version of the image on the recently popular. The statue gifted from the local sodality of the Children of Mary stayed at a Algerian monastery it was moved to a chapel built on a hill in the city in 1857 by the bishop. Following the July 1872 blessing of the new Cathedral of Algiers, the statue of Our Lady of Africa was installed there that May. Pope Pius IX authorized the crowning of the statue by the bishop on April 30, 1876.

5ᵀᴴ WEEK OF EASTER

First Reading: *Acts 16:1-10*
Responsorial Psalm: *Ps 100:1B-2, 3, 5*
Gospel Reading: *John 15:18-21*

APRIL 2016

s	m	t	w	t	f	s
					1	2
3	4	5	6	7	8	9
10	11	12	13	14	15	16
17	18	19	20	21	22	23
24	25	26	27	28	29	30

May
sunday
1

OUR LADY OF THE COURTS
Albacete, Spain
(1222)

On May 1, 1222, shepherd Francisco Alvarez was in the mountains of Cortes herding a flock of sheep which began to stir when a light like lightning passed over the oak.

A beautiful fragrance surround him and angelic music was heard as an image of Our Lady of Courts appeared, which he took to San Ignacio. The next morning the picture was gone. He returned to the oak and found the image of the Lady surrounded by a glowing and beautiful cloud.

Our Lady had asked him to build a temple where God's mercy and miracles would be shown. As a testimony to the truth of the events, his arm crippled from birth was healed.

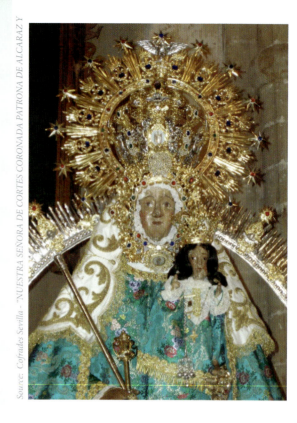

Source: Cofrades Sevilla - "NUESTRA SEÑORA DE CORTES CORONADA PATRONA DE ALCARAZ Y

MAY 2016

s	m	t	w	t	f	s
1	2	3	4	5	6	7
8	9	10	11	12	13	14
15	16	17	18	19	20	21
22	23	24	25	26	27	28
29	30	31				

6TH SUNDAY OF EASTER

First Reading: *Acts 15:1-2, 22-29*
Responsorial Psalm: *Ps 67:2-3, 5, 6, 8*
Second Reading: *Rev 21:10-14, 22-23*
Gospel Reading: *John 14:23-29*

May
monday

2

QUEEN OF THE ROSARY AND PEACE
Itapiranga, Brazil (1994)

Our Lady appeared as the Queen of the Rosary in Itapiranga in northern Brazil to the young man Edson Glauber, who describes Mary as a very beautiful seventeen year old girl.

Sometimes she appeared with the Child Jesus in the arms of St. Joseph who appears with a heart on his chest and in his heart there is a M with a cross, indicating the three hearts are together. The mission is to pray for the young, for their conversion, for peace and for the world.

Eventhough the apparitions continue, Archbishop Carillo Gritti of Itacoatiara in 2009 approved the supernatural character of the events (1994-1998).

MAY 2016

s	m	t	w	t	f	s
1	2	3	4	5	6	7
8	9	10	11	12	13	14
15	16	17	18	19	20	21
22	23	24	25	26	27	28
29	30	31				

6TH WEEK OF EASTER
Memorial of Saint Athanasius, Bishop and Doctor of the Church

First Reading: *Acts 16:11-15*
Responsorial Psalm: *Ps 149:1B-2, 3-4, 5-6A AND 9B*
Gospel Reading: *John 15:26—16:4A*

May
tuesday
3

OUR LADY OF MIRACLES
Jaffna patao, Sri Lanka (1614)

In 1614, Friar Francisco de S. Antonio, the Rector of Our Lady of Victory, wanted a statue for the church altar. The friar asked a local sculptor named Annacutti to carve a statue from a piece of wood he had brought with him from Cochin. The statue of the Virgin Mary, holding her infant son in her arms became known for miracles. People went to Annacutti's house to pray before the statue and many reported cures. Annacutti was amazed but dared not to proceed with the work asking for the unfinished statue to be taken to the church. On July 24, 1614, the statue was taken in a procession and placed on an altar. Due to numerous miracles she was called Puthumai Matha (Our Lady of Miracles) .

MAY 2016

s	m	t	w	t	f	s
	1	2	3	4	5	6	7
8	9	10	11	12	13	14
15	16	17	18	19	20	21
22	23	24	25	26	27	28
29	30	31

6TH WEEK OF EASTER
Feast of Saints Philip and James, Apostles

First Reading: *1 Corinthians 15:1-8*
Responsorial Psalm: *Ps 19:2-3, 4-5*
Gospel Reading: *John 14:6-14*

Source: Lazionatta - "Cori ricorda la Madonna del Soccorso"

OUR LADY OF THE BROOM
Cori, Italy (1521)

The sanctuary is the place where the Madonna went to rescue a three-year-old Olive during a storm, who was found only after eight days and when she had told her story, all the church with the clergy and magistrates, went in procession to the mountain, where they unearthed a fresco with the image of the Virgin on a throne holding the arm of the Child in blessing. The many times painted over fourteenth-century fresco probably belonged to an ancient chapel.

The first church was consecrated in 1537 to Our Lady of the Broom. The numerous miracles in the following years led to change of the title to Our Lady of Salvation and the construction of a new larger church, consecrated in 1639.

MAY 2016

s	m	t	w	t	f	s
1	2	3	4	5	6	7
8	9	10	11	12	13	14
15	16	17	18	19	20	21
22	23	24	25	26	27	28
29	30	31				

6TH WEEK OF EASTER

First Reading: *Acts 17:15, 22—18:1*
Responsorial Psalm: *Ps 148:1-2, 11-12, 13, 14*
Gospel Reading: *John 16:12-15*

May
thursday

5

BLESSED VIRGIN OF THE ADORATION
Fivizzano, Italy (1596)

In the small town of Fivizzano, a humble woman named Margaret lived the ordinary life of a mother, when she suddenly fell ill and confounding doctors who couldn't identify her illness, lay in bed for eighteen years with no hope of recovery.

On May 5, 1596, Margaret greeted a friend who was to bring to her a miraculous image of Our Lady, The Madonna della Ghiara. To her disappointment, he had forgotten, but looking up she saw the desired image appearing above her. With a cry of excitement and gratitude, she was healed.

The news spread throughout the town, and a shrine was built. To this day Our Lady is venerated under the title of "Our Lady of Adoration."

Source: Maria di Nazareth – "Beata Vergine dell'Adorazione Fivizzano"

MAY 2016

s	m	t	w	t	f	s
1	2	3	4	5	6	7
8	9	10	11	12	13	14
15	16	17	18	19	20	21
22	23	24	25	26	27	28
29	30	31				

6TH WEEK OF EASTER
Solemnity of the Ascension of the Lord

First Reading: *Acts 1: 1-11*
Responsorial Psalm: *Ps 47: 2-3.6-7.8-9 (6)*
Second Reading: *Eph 4: 1-13*
Gospel Reading: *Mark 16: 15-20*

Ass. di promozione sociale "Madonna delle Grazie"

Source: Santuario della Madonna Delle Grazie

OUR LADY OF GRACE
Piove di Sacco, Italy (1631)

During the four centuries of Venetian rule, the greatest problem for the people of Piove di Sacco was the plague, which in several occurrences over many years brought much misery. The plague of 1576 was long remembered for its many victims of Padova. Far more serious was the plague of 1631 in which in Padova alone 18,000 people lost their lives. When the plague continued to impact the people, a procession was made to the church of Saint Rocco but it did not stop. The death register recorded 362 deaths in three years. On April 26, 1631 the town council decided to ask for the help of the Virgin, and on May 6, there was a plague-ending procession to the church of the Madonna delle Grazie that is still remembered annually with a procession on that day.

MAY 2016

s	m	t	w	t	f	s
1	2	3	4	5	6	7
8	9	10	11	12	13	14
15	16	17	18	19	20	21
22	23	24	25	26	27	28
29	30	31				

6TH WEEK OF EASTER

First Reading: *Acts 18:9-18*
Responsorial Psalm: *Ps 47:2-3, 4-5, 6-7*
Gospel Reading: *John 16:20-23*

May
saturday
7

THE MOLCHENSKAYA ICON
Busynovo, Russia (17th c.)

In the 17th Century, a blind maiden lived in the village of Busynovo, in a house on the right bank of Busynka River. It happened that in a dream, the Mother of God appeared to her and told her to go with her mother to the river. The next day, following the instructions of the Mother of God, the girl went there and washed her eyes and received her sight. The next day, the Mother of God again appeared to the maiden and showed her where the miraculous icon of the Mother of God was to be excavated.

Soon, a chapel was erected on the site and a well was dug where the lame, crippled, and sick would come for healing from all over Russia.

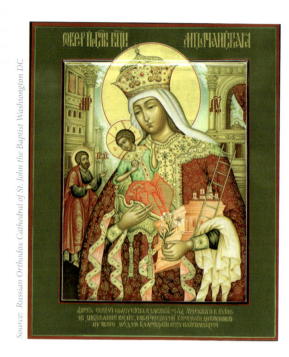

Source: Russian Orthodox Cathedral of St. John the Baptist Washington DC

MAY 2016

s	m	t	w	t	f	s
1	2	3	4	5	6	7
8	9	10	11	12	13	14
15	16	17	18	19	20	21
22	23	24	25	26	27	28
29	30	31				

6TH WEEK OF EASTER

First Reading: *Acts 18:23-28*
Responsorial Psalm: *Ps 47:2-3, 8-9, 10*
Gospel Reading: *John 16:23B-28*

Source: Wikipedia (Spanish) / Nuestra Señora de Luján

OUR LADY OF LUJÁN
Argentina (1630)

Around the year 1630, when a man from Portugal was transporting the statue and his mules stopped on the shores of the Luján River, he left it with a slave who for more than forty years was its guardian, building a brick chapel for the many pilgrims who came to venerate it. It was later moved to the location where it currently resides. In 1887 a basilica was built on the spot.

Among the Popes who have honored Our Lady of Luján are Clement XI, Clement XIV, Pius VI, Pius IX, Leo XIII, Pius XI, Pius XII, and John Paul II, who personally bestowed a Golden Rose on the statue of Our Lady.

7TH SUNDAY OF EASTER
Solemnity of the Ascension of the Lord

First Reading:	*Acts 1:1-11*
Responsorial Psalm:	*Ps 47:2-3, 6-7, 8-9*
Second Reading:	*Ephesians 1:17-23*
Gospel Reading:	*Luke 24:46-53*

MAY 2016

s	m	t	w	t	f	s
1	2	3	4	5	6	7
8	9	10	11	12	13	14
15	16	17	18	19	20	21
22	23	24	25	26	27	28
29	30	31				

May
monday
9

OUR LADY OF THE WOODS
Imbersago, Italy (1617)

Three shepherds, one named Peter, saw the Madonna near a large chestnut tree. Then they testified that the apparition rose up and disappeared into the sky.

They were believed because that chestnut was found full of fruit out of season. In 1632 a chapel was erected at the apparition site, then replaced with a real church in 1677. There sits an image called the Madonna del Bosco (The Our Lady of the Woods).

Two years before this occurrence, some had seen in the same place, a lady bathed in light hovering on top of those chestnut trees, and heard beautiful songs come from the spot of the apparition.

MAY 2016

s	m	t	w	t	f	s
1	2	3	4	5	6	7
8	9	10	11	12	13	14
15	16	17	18	19	20	21
22	23	24	25	26	27	28
29	30	31				

7TH WEEK OF EASTER

First Reading: *Acts 19:1-8*
Responsorial Psalm: *Ps 68:2-3AB, 4-5ACD, 6-7AB*
Gospel Reading: *John 16:29-33*

Source: Wikipedia (Croatian) - Crkva Gospe Trsatske

OUR LADY OF TRSAT
Croatia (1291)

According to pious legend, on May 10, 1291 the Holy House of Mary was carried on the wings of angels out of danger in Nazareth to Trsat, on a mountain of the Rjecina River gorge on the Adriatic. Even more famously, it was then miraculously flown by angels to Loreto, Italy, in 1294 according to legend. The house became the namesake for the Litany of Loreto, recounting many of the Virgin's titles of honor. Legendarily painted in oil by St. Luke the Evangelist, the Mother of Mercy in the style of *virgo lactans* was gifted to the shrine of Trsat in 1367 by Pope Urban V. It became the first image outside of Italy to receive a papal coronation in 1715. Our Lady of Trsat is processed through the streets on her feast day, May 10, and the Assumption, August 15. The Pope gave it the title of Basilica Minor in 1930.

7TH WEEK OF EASTER

First Reading:	*Acts 20: 17-27*
Responsorial Psalm:	*Ps 68: 10-11.20-21*
Gospel Reading:	*John 17: 1-11a*

MAY 2016

s	m	t	w	t	f	s
1	2	3	4	5	6	7
8	9	10	11	12	13	14
15	16	17	18	19	20	21
22	23	24	25	26	27	28
29	30	31				

May
wednesday

11

MADONNA OF THE ROCK
Calabria, Italy (1968)

Fratel Cosimo Fragomeni was born in Santa Domenica di Placanica, a village of Calabria, one of the poorest regions in Italy. On May 11th, 1968 he reported to the village priest, Don Rocco Gregorace that the Mother of God, appeared to him standing on a rock. The Virgin Mary asked Cosimo to transform the valley into a shrine in order to bring people closer to God.

Cosimo built a little chapel, that he called "Our Lady of The Rock". He also placed a marble statue of Our Lady on the rock of the apparitions. While no formal approval has been given, the local Bishop Mons. Morosini, approved the devotion for Faith Expression by declaring the "Scoglio" an official shrine on December 8, 2007.

Source: Nostra Signora dello Scoglio - madonnadelloscoglio.calabria.it

MAY 2016

s	m	t	w	t	f	s
1	2	3	4	5	6	7
8	9	10	11	12	13	14
15	16	17	18	19	20	21
22	23	24	25	26	27	28
29	30	31				

7TH WEEK OF EASTER

First Reading: *Acts 20: 28-38*
Responsorial Psalm: *Ps 68: 29-30.33-35a.35bc-36ab*
Gospel Reading: *John 17: 11b-19*

May
thursday

12

OUR LADY HELP OF CHRISTIANS
Pra, Italy (1874)

On May 12, 1874, the Blessed Virgin appeared to the shepherds Vincenzo Scossiera (12) and Angela Berruti (13). Angela first saw a lady high off the ground and on a cloud beckoning her to come closer, wearing a brown-colored dress and veil. Vincenzo came to the place and saw the lady in blue but he became scared and ran to the house.

Others including Magdalene Olivieri, and, Teresa Burnengo (36) saw the Madonna saw the Virgin as Angela had seen her. On October 25, Maria Pegollo (13) went to the site and saw the Virgin Mary dressed in black.

Our Lady said that she wanted a chapel in that place, which was built, amidst opposition from the authorities of Feglino.

Source: Cistemi Nobci & Territorio - "Festa in onore di Maria Ausiliatrice"

7TH WEEK OF EASTER

First Reading: *Acts 22: 30; 23:6-11*
Responsorial Psalm: *Ps 16: 1-2a&5.7-8.9-10.11*
Gospel Reading: *John 17: 20-26*

MAY 2016

s	m	t	w	t	f	s
1	2	3	4	5	6	7
8	9	10	11	12	13	14
15	16	17	18	19	20	21
22	23	24	25	26	27	28
29	30	31				

May
friday
13

OUR LADY OF THE ROSARY
Fatima, Portugal (1917)

While tending sheep in a field called the Cova de Iria, Lucia de Santos (10) and her two cousins, Francisco and Jacinta Marto, reported six apparitions of Mary, who identified herself as "Our Lady of the Rosary." Mary urged prayer of the rosary, penance for the conversion of sinners and the consecration of Russia to her Immaculate Heart. On October 13th, the great sun miracle of Fatima occurred. She gave the children three secrets, the third of which was revealed by Pope John Paul II with Sr. Lucia in attendance. He also beatified the two deceased seers, Jacinta and Francisco and made the feast day of Our Lady of Fatima universal by ordering it to be included in the Roman Missal.

Source: Wikipedia - Our Lady of Fátima

MAY 2016

s	m	t	w	t	f	s
1	2	3	4	5	6	7
8	9	10	11	12	13	14
15	16	17	18	19	20	21
22	23	24	25	26	27	28
29	30	31				

7TH WEEK OF EASTER

First Reading: *Acts 25: 13b-21*
Responsorial Psalm: *Ps 103: 1-2.11-12.19-20ab*
Gospel Reading: *John 21: 15-19*

May
saturday

14

OUR LADY OF THE PINE
Montagnaga, Italy (1729)

Domenica Targa (30) was busy watching her cattle which started running in all directions, when she cried: "Mary, Jesus, help me." The Virgin Mary appeared with a white veil and promised her help in exchange for her making a pilgrimage on the Ascension to St. Anne in Montagnaga that had an image by Caravaggio. She went and as she knelt in prayer the crowned Blessed Virgin appeared again in a golden robe, with Jesus in her arms, asking that the local priest be told of the apparition and that a feast be established.

In 1730, an ecclesiastical investigation began which had a positive result. A sanctuary was built and consecrated in 1750.

Source: Arcidiocesi di Trento - STORIA DEL SANTUARIO

7TH WEEK OF EASTER
Feast of Saint Matthias, Apostle

First Reading: *Acts 1:15-17, 20-26*
Responsorial Psalm: *Ps 113:1-2, 3-4, 5-6, 7-8*
Gospel Reading: *John 15:9-17*

MAY 2016

s	m	t	w	t	f	s
1	2	3	4	5	6	7
8	9	10	11	12	13	14
15	16	17	18	19	20	21
22	23	24	25	26	27	28
29	30	31				

May

sunday

15

OUR LADY OF THE HARBOR
Clermont-Ferrand, France (1614)

Continuous snow from November to Easter, froze the region of Clermont-Ferrand in 1614. With famine around the corner in a barren May, the town decided to process in the streets a wooden statue of Our Lady of the Port on followed by a prayerful crowd of over 8,000 people on Ascension Day, May 15, 1614. Starting the very next day, the weather turned warm and the door was opened for a successful harvest. After an inquiry by the bishop on May 6, 1616, he declared that the feast day of Notre-Dame du Port would be celebrated on May 15. The coronation of the statue occurred in a ceremony in 1875, and on May 15, 1881, Pope Leo XII declared the church a Minor Basilica.

Source: Mark Loopt - http://www.markloopt.nl

MAY 2016

s	m	t	w	t	f	s
1	2	3	4	5	6	7
8	9	10	11	12	13	14
15	16	17	18	19	20	21
22	23	24	25	26	27	28
29	30	31				

PENTECOST

First Reading: *Acts 2: 1-11*
Responsorial Psalm: *Ps 104: 1.24.29-30.31.34*
Second Reading: *1 Corinthians 12: 3b-7.12-13*
Gospel Reading: *John 20: 19-23*

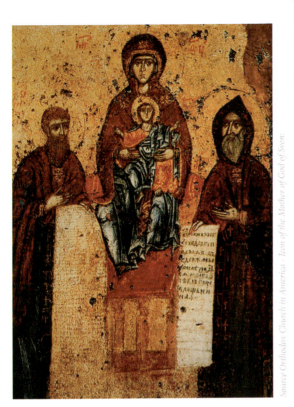

Source: Orthodox Church in America - Icon of the Mother of God of Sven:

THE SVEN CAVES ICON OF THE MOTHER OF GOD
Briansk, Russia (1288)

Prince Roman of Chernigov who became blind, requested that the icon be sent to him at Briansk. A priest went with the icon along the River Desna and after lodging for the night on the right bank of the River Svena, the icon was missing from the boat. It was found on a hill on the opposite bank, resting in the branches of an oak tree. The Prince came to the icon and was healed of his blindness. A wooden church was built in honor of the Dormition of the Most Holy Theotokos, and the tree on which the icon rested was cut up and used as wood for other icons.
The icon was glorified by healings of the blind and of the possessed, and has long been regarded as a protector from enemies.

MAY 2016

s	m	t	w	t	f	s
1	2	3	4	5	6	7
8	9	10	11	12	13	14
15	16	17	18	19	20	21
22	23	24	25	26	27	28
29	30	31				

7TH WEEK IN ORDINARY TIME

First Reading: *James 3:13-18*
Responsorial Psalm: *Ps 19:8, 9, 10, 15*
Gospel Reading: *Mark 9:14-29*

May
tuesday
17

IMMACULATE CONCEPTION
Marpingen, Germany (1876)

On July 3, 1876, one day after the coronation in Lourdes image of the Immaculate Conception, the Virgin Mary was said to appear on the top of a tree to three children, Katherina Hubertus, Margaretha Kunz, and Susanna Leist. Three days later, five adults also claimed to see her. A healing spring was found in the forest with miraculous curative powers. The Virgin identified herself as the Immaculate Conception and urged them to pray with faith and turn from sin. These facts were published in newspapers all over Germany and caused a massive influx of pilgrims which greatly worried the Prussian Parliament who imprisoned the children. On May 17, 1999, a new set of apparitions were claimed by three more children in Marpingen.

Source: Wikipedia (German) – Mariä Himmelfahrt (Marpingen)

MAY 2016

s	m	t	w	t	f	s
1	2	3	4	5	6	7
8	9	10	11	12	13	14
15	16	17	18	19	20	21
22	23	24	25	26	27	28
29	30	31				

7TH WEEK IN ORDINARY TIME

First Reading: *James 4:1-10*
Responsorial Psalm: *Ps 55:7-8, 9-10A, 10B-11A, 23*
Gospel Reading: *Mark 9:30-37*

Source: Immaculata - UNSERE LIEBE FRAU AUF DEM WESEMLIN

May
wednesday

18

OUR LADY OF WESEMLIN
Lucerne, Switzerland (1531)

During the night of Pentecost on May 18, 1531, the city councilor, Maurice von Mettenwyl, saw the Virgin Mary surrounded by a heavenly light and by arrows and the moon at her feet. Mary appeared crowned and carrying the Child Jesus on her left arm, while the right hand held a scepter.

Faced with this majestic appearance, the man was shocked and fell on his knees, promising to rebuild the chapel and put the portrait of Mary in her place, as she had appeared.

MAY 2016

s	m	t	w	t	f	s
1	2	3	4	5	6	7
8	9	10	11	12	13	14
15	16	17	18	19	20	21
22	23	24	25	26	27	28
29	30	31				

7TH WEEK IN ORDINARY TIME

First Reading: *James 4:13-17*
Responsorial Psalm: *Ps 49:2-3, 6-7, 8-10, 11*
Gospel Reading: *Mark 9:38-40*

May
thursday
19

VIRGIN OF PEÑA DE FRANCIA
El Cabaco, Spain (1434)

In 1425, Simon Rolan, a young Franciscan tertiary, was studying in Paris when he encountered an apparition of the Virgin, who instructed him to look for an image resembling her. After nine years of searching, another vision of the Virgin told him to go to the top of the mountain where he lifted a rock and unearthed a statue of a Black Virgin on May 19, 1434. All four men assisting him, each with their own ailments, were healed instantaneously. Construction was begun on the mountaintop chapel that same day and the young man then continued to build and care for the shrine. It became one of the great pilgrimage churches of Spain. The fiesta of the Virgin of Peña de Francia is celebrated in the province of Salamanca on the Nativity of Mary.

MAY 2016

s	m	t	w	t	f	s
1	2	3	4	5	6	7
8	9	10	11	12	13	14
15	16	17	18	19	20	21
22	23	24	25	26	27	28
29	30	31				

Source: Wordpress - elfarodeferia: LA VOZ DE FERIA: El Faro de Feria

7TH WEEK IN ORDINARY TIME

First Reading: *James 5:1-6*
Responsorial Psalm: *Ps 49:14-15AB, 15CD-16, 17-18, 19-20*
Gospel Reading: *Mark 9:41-50*

May
friday

20

MOTHER OF GOD
Zhyrovichy, Belarus
(14th c.)

One night around 1500, some herders noticed a wild pear tree radiating light from a small jasper oval carving of a woman and child in Eleousa (Tenderness) style and the Slavonic inscription of the Magnificat in the Orthodox liturgy, "More honorable than the cherubim, And more glorious beyond compare than the seraphim, In virginity you bore God the Word; True Mother of God, we magnify you." The herders took it to the landlord, Alexander Soltan, who put it in a chest, but it reappeared in the forest and Soltan built a wooden church there that burned down later. Some children passing the spot saw a radiant woman holding the stone icon. When a priest came, she had vanished, but the icon remained on that rock where she sat.

7TH WEEK IN ORDINARY TIME

First Reading: *James 5:9-12*
Responsorial Psalm: *Ps 103:1-2, 3-4, 8-9, 11-12*
Gospel Reading: *Mark 10:1-12*

MAY 2016

s	m	t	w	t	f	s
1	2	3	4	5	6	7
8	9	10	11	12	13	14
15	16	17	18	19	20	21
22	23	24	25	26	27	28
29	30	31				

May

saturday

21

OUR LADY OF THE ANGELS
Arcola, Italy (1556)

Baldassare Fiamberti and family attended Mass for Pentecost in the parish church of Arcola on May 21, 1556. The five daughters with permission of the family decided to visit the nearby forest, where they at times would like to go to play and then pray. They walked for a bit and then when the ringing of the church bells filled the air, they stopped to pray the rosary. Suddenly, a bright light and the choirs of angels surrounded the girls. The Virgin in bright white as the sun appeared saying: "Fear not. I am Mary, the Mother of Jesus, Queen of Angels. Go, tell the people to pray and do penance." The Bishop of Sarzana led an investigation that declared the event miraculous. The Shrine of Our Lady of Angels of Arcola was completed in 1558.

Source: Blogspot – La Meditazione di Cristo "Arcola e il Santuario di Nostra Signora degli Angeli"

Miracolosa immagine di N. S. degli Angeli
(Apparsa in Arcola il 21 Maggio 1556)
(Incoronata dal Capitolo Vaticano il 16 maggio 1910)

MAY 2016

s	m	t	w	t	f	s
1	2	3	4	5	6	7
8	9	10	11	12	13	14
15	16	17	18	19	20	21
22	23	24	25	26	27	28
29	30	31				

7TH WEEK IN ORDINARY TIME

First Reading: James 5:13-20
Responsorial Psalm: Ps 141:1-2, 3 AND 8
Gospel Reading: Mark 10:13-16

Source: Foros de la Virgen - "Nuestra Señora de la Misericordia de Bovegno, Italia"

sunday

22

OUR LADY OF MERCY
Croce di Savenone, Italy (1527)

On May 14, 1527 Mary Amadini, a 22 year old from a poor family, who worried how to feed her family and care for her twelve year old sore-stricken brother Andrea, came home early to go to collect firewood and bring to the bakery hoping to get some bread. While gathering, she discovered some silver coins and filled her apron before returning.

On May 22, she prayed in gratitude to the Virgin who appeared to her and made known the impending punishment of her Son which could be abated by three Saturdays of fasting and penance. To prove the veracity of the apparition, Our Lady cured the leprosy of her brother. The people decided to build a Shrine where many miracles later occurred.

MAY 2016

s	m	t	w	t	f	s
1	2	3	4	5	6	7
8	9	10	11	12	13	14
15	16	17	18	19	20	21
22	23	24	25	26	27	28
29	30	31				

8TH SUNDAY IN ORDINARY TIME
The Solemnity of the Most Holy Trinity

First Reading: *Proverbs 8:22-31*
Responsorial Psalm: *Ps 8:4-5, 6-7, 8-9*
Second Reading: *Romans 5:1-5*
Gospel Reading: *John 16:12-15*

May
monday
23

VIRGIN OF GRACE
Aés, Spain (1575)

On May 23, 1575, as widow María Saínz de Quijano said the rosary while watching sheep on Hedilla Mountain, she saw the Virgin appear. She asked that a chapel be built on that spot. To the woman's objection that people wouldn't believe her, the Virgin promised that she would help. The woman found she could not get up, calling for her daughter Juana, who carried her mother home on her back. María asked her to get the vicar, who dismissed it, saying the shepherdess must have been dreaming and suddenly he went blind. The vicar dictated a letter to the Archbishop, asking him to construct a chapel so to regain his sight. The chapel was built and renovated several times over the centuries. An annual romería to the shrine occurs on May 23.

Source: Olivia de la Frontera "Santuario De Nuestra Señora Virgen De Gracia"

MAY 2016

s	m	t	w	t	f	s
1	2	3	4	5	6	7
8	9	10	11	12	13	14
15	16	17	18	19	20	21
22	23	24	25	26	27	28
29	30	31				

8TH WEEK IN ORDINARY TIME

First Reading: *1 Peter 1:3-9*
Responsorial Psalm: *Ps 111:1-2, 5-6, 9 AND 10C*
Gospel Reading: *Mark 10:17-27*

Source: Catholic Tradition - "The Virgin of Passau Germany"

May
tuesday

24

AUXILIUM CHRISTIANORUM / OUR LADY, HELP OF CHRISTIANS
Germany (1861)

Invoking Mary under this title, Catholics recalled Mary's help against Islamic forces at Vienna (1683) and earlier at Lepanto (1571) where forces of the Holy League defeated the Ottomans behind the prayers of the Rosary of all of Europe in one of the most impactful naval battles in all of history. In 1815, after Waterloo, Pope Pius VII instituted the feast of Mary, Help of Christians for the Papal States, recalling the date he returned to Rome after captivity under Napoleon: May 24, 1814.

8TH WEEK IN ORDINARY TIME

First Reading:	*1 Peter 1:10-16*
Responsorial Psalm:	*Ps 98:1, 2-3AB, 3CD-4*
Gospel Reading:	*Mark 10:28-31*

MAY 2016

s	m	t	w	t	f	s
1	2	3	4	5	6	7
8	9	10	11	12	13	14
15	16	17	18	19	20	21
22	23	24	25	26	27	28
29	30	31				

May
wednesday
25

OUR LADY OF THE MEADOW
Ciudad Real, Spain
(1088)

According to tradition, on 25 May 1088, the Romanesque image of the Virgen del Prado came as part of the royal entourage of Alfonso VI to a small settlement called La Mancha Don Pozuelo. The locals, after the alleged appearance of the Virgin, asked their king to provide a sacred image to be venerated there. At the center of the settlement, which four centuries later would be called Ciudad Real, there was a small shrine of little importance built there. When in 1195 he lost the battle of Alarcos against the Almohads, the Castilian King Alfonso VIII constructed a new church on the site of the chapel, within walking distance of Ciudad Real.

Source: Wikipedia (Spanish) - Nuestra Señora del Prado

MAY 2016

s	m	t	w	t	f	s
1	2	3	4	5	6	7
8	9	10	11	12	13	14
15	16	17	18	19	20	21
22	23	24	25	26	27	28
29	30	31				

8TH WEEK IN ORDINARY TIME

First Reading: *1 Peter 1:18-25*
Responsorial Psalm: *Ps 147:12-13, 14-15, 19-20*
Gospel Reading: *Mark 10:32-45*

Source: Wolfgang Moroder – Wikipedia "Our Lady of Caravaggio"

OUR LADY OF CARAVAGGIO
Italy (1432)

In 1879, Italians from Lombardy built a chapel for their settlement in southern Brazil. Lacking sacred art, they dedicated the chapel around an available image, that of Madonna di Caravaggio. Today the shrine hosts over a million pilgrims annually. The pilgrimage to Farroupilha on the fourth Sunday in May commemorates an apparition that took place on May 26, 1432 near the Lombard town of Caravaggio. Giannetta De' Vacchi Varoli was cutting hay in a field when the Virgin appeared. After Signora Varoli told the townsfolk of the Virgin's requests for penance and a chapel, a new healing spring arose. The apparition anniversary became a day of pilgrimage to the shrine of Santa Maria del Fonte, and devotion to the Madonna of Caravaggio spread.

8TH WEEK IN ORDINARY TIME
Memorial of Saint Philip Neri, Priest

First Reading: *1 Peter 2:2-5, 9-12*
Responsorial Psalm: *Ps 100:2, 3, 4, 5*
Gospel Reading: *Mark 10:46-52*

MAY 2016

s	m	t	w	t	f	s
1	2	3	4	5	6	7
8	9	10	11	12	13	14
15	16	17	18	19	20	21
22	23	24	25	26	27	28
29	30	31				

May
friday
27

VIRGIN OF SORROWS
La Codosera, Spain
(1945)

At 3 pm on May 27, 1945, a girl Marcelina Exposito Barroso and her cousin Agustina Gonzalez, were walking to the next village to run an errand. They had gone about two miles, when Marcelina noticed something off the road. Our Lady of Sorrows, was half way up the trunk of a tree, with black cloak embroidered with stars, hands together, and a beautiful but sorrowful face. The vision disappeared, and the girl ran to the village and told her mother what had happened, and word spread. On June 4, the Blessed Virgin told her to walk on her knees which she did without a scratch. The diocesan curia of Badajoz has not yet officially pronounced on these facts, but allowed the construction of the Shrine.

Source: Cofrades - "las apariciones de la virgen de los dolores en chandavila"

MAY 2016

s	m	t	w	t	f	s
1	2	3	4	5	6	7
8	9	10	11	12	13	14
15	16	17	18	19	20	21
22	23	24	25	26	27	28
29	30	31				

8TH WEEK IN ORDINARY TIME

First Reading: *1 Peter 4:7-13*
Responsorial Psalm: *Ps 96:10, 11-12, 13*
Gospel Reading: *Mark 11:11-26*

May
saturday

28

OUR LADY OF THE BURNING FIRE
Arras, France (1105)

In 1105, a major epidemic of a raging fever began in the region of Arras that was claiming hundreds of lives. On May 28, when the people called upon her praying, the Holy Mother of Heaven appeared from the bell tower of the church and the bishop held out a large candle, symbol of both faith and healing. Whoever had drunk a little bit of this candle wax dissolved in water would be saved from the plague. Despite the widespread use, the candle has not been consumed and never even went out throughout the period of the epidemic.

In 1140, in gratitude for the miraculous intervention of the Holy Virgin, the first votive chapel was erected in honor of "Notre Dame des Ardents (Our Lady of the Burning Fire)".

Source: images saintes "Notre Dame des Ardents" 1

8TH WEEK IN ORDINARY TIME

First Reading: *Jude 17, 20B-25*
Responsorial Psalm: *Ps 63:2, 3-4, 5-6*
Gospel Reading: *Mark 11:27-33*

MAY 2016

s	m	t	w	t	f	s
1	2	3	4	5	6	7
8	9	10	11	12	13	14
15	16	17	18	19	20	21
22	23	24	25	26	27	28
29	30	31				

May
sunday
29

OUR LADY OF GOOD DELIVERY
Paris, France
(14th c.)

The Marian title for the patroness of Easy Childbirth, which is quite popular throughout western Europe, is traditionally celebrated on May 29. The title is also known as Our Lady of the Milk and Happy Delivery. One of the most celebrated Madonnas in Paris if the 14th century image carved from a single block of hard limestone known by the title La Vierge Noire de Paris. It was saved from destruction during the Revolution and is now preserved in the Church of St. Etienne de Gres. The Institution of the Confraternity of Our Lady of Deliverance was established at the Church of St. Etienne de Gres in 1533 or 1583.

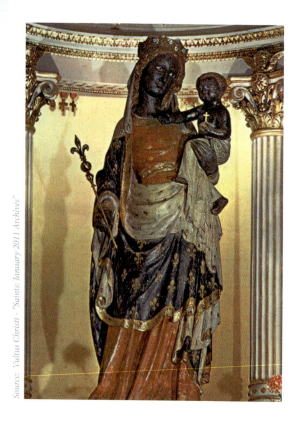

Source: Vultus Christi - "Saints: January 2011 Archives"

MAY 2016

s	m	t	w	t	f	s
1	2	3	4	5	6	7
8	9	10	11	12	13	14
15	16	17	18	19	20	21
22	23	24	25	26	27	28
29	30	31				

9TH SUNDAY IN ORDINARY TIME
The Solemnity of the Most Holy Body and Blood of Christ

First Reading: *Genesis 14:18-20*
Responsorial Psalm: *Ps 110:1, 2, 3, 4*
Second Reading: *1 Corinthians 11:23-26*
Gospel Reading: *Luke 9:11B-17*

May
monday

30

OUR LADY OF THE LITTLE BRIDGE
San Marino di Carpi, Italy (16th c.)

Source: Diocesi di Carpi - Con Maria nel mese di maggio

The image of the Madonna and Child named after the town river is a fresco dating from the sixteenth century attributed to Loschi Bernardino. In the beginning of the seventeenth century, the church containing the fresco of the Madonna of Bridges which is accessed via two lateral stairways. In May 2005, two works were added from the painter Alberto Carpi Rustichelli illustrating scenes of the miracle of Ponticelli. It was elevated to the title of diocesan shrine in 1935.

9TH WEEK IN ORDINARY TIME

First Reading: *2 Peter 1:2-7*
Responsorial Psalm: *Ps 91:1-2, 14-15B, 15C-16*
Gospel Reading: *Mark 12:1-12*

MAY 2016

s	m	t	w	t	f	s
1	2	3	4	5	6	7
8	9	10	11	12	13	14
15	16	17	18	19	20	21
22	23	24	25	26	27	28
29	30	31				

May

tuesday

31

OUR LADY OF THE STARS
Cellatica, Italy
(1536)

On May 31, 1536 the Blessed Virgin appeared to Antonio de 'Antoni, a poor deaf-mute shepherd of Gardone Val Trompia. who was tending the flock of a landowner of San Vigilio,and reciting the Holy Rosary; Suddenly, he received an apparition of Our Lady with the Child in her arms. She said to invite the inhabitants of the surrounding villages to dedicate a temple in that place. Mary encouraged him, assuring him that she herself would have confirmed his request with miracles and graces.

Pope Paul III granted the building of the sanctuary, on which work began in 1537 and ended in 1539.

Source: Eco delle Valli "Il Festival del Romanino arriva al santuario della stella"

MAY 2016

s	m	t	w	t	f	s
1	2	3	4	5	6	7
8	9	10	11	12	13	14
15	16	17	18	19	20	21
22	23	24	25	26	27	28
29	30	31				

9TH WEEK IN ORDINARY TIME
Feast of the Visitation of the Blessed Virgin Mary

First Reading: *Zephaniah 3:14-18A*
Responsorial Psalm: *Isaiah 12:2-3, 4BCD, 5-6*
Gospel Reading: *Luke 1:39-56*

Source: Altervista: Leiniaccun - "Santuario Madonna delle Grazie" Photo by Paolo Bolognesi

OUR LADY OF GRACE
Leini, Italy
(1630)

The town of Leini was devastated by famine and plague, decimating the population. A deaf and mute man returned from the fields on June 1, 1630. He began to pray before the image of the Virgin: "Save Leini, Mary, hear our prayer, save us ..." The Madonna appeared with a smile and placed a rosary around his neck. Miraculously his speech was restored and he began to sing praises. The Blessed Mother's voice was the first he ever heard: "go build a church here and I will ask my Son to stop the plague". The streets were filled with his shouts of joy, announcing that the plague had ceased. The survivors heard him and joined in a prayer of thanksgiving. From that day the plague stopped, the sick were cured, and those alive were able to build a sanctuary as promised.

JUNE 2016

s	m	t	w	t	f	s
			1	2	3	4
5	6	7	8	9	10	11
12	13	14	15	16	17	18
19	20	21	22	23	24	25
26	27	28	29	30		

9TH WEEK IN ORDINARY TIME
Memorial of Saint Justin, Martyr

First Reading: *2 Timothy 1:1-3, 6-12*
Responsorial Psalm: *Ps 123:1B-2AB, 2CDEF*
Gospel Reading: *Mark 12:18-27*

June
thursday

2

MADONNA OF THE TEARS
Ponte Nossa, Italy
(1511)

According to tradition, on June 2, 1511, a shepherdess was staring at a Marian icon and saw the face change, open and close her eyes to weep blood. She heard a voice that told her to call the other people in order to observe the miracle, as well as to build a new church. The witness' testimony was then collected by a notary and put in writing. The new sacred building, begun in 1525 and completed in 1533, was built alongside the existing church dedicated to Santa Maria Assunta. Consecrated in 1575 and elevated to the rank of a parish in 1583, when separated from Premolo, the church featured the fresco became as a side altar. The previous church was then demolished in 1716 in order to make room for the new sacristy.

Source: Panoramio - Madonna Delle Lacrime di Ponte Nossa

JUNE 2016

s	m	t	w	t	f	s
			1	2	3	4
5	6	7	8	9	10	11
12	13	14	15	16	17	18
19	20	21	22	23	24	25
26	27	28	29	30		

9TH WEEK IN ORDINARY TIME

First Reading: *2 Timothy 2:8-15*
Responsorial Psalm: *Ps 25:4-5AB, 8-9, 10 AND 14*
Gospel Reading: *Mark 12:28-34*

Source: Collection — GTG "Tretyakov State Gallery"

June
friday

3

OUR LADY OF VLADIMIR
Moscow, Russia (1395)

The Mother of God of Vladimir is an icon of the *Eleusa* or Tenderness type and is one of the world's most beloved and well-known Marian images. The Virgin of Vladimir is said to have been moved from Jerusalem to Constantinople in 450. When he became ruler of Vladimir, the prince brought the tempera panel from Kiev and placed it in the Dormition Cathedral. The end of Tamerlane's siege, a miracle commemorated annually on September 8 is credited to the icon when it was carried to Moscow in 1395. After a victory over the Tatars in 1480, Moscow became the permanent home of the image. The icon hung in Moscow's Church of Annunciation until 1918. June 3rd (May 21 Julian calendar) remembers Moscow's deliverance from Khan Mahmet Ghirei in 1521.

JUNE 2016

s	m	t	w	t	f	s
			1	2	3	4
5	6	7	8	9	10	11
12	13	14	15	16	17	18
19	20	21	22	23	24	25
26	27	28	29	30		

9TH WEEK IN ORDINARY TIME
Solemnity of the Most Sacred Heart of Jesus

First Reading: *Ezekiel 34:11-16*
Responsorial Psalm: *Ps 23:1-3A, 3B-4, 5, 6*
Second Reading: *Romans 5:5B-11*
Gospel Reading: *Luke 15:3-7*

June

saturday

4

VIRGIN MARY THE PLANTER
Hurlingham, Argentina (17th c.)

The image of Virgen Maria Sembradora (Virgin Mary the Planter) is housed in the parish San Carlos Borromeo in Hurlingham, Buenos Aires, Argentina. The Virgin carries in her right hand the Seeds of the Word, planting it in the hearts of the faithful. Her left hand is in a posture of blessing and protection.

A novena is begun on May 25th and, on the 4th of June every year, the statue is carried out in procession at 4:30 PM.

Source: Arcangelgabriel.com - Maria Sembradora

JUNE 2016

s	m	t	w	t	f	s
				1	2	3	4
5	6	7	8	9	10	11
12	13	14	15	16	17	18
19	20	21	22	23	24	25
26	27	28	29	30		

9TH WEEK IN ORDINARY TIME
Memorial of the Immaculate Heart of the Bl. Virgin Mary

First Reading: *2 Timothy 4:1-8*
Responsorial Psalm: *Ps 71:8-9, 14-15AB, 16-17, 22*
Gospel Reading: *Luke 2:41-51*

Source: Chiesa di Gorgonzola Santuario Madonna dell'Aiuto

June

sunday

5

OUR LADY OF HELP
Bobbio, Italy
(15th c.)

Adriano Repetino, who had a vineyard in fields of Corgnate outside Bobbio, built a wall along the road, and in it a niche with an image of a seated Mary with the Child in the 15th century. The image became a focus of local devotion: there were healings, and the picture changed its appearance in 1472. After an investigation, Church authorities decided the site merited a chapel. The building dedicated to the Annunciation was constructed on the property donated by Adriano. The miracles of the image resumed on June 5, 1611. When the icon was discovered to sweat, the Bishop named the image the "Blessed Virgin of Help." A larger church was consecrated in 1738. In 1947, the icon was crowned and Pope Paul VI elevated the church to Basilica Minor in 1970.

10ᵀᴴ SUNDAY IN ORDINARY TIME

First Reading: *1 Kings 17:17-24*
Responsorial Psalm: *Ps 30:5-6, 11, 12, 13*
Second Reading: *Galatians 1:11-14A, 15AC, 16A, 17, 19*
Gospel Reading: *Luke 7:11-17*

JUNE 2016

s	m	t	w	t	f	s
			1	2	3	4
5	6	7	8	9	10	11
12	13	14	15	16	17	18
19	20	21	22	23	24	25
26	27	28	29	30		

June

monday

6

VIRGIN OF THE ROSARY
Villarreal de Huerva, Spain
(13th c.)

The festivities in honor of Our Lady of the Rosary take place during the 6th and 7th of June.

The five foot tall statue, a Polychrome carving of the Virgin of the Rosary with the child, by an unknown sculptor in the thirteenth century, from the Romanesque period is kept in the parish church of Huerva Villarreal.

It was restored by Natalia de la Serna in 1997.

Source: Xiloca - Virgen del Rosario (Villarreal de Huerva)

JUNE 2016

s	m	t	w	t	f	s
			1	2	3	4
5	6	7	8	9	10	11
12	13	14	15	16	17	18
19	20	21	22	23	24	25
26	27	28	29	30		

10ᵀᴴ WEEK IN ORDINARY TIME

First Reading: *1 Kings 17:1-6*
Responsorial Psalm: *Ps 121:1BC-2, 3-4, 5-6, 7-8*
Gospel Reading: *Matthew 5:1-12*

Source: lameziainstrada.it – Viaggio per i santuari di Calabria

June
tuesday

7

OUR LADY OF THE OAK
Visora di Conflenti, Italy (1578)

The Mother of God appeared on June 7, 1578 to a lowly shepherd, named Lorenzo Folino. The young man was resting in the shade when he heard sweet music and saw the Virgin Mary surrounded by angels in a large oak tree. She asked him to tell the priest to build a church. After apparitions to others, the church was finally built.

The place became a place of pilgrimage, and there arose votive icons, in one of them was a large stone in the shape of a foot referred to as "The Lady of the Tread." In 1921 a fire destroyed the shrine but in 1958, it was rebuilt in the same place as it is today. Our Lady of Visora is venerated with the title of "Madonna della Quercia".

10TH WEEK IN ORDINARY TIME

First Reading: *1 Kings 17:7-16*
Responsorial Psalm: *Ps 4:2-3, 4-5, 7B-8*
Gospel Reading: *Matthew 5:13-16*

JUNE 2016

s	m	t	w	t	f	s
			1	2	3	4
5	6	7	8	9	10	11
12	13	14	15	16	17	18
19	20	21	22	23	24	25
26	27	28	29	30		

June
wednesday

8

OUR LADY OF SUNDAY
Saint-Bauzille-de-la-Sylve, France (1873)

Although it was Sunday the feast of the Trinity, the wine maker Augustus Arnaud worked in his vineyard. Suddenly, according to local legend, Augustus saw a bright light in the middle of the field that manifested itself in the figure of the Blessed Virgin Mary. She urged the farmer to erect a cross, to place a statue of the Madonna in the vineyard and venerate it with his neighbors. Exactly one month later, she reappeared near the recently installed cross and said: "You must never work on Sunday! Blessed are those who believe." In 1876, the diocesan bishop, Bishop De Cabrières, after the establishment of a commission of inquiry and having questioned the seer, recognized the supernatural origin of the apparitions.

Source: http://immaculata.ch - Notre Dame du Dimanche

JUNE 2016

s	m	t	w	t	f	s
			1	2	3	4
5	6	7	8	9	10	11
12	13	14	15	16	17	18
19	20	21	22	23	24	25
26	27	28	29	30		

10TH WEEK IN ORDINARY TIME

First Reading: *1 Kings 18:20-39*
Responsorial Psalm: *Ps 16:1B-2AB, 4, 5AB AND 8, 11*
Gospel Reading: *Matthew 5:17-19*

Source: sabina.it - La Chiesa di S.Maria della Noce a Tarano

 June
thursday

9

HOLY MARY OF THE WALNUT
Rieti, Italy (1505)

A young man prayed fervently to the Blessed Virgin Mary for the healing of his brother who was very sick. One day on June 9, 1505 Mary appeared to him and promised him that his brother would be cured. In fact, shortly after it happened, in gratitude he erected a church; A statue of Our Lady of Grace was placed inside. In 1690, the coronation of the statue was celebrated. The Sanctuary of the Madonna di Tirano remains in this town even today.

10TH WEEK IN ORDINARY TIME

First Reading: *1 Kings 18:41-46*
Responsorial Psalm: *Ps 65:10, 11, 12-13*
Gospel Reading: *John 13:34*

JUNE 2016

s	m	t	w	t	f	s
			1	2	3	4
5	6	7	8	9	10	11
12	13	14	15	16	17	18
19	20	21	22	23	24	25
26	27	28	29	30		

June
friday
10

OUR LADY OF LAPA
Sernancelhe,
Portugal (1498)

According to legend, a statue of the Virgin in the cleft of a rock was found by a mute girl herding her flock. Much to the displeasure of her mother, she devotedly venerated the image. Thinking the statue to be a silly doll, the mother threw the statue in the fire. The girl desperately reached into the flames and recovered the unburnt image out of the fire. Strangely, she was cured, but her mother's arm became stricken with paralysis. After some prayer, the mother began to use her arm again. The priest took the image to the parish church but it by some miracle it returned to its original spot three times. There on the spot a chapel was built later to become a major pilgrimage destination. In 1575, Pope Gregory XIII approved the transfer to the shrine to the Society of Jesus at the request of King Sebastian.

Source: Wikipedia (Portuguese) – Nossa Senhora da Lapa

JUNE 2016

s	m	t	w	t	f	s
			1	2	3	4
5	6	7	8	9	10	11
12	13	14	15	16	17	18
19	20	21	22	23	24	25
26	27	28	29	30		

10TH WEEK IN ORDINARY TIME

First Reading: *1 Kings 19:9A, 11-16*
Responsorial Psalm: *Ps 27:7-8A, 8B-9ABC, 13-14*
Gospel Reading: *Matthew 5:27-32*

Source: Lebanon Road – Shrine of Our Lady Mantara in Maghdouche: Saydet Al Mantara

June
saturday

11

OUR LADY OF MANTARA
Maghdouché, Lebanon (1721)

According to tradition, Mary is said to have waited in the cave of Mantara, while Jesus preached in Sidon. The place was memorialized as a shrine by Emperor Constantine's mother Helena. With a Muslim ruler's possession of the territory 3 centuries later, Christians fled Maghdouché after sealing the cave. In 1683, descendants of the exiles returned to their homeland. On September 8, 1721, a goat herder went down a hole in the rock where one of his flock had fallen and discovered St. Helen's icon. On September 8, Christians now celebrate its recovery annually. On June 11, 1911, 400 people saw a silent apparition of the Madonna and Child near this cave. The shrine has become a popular baptismal site as Our Lady of Mantara is invoked for the healing and protection of children.

JUNE 2016

s	m	t	w	t	f	s
			1	2	3	4
5	6	7	8	9	10	11
12	13	14	15	16	17	18
19	20	21	22	23	24	25
26	27	28	29	30		

10TH WEEK IN ORDINARY TIME
Memorial of Saint Barnabas, Apostle

First Reading: *Acts 11: 21b-26; 13: 1-3*
Responsorial Psalm: *Ps 98: 1.2-3ab.3cd-4.5-6*
Gospel Reading: *Matthew 5:33-37*

June
sunday
12

OUR LADY OF MONTALTO
Messina, Sicily, Italy (1294)

One night a humble friar named Nicholas dreamed of the Virgin Mary who told him to go the next day to the Senate of Messina and inform them that Our Lady of the High Mountain wanted a temple built. When he awoke, he ignored the dream. The next night, the Virgin appeared again, scolding him for disobedience. The monk then asked him how he could get himself heard by the Senate. Our Lady told him not to despair, and the next day at noon, a dove was outlined in snow on the hill site to indicate the location. On June 12, 1294, the hill was full of people of Messina, and the white dove marked out the spot. Fra Nicholas went to Matagrifone castle to find the Queen Constance who promised her help and laid the first stone in 1295.

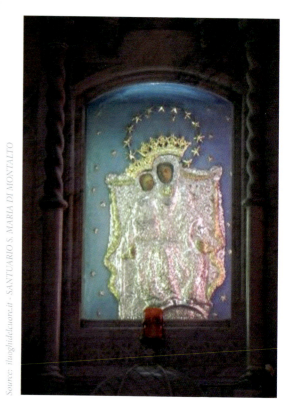

Source: *iluoghidelcuore.it - SANTUARIO S. MARIA DI MONTALTO*

JUNE 2016

s	m	t	w	t	f	s
			1	2	3	4
5	6	7	8	9	10	11
12	13	14	15	16	17	18
19	20	21	22	23	24	25
26	27	28	29	30		

11TH SUNDAY IN ORDINARY TIME

First Reading: *2 Samuel 12:7-10, 13*
Responsorial Psalm: *Ps 32: 5, 7, 11*
Second Reading: *Galatians 2:16A, 19B-20*
Gospel Reading: *Luke 7:36-50*

Source: Blogspot Caravanista "ORNES - FERREIRA DO ZÊZERE"

OUR LADY OF TEARS
Espinhal, Portugal
(13th c.)

At the time King Dinis ruled Portugal, in a village called Vats, the overseer of the land, William of Pavia, heard sorrowful moans coming from the woods. He gave the news to the Queen that he heard these moans and she told him to return and seek an image of Our Lady that he should take to church in Vats. William heard the cries again, searched the woods and found a very heavy stone image of the Virgin, needing to be transported to the river in a cart. William did not neglect to go to Coimbra to break the news to the Queen, the saintly Isabel, who immediately hastened to come to Vats to be the first of pilgrims to pray before the image of Our Lady of Tears. Miracles, including the end of a drought, began to happen.

11TH WEEK IN ORDINARY TIME
Memorial of St. Anthony of Padua, Priest & Doctor of the Church

First Reading: *1 Kings 21:1-16*
Responsorial Psalm: *Ps 5:2-3AB, 4B-6A, 6B-7*
Gospel Reading: *Matthew 5:38-42*

JUNE 2016

s	m	t	w	t	f	s
			1	2	3	4
5	6	7	8	9	10	11
12	13	14	15	16	17	18
19	20	21	22	23	24	25
26	27	28	29	30		

June

tuesday

14

OUR LADY OF THE ARBOR
Lille, France (1234)

On June 14, 1234, 53 cripples were cured upon praying before the statue of Our Lady of the Trellis, installed behind a latticework fence in St. Peter's Collegiate Church. A procession held annually on the second Sunday after Pentecost commemorates the miracles. Saved during the destruction of St. Peter's Church in the French Revolution, the statue moved afterwards to St. Catherine's Church. Devotion to Our Lady of the Trellis revived in the mid-1800s, and a grand neo-Gothic church arose in her honor, where the statue was installed in 1872 and canonically crowned in 1874. After the theft of the original in 1959, sculptor Marie Madeleine Weerts carved the image now displayed in Lille's Catholic Cathedral, the Basilica of Notre-Dame de la Treille.

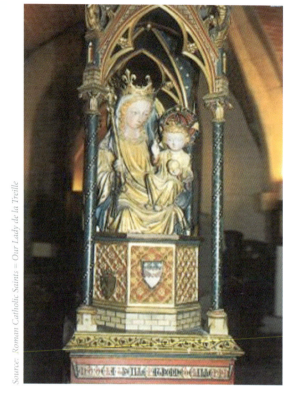

Source: Roman Catholic Saints = Our Lady de la Treille

JUNE 2016

s	m	t	w	t	f	s
			1	2	3	4
5	6	7	8	9	10	11
12	13	14	15	16	17	18
19	20	21	22	23	24	25
26	27	28	29	30		

11TH WEEK IN ORDINARY TIME

First Reading: *1 Kings 21:17-29*
Responsorial Psalm: *Ps 51:3-4, 5-6AB, 11 AND 16*
Gospel Reading: *Matthew 5:43-48*

Source: Orthodox Church in America "Icon of the Mother of God 'Kiev-Bratsk'"

June
wednesday

15

ICON OF THE MOTHER OF GOD Kiev-Bratsk, Russia (1654)

The Kiev-Bratsk Icon was at first in the church of Sts. Boris and Gleb in the city of Vyshgorod (Kiev), where it miraculously appeared in the year 1654. In 1662, the temple of the holy Passion-Bearers Boris and Gleb was destroyed in war and defiled. The wonderworking icon was taken out of the church and sent down the river to the Bratsk monastery.

The Kiev-Bratsk Icon of the Mother of God is commemorated four times during the year on days dedicated to the miraculous appearance of the holy icon in 1654. The original icon has not been preserved. The copy was painted from it "measure for measure," and is at present located in the Kiev monastery of the Protection of the Mother of God.

11ᵀᴴ WEEK IN ORDINARY TIME

First Reading: *2 Kings 2:1, 6-14*
Responsorial Psalm: *Ps 31:20, 21, 24*
Gospel Reading: *Matthew 6:1-6, 16-18*

JUNE 2016

s	m	t	w	t	f	s
			1	2	3	4
5	6	7	8	9	10	11
12	13	14	15	16	17	18
19	20	21	22	23	24	25
26	27	28	29	30		

June

thursday

16

BLESSED VIRGIN OF SORROWS
Campocavallo, Italy (1892)

In the 1870s, a small country chapel was built three miles from Osimo, a town just inland from the Adriatic near the world-famous shrine of Loreto. An oleograph of the Pietà bought from a traveling salesman was hung there. On June 16, 1892, a few women who stayed to pray after mass saw the eyes of the Sorrowful Virgin move and blink. News of the "prodigy" traveled rapidly and widely. On July 7, a blind woman regained sight. The same year, the present magnificent sanctuary was built and consecrated in 1905. It is the focus of the Festa del Covo, a Nativity-themed harvest festival the first Sunday of August, and the Festa dell'Addolorata the third Sunday of September.

Source: Santuario B.V. Addolorata

JUNE 2016

s	m	t	w	t	f	s
			1	2	3	4
5	6	7	8	9	10	11
12	13	14	15	16	17	18
19	20	21	22	23	24	25
26	27	28	29	30		

11TH WEEK IN ORDINARY TIME

First Reading: *Sirach 48:1-14*
Responsorial Psalm: *Ps 97:1-2, 3-4, 5-6, 7*
Gospel Reading: *Matthew 6:7-15*

Source: Wikipedia (German) "Grafenstein"

MARY IN THE FOREST
Dolina, Austria
(1849)

The Blessed Virgin Mary appeared as the Immaculate Conception on June 17, 18 and 19 to three shepherdesses to prepare the public proclamation of the dogma (1854). Thus began an influx of pilgrims into the woods to the place where she had appeared. A wooden chapel was built and a painting created from the testimony of the children.

A local artist painted a picture called the Madonna del Bosco, inspired by the descriptions of the three shepherdesses. This painting was a picture of grace that inspired the faith and devotion of many.

11TH WEEK IN ORDINARY TIME

First Reading: *2 Kings 11:1-4, 9-18, 20*
Responsorial Psalm: *Ps 132:11, 12, 13-14, 17-18*
Gospel Reading: *Matthew 6:19-23*

JUNE 2016

s	m	t	w	t	f	s
			1	2	3	4
5	6	7	8	9	10	11
12	13	14	15	16	17	18
19	20	21	22	23	24	25
26	27	28	29	30		

June

saturday

18

OUR LADY OF IGOR
Kiev, Ukraine (1147)

In 1146, an uprising unseated Prince Igor Olegovich who had recently ascended the Kievan throne. Becoming a monk of St. Theodore's in Kiev after his defeat, the prince prayed in his cell before an icon of the Mother of God. Soon his enemies found, captured, tortured, and martyred him in his cell. On September 19, 1147, his small icon of the Tenderness style with the Child against her cheek as in the contemporaneous icon of Vladimir, began to be known for miracles. The feast day of the Our Lady of Igor was established for June 18 (June 3 in the Julian calendar), the date Prince Igor's remains were interred with honor in 1150. The original painting was located in the Dormition Cathedral at the Kiev Cave Monastery, but only replicas exist.

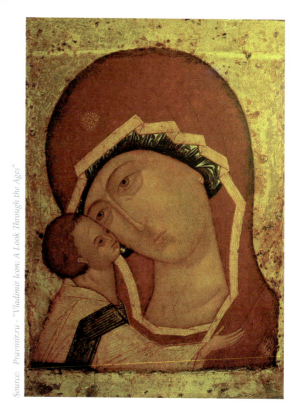

Source: Pravmir.ru – "Vladimir Icon: A Look Through the Ages"

JUNE 2016

s	m	t	w	t	f	s
			1	2	3	4
5	6	7	8	9	10	11
12	13	14	15	16	17	18
19	20	21	22	23	24	25
26	27	28	29	30		

11TH WEEK IN ORDINARY TIME

First Reading: *2 Chronicles 24:17-25*
Responsorial Psalm: *Ps 89:4-5, 29-30, 31-32, 33-34*
Gospel Reading: *Matthew 6:24-34*

Source: days.pravoslavie.ru – "KAZAN ICON OF THE MOTHER OF GOD"

June
sunday
19

KAZAN ICON OF THE MOTHER OF GOD
Moscow, Russia (1701)

In 1689,hymns had been sung at the Ascension Monastery in Moscow and someone forgot to extinguish the candle before leaving the church. The candle fell, and the flames burned the church but the Kazan Icon did not suffer any damage. In a fire in the Kremlin on June 19, 1701, the Palace and Ascension Monastery were consumed by flames. During that fire, the daughter of the deceased prince, entered his tomb and prayed before the Kazan Icon. The Icon remained behind. In the course of an inventory taken to see whether everything had been removed from the church, they found the Kazan Icon. No one knew how it got there, as no one had taken it from the church. It later miraculously returned to its original spot.

12TH SUNDAY IN ORDINARY TIME

First Reading: *Zechariah 12:10; 13:1*
Responsorial Psalm: *Ps 63:3-4, 5-6, 8-9*
Second Reading: *Galatians 3:26-29*
Gospel Reading: *Luke 9:18-24*

JUNE 2016

s	m	t	w	t	f	s
			1	2	3	4
5	6	7	8	9	10	11
12	13	14	15	16	17	18
19	20	21	22	23	24	25
26	27	28	29	30		

June

monday

20

OUR LADY OF CONSOLATION
Turin, Italy (1104)

A Byzantine-style icon legendarily painted by St. Luke, La Consolata (Our Lady of Consolation), was given to St. Maximus, Bishop of Turin, by St. Eusebius. It was later hidden during the iconoclastic period. The Marquis of Ivrea received a apparition of the Mother of God at his sickbed in 1014, requesting a chapel to "La Consolata" in St. Andrew's Church. When he accomplished what she asked, his health returned and he then discovered the old icon. In 1104 civil war left St. Andrew's in ruins. A blind man in France dreamed of discovering an icon of the Virgin in the rubble of a church. Being called to this endeavor and believing he would be healed, the man went to Italy and convinced others to excavate in search of the icon. On June 20, 1104, they uncovered the remains of the chapel and the undamaged icon.

Source: Amico – Maria Consolata, Regina dei missionari

JUNE 2016

s	m	t	w	t	f	s
			1	2	3	4
5	6	7	8	9	10	11
12	13	14	15	16	17	18
19	20	21	22	23	24	25
26	27	28	29	30		

12ᵀᴴ WEEK IN ORDINARY TIME

First Reading: *2 Kings 17:5-8, 13-15A, 18*
Responsorial Psalm: *Ps 60:3, 4-5, 12-13*
Gospel Reading: *Matthew 7:1-5*

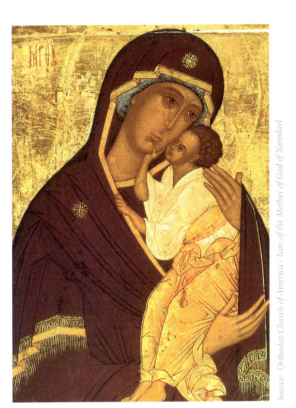

Source: Orthodox Church of America – Icon of the Mother of God of Yaroslavl

tuesday

21

ICON OF THE MOTHER OF GOD OF YAROSLAVL
Russia (1501)

Princes Vassily and Konstantin Vsevoiodovich of Yaroslavl made a great effort to reconstruct and restore many Orthodox churches in the 13th century after the Tatar invasions under Khan Bam. Grand Duke Ivan the Great of Moscow ordered in 1501 a stone church built in honor of the two saints, featuring the icon they were devoted to displayed above their incorrupt bodies. One of these icons was a depiction of the Virgin Mary and the image became known as the Yaroslavl Mother of God. Her feast day is celebrated on June 21 (June 8 in the Julian calendar).

12TH WEEK IN ORDINARY TIME
Memorial of Saint Aloysius Gonzaga, Religious

First Reading: *2 Kings 19:9B-11, 14-21, 31-35A, 36*
Responsorial Psalm: *Ps 48:2-3AB, 3CD-4, 10-11*
Gospel Reading: *Matthew 7:6, 12-14*

JUNE 2016

s	m	t	w	t	f	s
			1	2	3	4
5	6	7	8	9	10	11
12	13	14	15	16	17	18
19	20	21	22	23	24	25
26	27	28	29	30		

June
wednesday
22

OUR LADY OF THE CAPE
Quebec, Canada (1879)

Notre-Dame-du-Cap is most famous for two miracles. In 1879 the pastor instructed his congregation to pray the rosary in order to obtain ice to cross the river so that materials and tools could be brought to the site. Pieces of ice floated downstream from Lake St-Pierre, forming a "rosary bridge" across the St. Lawrence River. On June 22, 1888, three men were in the chapel in prayer when they witnessed the eyes of the statue open and close. News of the event quickly spread and the fame of the miraculous image spread. The feast day of Notre-Dame-du-Cap is celebrated on August 15th.

Source: Wikipedia - Our Lady of the Cape

JUNE 2016

s	m	t	w	t	f	s
			1	2	3	4
5	6	7	8	9	10	11
12	13	14	15	16	17	18
19	20	21	22	23	24	25
26	27	28	29	30		

12TH WEEK IN ORDINARY TIME

First Reading: *2 Kings22:8-13; 23:1-3*
Responsorial Psalm: *Ps 119:33, 34, 35, 36, 37, 40*
Gospel Reading: *Matthew 7:15-20*

Source: La thotokos - BIBBIENA (ITALIA)

June
thursday
23

OUR LADY OF THE STONE
Bibbiena, Italy (1347)

On June 23, 1347, seven year-old Catherine experienced a vision of a beautiful lady dressed in white. The woman gave some her pods, found that evening to be full of blood: an omen of the bubonic plague of the following year, from which the city of Bibbiena and surrounding areas in Italy were largely spared.

The place of the rock formation where Catherine witnessed the Madonna became the base structure of the Sanctuary of the Madonna of the Rock. Around 1435, Bicci di Lorenzo created a fresco for the main altarpiece against its top. In the year 1942, the church was elevated to the status of minor basilica.

12TH WEEK IN ORDINARY TIME

First Reading: *2 Kings 24:8-17*
Responsorial Psalm: *Ps 79:1B-2, 3-5, 8, 9*
Gospel Reading: *Matthew 7:21-29*

JUNE 2016

s	m	t	w	t	f	s
			1	2	3	4
5	6	7	8	9	10	11
12	13	14	15	16	17	18
19	20	21	22	23	24	25
26	27	28	29	30		

June
friday
24

OUR LADY OF THE SHIP
Chioggia, Italy (1508)

Historical records of the town of Chioggia recount a very gloomy afternoon on June 24, 1508 when a violent storm broke out. The townspeople prayed desperately for the fishermen caught at sea but only towards evening did the storm subside. An old guard dejectedly came out of his lighthouse and suddenly he heard a voice from the shore calling him. He turned and saw a majestic lady dressed in a black robe sitting on a trunk of a beechwood tree. The Mother of God said that she was deeply saddened by the sinful lives led by the people of Chioggia. The hurricane was a warning of a worse cataclysm, if people didn't repent. She called for a crusade of prayer and penance. On the site was quickly built a small chapel and, later, a church.

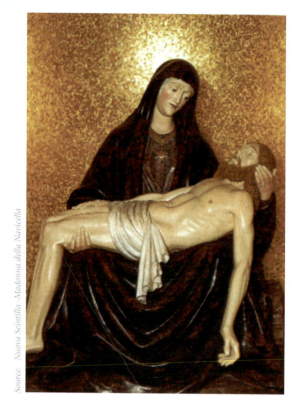

Source: Nuova Scintilla -Madonna della Navicella

JUNE 2016

s	m	t	w	t	f	s
			1	2	3	4
5	6	7	8	9	10	11
12	13	14	15	16	17	18
19	20	21	22	23	24	25
26	27	28	29	30		

12TH WEEK IN ORDINARY TIME
Solemnity of the Nativity of Saint John the Baptist

First Reading: *Isaiah 49: 1-6*
Responsorial Psalm: *Ps 139: 1b-3.13-14ab.14c-15*
Second Reading: *Acts 13: 22-26*
Gospel Reading: *Luke 1: 57-66.80*

Source: Wikipedia Medjugorje

June
saturday
25

QUEEN OF PEACE
Medjugorje, Bosnia and Herzegovina (1981)
* Under Vatican Investigation 2010

After Fatima, this remote spot, formerly in Yugoslavia and Croatia, is perhaps the most famous and visited Marian apparition site of the 20th century, although it has not been approved as supernatural by Church authorities. On June 24, 1981, "Kraljice Mira," Queen of Peace, first allegedly with the Christ-child appeared to six young people of Medjugorje but they quickly left fearfully. The next day, four of them returned to that location along with two friends, again ascending what became known as "Apparition Hill". The apparitions of the Gospa have continued to be claimed to this day and over 30 million pilgrims have traveled to the spot. June 25 is celebrated as the anniversary in Medjugorje.

JUNE 2016

s	m	t	w	t	f	s
			1	2	3	4
5	6	7	8	9	10	11
12	13	14	15	16	17	18
19	20	21	22	23	24	25
26	27	28	29	30		

12TH WEEK IN ORDINARY TIME

First Reading: *Lamentations 2:2, 10-14, 18-19*
Responsorial Psalm: *Ps 74:1B-2, 3-5, 6-7, 20-21*
Gospel Reading: *Matthew 8:5-17*

June

sunday

26

THE BLESSED VIRGIN OF POWER
Trompone, Italy (1562)

Cigliano, a poor sickly woman was almost unable to speak, living her life in pain and sorrow, consoled only by prayer. One day, while praying, she saw the Blessed Virgin, with the Infant Jesus in her arms who spoke saying that she wished to erect a Church in Trompone. Cigliano was completely healed. The news of the miracle spread quickly in neighboring countries. People flocked to Trompone to pray to Our Lady and to bring their sick to the site of the apparition. New miracles soon occurred: healing of the blind, the lame, and people affected by various ills.

A few months later, on August 19, 1562 the clergy and people went in procession to Trompone, and the foundation was laid for a small church.

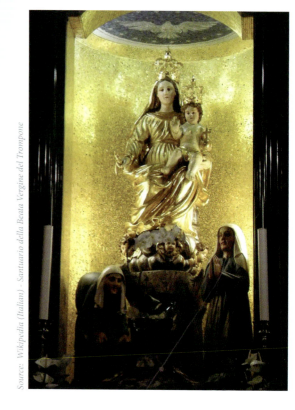

Source: Wikipedia (Italian) - Santuario della Beata Vergine del Trompone

JUNE 2016

s	m	t	w	t	f	s
			1	2	3	4
5	6	7	8	9	10	11
12	13	14	15	16	17	18
19	20	21	22	23	24	25
26	27	28	29	30		

13TH SUNDAY IN ORDINARY TIME

First Reading: *1 Kings 19:16B, 19-21*
Responsorial Psalm: *Ps 16:1-2 AND 5, 7-8, 11*
Second Reading: *Galatians 5:1A, 13-14, 16A, 18*
Gospel Reading: *Luke 9:51, 57-62*

Source: Mary Pages – Holy Mother of Gietzwald

June
monday
27

MOTHER OF GOD OF GIETRZWALD
Poland (1877)

Our Lady appeared as the "Immaculate Conception" to Justyna Szafrynska (13) when she was returning home from school. The next day, Barbara Samulowska (12) also saw the 'Bright Lady' sitting on the throne with the Christ-child among angels over a maple tree. Our Lady requested that the rosary be said everyday.

In 1967, Primate of Poland Cardinal Stefan Wyszynski visited the shrine to commemorate the ninetieth anniversary of the apparitions and crowned the miracle icon. On the one hundredth anniversary of the apparitions in Gietrzwald, the Episcopal Conference of Poland headed by Cardinal Karol Wojtyla (future St. John Paul II) celebrated a mass. The Warmian Bishop, Jozef Drzazga, confirmed the supernatural nature of the events.

JUNE 2016

s	m	t	w	t	f	s
			1	2	3	4
5	6	7	8	9	10	11
12	13	14	15	16	17	18
19	20	21	22	23	24	25
26	27	28	29	30		

13TH WEEK IN ORDINARY TIME

First Reading: *Amos 2:6-10, 13-16*
Responsorial Psalm: *Ps 50:16BC-17, 18-19, 20-21, 22-23*
Gospel Reading: *Matthew 8:18-22*

June

tuesday

28

OUR LADY OF LONGING
Matka Boza Teskniaca, Warsaw, Poland (1998)

One of the oldest churches in the Archdiocese of Warsaw is St. Elizabeth Powsin. Located on the main altar is a painting of Our Lady of Longing - artist unknown - from the first half of the seventeenth century. At either side, the image is surrounded by statues of Saints Adalbert and Stanislaus - Polish bishops and martyrs. The testimony of miracles and graces relating to the Our Lady of Longing icon have been collected at least since the mid-seventeenth century.

On June 28, 1998, the image became the fourth image of Mary in the Archdiocese of Warsaw to be canonically crowned.

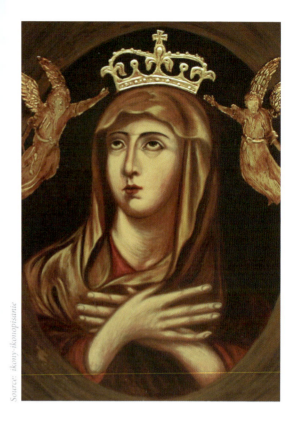

Source: ikony-ikonopisanie

JUNE 2016

s	m	t	w	t	f	s
			1	2	3	4
5	6	7	8	9	10	11
12	13	14	15	16	17	18
19	20	21	22	23	24	25
26	27	28	29	30		

13TH WEEK IN ORDINARY TIME
Memorial of Saint Irenaeus, Bishop and Martyr

First Reading: *Amos 3:1-8; 4:11-12*
Responsorial Psalm: *Ps 5:4B-6A, 6B-7, 8*
Gospel Reading: *Matthew 8:23-27*

Source: 2 LA PURISIMA CONCEPCIÓN DE LINARES EN CÓRDOBA. LA VIRGEN CAPITANA"

June
wednesday
29

OUR LADY OF LINARES
Spain (1808)

The first time the image of Our Lady of Linares was moved to Córdoba was in 1808, when the French invasion, whose troops, under General Dupont, were about to enter the city. In the afternoon of Saturday June 4, 1808, at the sanctuary of Our Lady of Help, many priests and people came through the door processed with the image of Our Lady of Linares along with Saint Fernando and accompanied by all the inhabitants of the province, including soldiers, cheered to the ringing of bells and proclaimed her "The Invincible General." The procession went through the Cross Trail to the parish of St. Peter, in whose church the images were deposited. The feast day is celebrated on June 29 to commemorate Reconquista in 1236.

13TH WEEK IN ORDINARY TIME
Solemnity of Saints Peter and Paul, Apostles

First Reading: *Acts 12: 1-11*
Responsorial Psalm: *Ps 34: 2-3.4-5.6-7.8-9v*
Second Reading: *2 Timothy 4: 6-8.17-18*
Gospel Reading: *Matthew 16: 13-19*

JUNE 2016

s	m	t	w	t	f	s
			1	2	3	4
5	6	7	8	9	10	11
12	13	14	15	16	17	18
19	20	21	22	23	24	25
26	27	28	29	30		

June
thursday
30

OUR LADY OF GOOD SUCCOR
Montréal, Canada (1672)

In 1672, St. Marguerite Bourgeoys, a French missionary in Canada, obtained a small statue carved from the sacred oak of Montaigu in Belgium and brought the wooden image back to Montréal. It was placed in a reliquary in Notre-Dame de Bon Secours, Our Lady of Good Help, a stone chapel dedicated on June 30, 1675. This pilgrimage sanctuary outside the original settlement went up in flames in 1754 but the statuette was saved from the burning building. A new chapel still used to this day was constructed in 1771 and the statue placed on a side altar. This "Sailors' Church," features model ships hung from the ceiling given by mariners in gratitude for Our Lady's intercession. The body of St. Marguerite was interred below the statue in 2005.

JUNE 2016

s	m	t	w	t	f	s
			1	2	3	4
5	6	7	8	9	10	11
12	13	14	15	16	17	18
19	20	21	22	23	24	25
26	27	28	29	30		

13TH WEEK IN ORDINARY TIME

First Reading: *Amos 7:10-17*
Responsorial Psalm: *Ps 19:8, 9, 10, 11*
Gospel Reading: *Matthew 9:1-8*

Source: Blogspot - Ofrilio Vidual "XII Procesión Marítima Virgen de la Guía 2009"

July
friday

1

OUR LADY THE GUIDE
Portugalete, Spain (13th c.)

On either side of Coscojales Street in Portugalete, the harkening back to a mariners' celebration features two big rag dolls hung from a rope tied to balcony railings in the first hours of day with an opening volley and the traditional sally of the Dominguines. The faithful simultaneously offer flowers to the Blessed Virgin, whose statue is a in a niche on the façade of Market Square at the end of the street. The fiesta is replete with the fanfare of drumming, accordions, and masks filling the streets. The devotees of the Virgin Guide at midnight process from the street's beginning, following the Municipal Band's march. A concluding volley is the culmination of the event with a serenade.

13TH WEEK IN ORDINARY TIME

First Reading: *Amos 8:4-6, 9-12*
Responsorial Psalm: *Ps 119:2, 10, 20, 30, 40, 131*
Gospel Reading: *Matthew 9:9-13*

JULY 2016

s	m	t	w	t	f	s
					1	2
3	4	5	6	7	8	9
10	11	12	13	14	15	16
11	18	19	20	21	22	23
24	25	26	27	28	29	30
31						

July
saturday

2

OUR LADY OF MADHU
Wanni, Sri Lanka (16th c.)

In 1583, Catholics in Mannar to escape persecution went to a safer locale in Maruda Madhu along with a statue of Our Lady of the Rosary and were joined by migrants from Jaffna peninsula in Wanni forests. These two communities met in Madhu, and built a Shrine which started to attract pilgrims from all over the country. Soon the devotion spread and people believed that they were not harmed by animals and poisonous reptiles due to the miraculous statue, and the soil was used as a remedy for snake bites. The Madhu Shrine is not only a place of solace for Catholics, but also a symbol of racial harmony where Tamils from the North and East and Sinhalese from the South and other parts of the country meet together like one family to pray.

Source: Homestead - Tamil Church "Our Lady of Madhu"

OUR LADY OF MADU
PRAY FOR CEYLON

JULY 2016

s	m	t	w	t	f	s
					1	2
3	4	5	6	7	8	9
10	11	12	13	14	15	16
11	18	19	20	21	22	23
24	25	26	27	28	29	30
31						

13TH WEEK IN ORDINARY TIME

First Reading: *Amos 9:11-15*
Responsorial Psalm: *Ps 85:9AB AND 10, 11-12, 13-14*
Gospel Reading: *Matthew 9:14-17*

Source: I CAVALIERI TEMPLARI "I FRATI CHE RINVENNERO IL TESORO DI ALARICO"

sunday

3

HODEGETRIA
Mt. Athos, Greece
(16th c.)

An icon depicting the Mother of God gesturing toward the Child on her lap is known as the *Hodegetria* or "Directress" type. This treasured icon mysteriously was gone from the Vatopedi monastery on Mt. Athos In 1730, with the resident monks assuming it stolen behind locked doors. Three hours away at the Xenophon Monastery, the image turned up and the monks from Vatopedi went to return it to its home at Mt. Athos; but after the same sequence of events happened two more times, the monks discerned that it was the Holy Virgin's will to remain there in the new location. The feast of the All-Holy Hodegetria is celebrated at the monastery on the first Sunday in October. Russian and Serbian Orthodox churches honor this icon on June 20 in the old calendar, July 3 in the new.

JULY 2016

s	m	t	w	t	f	s
					1	2
3	4	5	6	7	8	9
10	11	12	13	14	15	16
11	18	19	20	21	22	23
24	25	26	27	28	29	30
31						

14TH SUNDAY IN ORDINARY TIME

First Reading: *Isaiah 66:10A, 12B-13*
Responsorial Psalm: *Ps 66:1-3, 4-5, 6-7*
Second Reading: *Galatians 6:14, 16-18*
Gospel Reading: *Luke 10:1-9*

July
monday

4

OUR LADY OF THE REFUGE
Matamoros, Mexico (1720)

In 1720, a painting of Our Lady, Refuge of Sinners was transported by Jesuit missionary Juan José Güica from Italy to Mexico. When the Virgin told him in a dream to ask the Franciscans of Zacatecas to use and promote the image, they distributed over 150 copies. In 1793 Franciscan friars came to the new settlement and renamed it "Nuestra Señora del Refugio de los Esteros Hermosos" (Our Lady of the Refuge of the Lovely Marshes) later to become Matamoros. An 1886 painting of Our Lady of Refuge was hung in the cathedral of the same name built in 1832. Celebrated across Mexico, her fiesta commemorates the coronation of the original "Refugium Peccatori" in the Jesuit church of Frascati, Italy, on July 4, 1717.

Source: Robert Morrisey – Antiques and Fine Art "Our Lady, Refuge of Sinners"

JULY 2016

s	m	t	w	t	f	s
					1	2
3	4	5	6	7	8	9
10	11	12	13	14	15	16
11	18	19	20	21	22	23
24	25	26	27	28	29	30
31						

14TH WEEK IN ORDINARY TIME

First Reading: *Hosea 2:16, 17C-18, 21-22*
Responsorial Psalm: *Ps 145:2-3, 4-5, 6-7, 8-9*
Gospel Reading: *Matthew 9:18-26*

Source: *matntalthos.gr"Oikonomissa – Megiste Lavra Monastery"*

tuesday

5

ECONOMISSA ICON OF THE MOST HOLY THEOTOKOS
Great Lavra, Greece (8th c.)

In the 900s, the unfinished Great Monastery on Mount Athos ran out of funds, and the starving monks had to leave. Finally the monastery founder, St. Athanasius, left too in search of help. On the road he met a woman in a long blue veil. When Athanasius asked the lady's name, she answered, "I am the mother of your Lord." The abbot asked for a sign. "Strike the rock with your staff." As water flowed from the rock, she vanished. Athanasius returned to find the building completed and stocked with supplies. Soon it was full of monks as well. In the monastery church, the Economissa icon depicts many saints connected with the monastery. Our Lady the Steward is honored along with St. Athanasius on his feast day, July 5.

JULY 2016

s	m	t	w	t	f	s
					1	2
3	4	5	6	7	8	9
10	11	12	13	14	15	16
11	18	19	20	21	22	23
24	25	26	27	28	29	30
31						

14TH WEEK IN ORDINARY TIME

First Reading: *Hosea 8:4-7, 11-13*
Responsorial Psalm: *Ps 115:3-4, 5-6, 7AB-8, 9-10*
Gospel Reading: *Matthew 9:32-38*

July
wednesday
6

HOLY MOTHER OF AKITA
Japan (1973)

In Akita, Japan, Sister Agnes Sasagawa of the Institute of the Handmaids of the Eucharist on the night of July 6, 1973 was drawn to the chapel by a supernatural light and saw an angel. Both her hand and the right hand of a wooden statue of Our Lady of All Nations began to bleed simultaneously. Locutions began to emanate from the statue, including the promise to Sister Agnes that her deafness would be cured, and the request that she pray, especially for the Catholic clergy. All in all, 101 messages were spoken by the bleeding wooden statue. In a pastoral letter from Bishop John Shoojiroo Ito of Niigata that was allowed by the CDF's Joseph Cardinal Ratzinger to be disseminated to the faithful, the events were declared supernatural in 1984.

Source: John Haffert "The Miraculous Image of Our Lady of Akita"

JULY 2016

s	m	t	w	t	f	s
					1	2
3	4	5	6	7	8	9
10	11	12	13	14	15	16
11	18	19	20	21	22	23
24	25	26	27	28	29	30
31						

14TH WEEK IN ORDINARY TIME

First Reading: Hosea 10:1-3, 7-8, 12
Responsorial Psalm: Ps 105:2-3, 4-5, 6-7
Gospel Reading: Mark 1:15

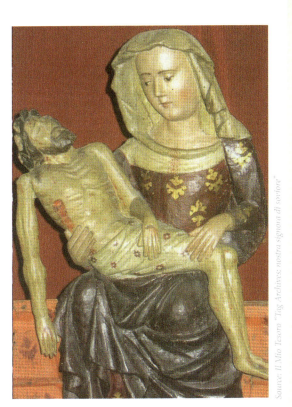

Source: Il Mio Tesoro "Tag Archives: nostra signora di soviore"

OUR LADY OF SOVIORE
Italy (740)

As the Lombard hordes approached in 641, villagers of Soviore buried their statue of the Madonna and fled toward the Mediterranean. A hundred years later, on July 7, 740, the parish priest was hunting at dawn, when he noticed a dove fly into a hole. Unsuccessful at uncovering the spot, he returned the next day with three helpers with shovels, who unearthed a wooden statue. When the priest tried to carry it home, it was too heavy to move, so he left it there. On the following day, people found that the statue had moved to the top of a nearby chestnut tree. When it repeatedly returned after being moved, the villagers built a chapel at that spot. The statue was crowned on August 10, 1749. Nostra Signora di Soviore is celebrated on the Feast of the Assumption, August 15th.

JULY 2016

s	m	t	w	t	f	s
					1	2
3	4	5	6	7	8	9
10	11	12	13	14	15	16
11	18	19	20	21	22	23
24	25	26	27	28	29	30
31						

14TH WEEK IN ORDINARY TIME

First Reading: *Hosea 11:1-4, 8E-9*
Responsorial Psalm: *Ps 80:2AC AND 3B, 15-16*
Gospel Reading: *Matthew 10:7-15*

July
friday

8

OUR LADY OF THE SNOW
Adro, Italy (1519)

On July 8, 1519, the Virgin appeared asking a deaf mute to build a church in her honor and make amends for his sins. Miraculously he spoke.

The people of Adro had to build a church at the place of occurrence, change their sinful ways, sanctify the holidays, not blaspheme the holy name of God and refrain from other sins.

The central feast of Our Lady of the Snows is celebrated on August 5. In the first half century, immediately after the occurrence, she was not called "Virgen de las Nieves", but instead "Madonna della Cava," the place where the Virgin had appeared to the shepherd, and the feast was celebrated on July 8, the anniversary of the occurrence.

JULY 2016

s	m	t	w	t	f	s
					1	2
3	4	5	6	7	8	9
10	11	12	13	14	15	16
11	18	19	20	21	22	23
24	25	26	27	28	29	30
31						

14TH WEEK IN ORDINARY TIME

First Reading: *Hosea 14:2-10*
Responsorial Psalm: *Ps 51:3-4, 8-9, 12-13, 14 AND 17*
Gospel Reading: *Matthew 10:16-23*

Source: Wikipedia (Spanish) - Virgen de Itatí

saturday

9

OUR LADY OF ITATÍ
Corrientes, Argentina
(1615)

Our Lady of Itatí is a celebrated wooden representation of Virgin Mary in the city of Itatí, Corrientes Province, Argentina. Spanish Jesuit missionary Friar Luis de Bolaños and a group of locals who converted to the Catholic faith were saved from an attack by another tribe after they prayed the rosary. According to the story, a passage was opened through Yaguari River and the people of Itati were saved due to the intercession of the Blessed Mother.

From the time of the solemn papal coronation in 1900, the feast day was established to be celebrated on July 9 while July 16 is the day of the great annual pilgrimage. The Basilica of Itatí is the destination for the faithful as a major Catholic pilgrimage center of the country.

JULY 2016

s	m	t	w	t	f	s
					1	2
3	4	5	6	7	8	9
10	11	12	13	14	15	16
11	18	19	20	21	22	23
24	25	26	27	28	29	30
31						

14TH WEEK IN ORDINARY TIME

First Reading: *Isaiah 6:1-8*
Responsorial Psalm: *Ps 93:1AB, 1CD-2, 5*
Gospel Reading: *Matthew 10:24-33*

July
sunday
10

MOTHER OF GOD OF BISTRICA
Croatia (13th c.)

The statue of the Mother of God of Bistrica is a Black Madonna of the late 1400s, buried for safekeeping from the Turks in 1545 and rediscovered, with the aid of supernatural light, in 1588. Again forgotten and walled in, it was rediscovered July 15, 1684. The Bishop of Zagreb dedicated a new church to the Mother of God in Marija Bistrica on July 15, 1731. The shrine's pilgrimage season begins on Pentecost and includes pilgrimages from the county of Varaždin on the Sunday after St. Peter's day (June 29), from Zagreb on the Sunday before St. Margaret's day (July 13), and on the feast of the Assumption (August 15). The Archbishop of Zagreb crowned the Mother of God of Bistrica Queen of Croatia in 1935.

JULY 2016

s	m	t	w	t	f	s
					1	2
3	4	5	6	7	8	9
10	11	12	13	14	15	16
11	18	19	20	21	22	23
24	25	26	27	28	29	30
31						

15TH SUNDAY IN ORDINARY TIME

First Reading: *Deuteronomy 30:10-14*
Responsorial Psalm: *Ps 19:8, 9, 11*
Gospel Reading: *Colossians 1:15, 16ABD,17-18A*

monday

11

Source: Wikipedia (Italian) - Santuario della Madonna del Carmine di Combarbio

OUR LADY OF MOUNT CARMEL
Combarbio di Anghiari, Italy (1536)

A 12-year-old shepherdess, Marietta Del Mazza, reported apparitions of the Virgin on July 11, 1536 and days following. When news spread through the region, along with reports of miracles attributed to the Virgin's intercession, the bishops of Arezzo and Sansepolcro conducted an investigation and authorized a shrine at the apparition site. Completed in 1539, the sanctuary was staffed by the Franciscan order at first, then by the Carmelites until 1782. Since 1987 it has been under the jurisdiction of the local bishop. Like many contemporary works of the Florentine school, the miraculous painting shows the infant St. John the Baptist pointing to the Child Jesus.

15TH WEEK IN ORDINARY TIME
Memorial of Saint Benedict, Abbot

First Reading: *Isaiah 1:10-17*
Responsorial Psalm: *Ps 50:8-9, 16BC-17, 21 AND 23*
Gospel Reading: *Matthew 10:34-11:1*

JULY 2016

s	m	t	w	t	f	s
					1	2
3	4	5	6	7	8	9
10	11	12	13	14	15	16
11	18	19	20	21	22	23
24	25	26	27	28	29	30
31						

July
tuesday
12

KASPEROV ICON OF THE MOTHER OF GOD
Kherson, Ukraine (1840)

In 1840, late one night in a village on the Dniepr, Mrs. Kasperov was praying before her old and darkened icon when she saw an illumination of vestiges of the Mother and Child. The icon was soon restored to its original beauty, and miracles of healing began to occur. Devotion to the icon spread, resulting in an annual procession in the town with it on the Feast of the Ascension. After the Crimean War, the procession moved from the city of Odessa, which to an annual rotation between Odessa, Kherson, and the towns of Nikolaev and Kasperovka. July 12 (June 29 in the old calendar), the icon's last day in Kherson, is celebrated as its feast, along with October 1 and the Wednesday after Easter.

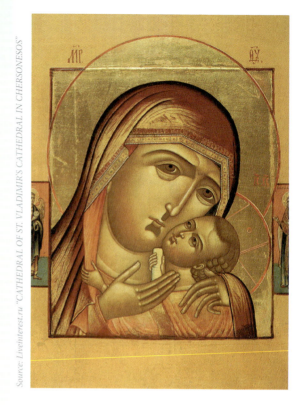

JULY 2016

s	m	t	w	t	f	s
					1	2
3	4	5	6	7	8	9
10	11	12	13	14	15	16
11	18	19	20	21	22	23
24	25	26	27	28	29	30
31						

15TH WEEK IN ORDINARY TIME

First Reading: *Isaiah 7:1-9*
Responsorial Psalm: *Ps 48:2-3A, 3B-4, 5-6, 7-8*
Gospel Reading: *Matthew 11:20-24*

Source: Don Bosco – Garessio Valsor (Cuneo): PORTAMI IL VESTITO PIÙ' BELLÒn

wednesday

13

OUR LADY OF GRACE
Garessio Valsorda, Italy (1653)

On Sunday, July 13, 1653, Mary, a young deaf and mute, with no parents, was laying flowers in front of a Marian image when for the first time heard a voice "Go and bring me the most beautiful dress in your clothing trunk." The news of the miraculous voice spread quickly, and people ran to venerate the Virgin Mary in the small chapel on the top of the hill. Nine years later, on Whit Monday of 1662, the image of Our Lady was solemnly crowned.

On April 3, 1858, another miracle happened: the healing of a paralytic Magdalene Ghirardi, who after years of immobility, was healed in the Sanctuary.

Cholera epidemics were averted in 1630 and 1835 through the intercession of Our Lady of Grace.

JULY 2016

s	m	t	w	t	f	s
					1	2
3	4	5	6	7	8	9
10	11	12	13	14	15	16
11	18	19	20	21	22	23
24	25	26	27	28	29	30
31						

15TH WEEK IN ORDINARY TIME

First Reading: *Isaiah 10:5-7, 13B-16*
Responsorial Psalm: *Ps 94:5-6, 7-8, 9-10, 14-15*
Gospel Reading: *Matthew 11:25-27*

July
thursday
14

MOTHER OF GOD OF CANÒLICH
Andorra (1223)

On July 14, 1223, a shepherd was pasturing his flock near the village of Canòlich in southern Andorra, when suddenly a bird with brilliant plumage showed itself. The shepherd caught the bird with no trouble, and carried it to his house. The next day the bird had disappeared, and again he found it in the field. The sequence recurred three times, but the last time, the shepherd found an image of the Virgin Mary in a niche in the rock. In response to this prodigy, the people decided to build a shrine to the Virgin where her statue was found. The wooden statue from the late 1100s was crowned by the Vatican in 1999. On the last Saturday in May, parishioners gather in Sant Julià de Lòria for fireworks and mass in the Virgin's honor followed by dancing, and blessing and distribution of bread.

JULY 2016

s	m	t	w	t	f	s
					1	2
3	4	5	6	7	8	9
10	11	12	13	14	15	16
11	18	19	20	21	22	23
24	25	26	27	28	29	30
31						

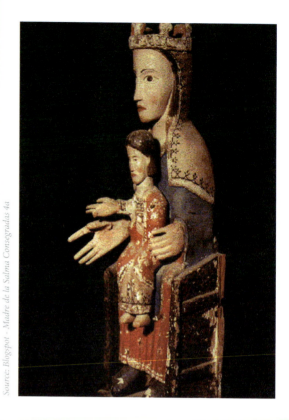

Source: Blogspot – Madre de la Salma Consegradas 4u

15TH WEEK IN ORDINARY TIME
Memorial of Saint Kateri Tekakwitha, Virgin

First Reading: Isaiah 26:7-9, 12, 16-19
Responsorial Psalm: *Ps 102:13-14AB AND 15, 16-18, 19-21*
Gospel Reading: *Matthew 11:28-30*

July
friday

15

AKHTYRSKAYA ICON OF THE MOTHER OF GOD
Croydon, Australia (1739)

A priest ran into an illuminated icon in the tall grass when he was mowing hay near his church in Akhtyrka, Russia on July 15, 1739. For three years he kept the icon in his house. When the painting lit up again, the Virgin Mary appeared to him in a dream, telling him to wash the icon. When finished, he went to empty the water in the river, but the Mother of God told him to use it to bless the sick instead. When his own daughter drank some, she soon recovered from her illness. An investigation in 1751 looked into the miracles of the icon, recognizing it as "wonder-working". After an exile, it was later moved to the Russian Orthodox Archdiocese of Australia. The feast day is July 15 (July 2 in the old calendar).

Source: Russian Church Chelonham "Pozhayskoy, Feodotevskoy and Akhtyrka Mother of God Icons"

JULY 2016

s	m	t	w	t	f	s
					1	2
3	4	5	6	7	8	9
10	11	12	13	14	15	16
11	18	19	20	21	22	23
24	25	26	27	28	29	30
31						

15TH WEEK IN ORDINARY TIME
Memorial of St. Bonaventure, Bishop and Doctor of the Church

First Reading: *Isaiah 38:1-6, 21-22, 7-8*
Responsorial Psalm: *Isaiah 38:10, 11, 12ABCD, 16*
Gospel Reading: *Matthew 12:1-8*

July
saturday
16

OUR LADY OF MT. CARMEL
Aylesford, England (1251)

In answer to St. Simon Stock's appeal for help for his oppressed order, the Virgin Mary appeared to him with a scapular in her hand. It is the sign of salvation, a safeguard in dangers, a pledge of peace and of the covenant. Soon after, he instituted the confraternity of the Brown Scapular. He received a confirmation of the Rule of his Order by Pope Honorius III, Gregory IX, and Pope Innocent IV, and the order was received under the special protection of the Holy See in 1251. St. Simon Stock has never been officially canonized by the Church but his feast day has been sanctioned.

The celebration of the Feast of Our Lady of Mt. Carmel on July 16 was extended to the universal Church by Pope Benedict XIII.

Source: From the Pulpit of My Life "Novena in Honor of Our Lady of Mount Carmel — Day 9"

JULY 2016

s	m	t	w	t	f	s
					1	2
3	4	5	6	7	8	9
10	11	12	13	14	15	16
11	18	19	20	21	22	23
24	25	26	27	28	29	30
31						

15TH WEEK IN ORDINARY TIME

First Reading: *Micah 2:1-5*
Responsorial Psalm: *Ps 10:1-2, 3-4, 7-8, 14*
Gospel Reading: *Matthew 12:14-21*

Source: http://www.donbosco-torino.it/image/Archivio/index3-Maria-di-Nazaret.htmla

OUR LADY OF HUMILITY
Pistoia, Italy (1490)

The chapel of Santa Maria Forisportam (St. Mary Outside the Gate) had a fresco of the Madonna of Humility installed in 1383 painted by Paolo Serafini. When Pistoia erupted in bloody conflict a century later, a group of people took refuge in the chapel. On July 17, 1490 while praying, the clothing of the Mother of God became wet with drops of sweat pouring from her face. The news spread when the witnesses ran and sounded the church bell. When both opposing sides dropped their weapons and ran to see the miraculous icon, the civil strife came to an abrupt halt. On December 31, 1582, a beautiful new sanctuary was dedicated and named for the painting. The *Madonna lactans* image shows the Madonna seated on a cushion on the floor, with the Christ-child.

JULY 2016

s	m	t	w	t	f	s
					1	2
3	4	5	6	7	8	9
10	11	12	13	14	15	16
11	18	19	20	21	22	23
24	25	26	27	28	29	30
31						

16TH SUNDAY IN ORDINARY TIME

First Reading: *Genesis 18:1-10A*
Responsorial Psalm: *Ps 15:2-3, 5*
Second Reading: *Colossians 1:24-28*
Gospel Reading: *Luke 10:38-42*

July
monday
18

OUR LADY OF GOOD DELIVERANCE
Neuilly-sur-Seine, France (14th c.)

Since the 1000s, the Church of Saint-Etienne-des-Grès in the old Latin Quarter of Paris had a confraternity and chapel to Our Lady of Good Deliverance, where pilgrims sought her help. In 1790, the anti-Catholic government closed the Church of Saint-Etienne-des-Grès a countess, Madame de Carignan Saint Maurice, bought the statue and took it to Paris. The following year, St.-Etienne's was destroyed. In 1793, the countess went to prison, where she met the Sisters of St. Thomas of Villanova who installed the statue in their chapel now moved to the suburb of Neuilly-sur-Seine. The feast of Our Lady of Good Deliveranceis July 18, commemorating the Vatican officially approved the congregation of Soeurs de Saint Thomas de Villeneuve in 1873.

JULY 2016

s	m	t	w	t	f	s
					1	2
3	4	5	6	7	8	9
10	11	12	13	14	15	16
11	18	19	20	21	22	23
24	25	26	27	28	29	30
31						

Source: Center Blog – Litanie de Notre Dame de la Délivrance

16TH WEEK IN ORDINARY TIME

First Reading: *Micah 6:1-4, 6-8*
Responsorial Psalm: *Ps 50:5-6, 8-9, 16BC-17, 21 AND 23*
Gospel Reading: *Matthew 12:38-42*

Source: Center Blog · Litanie de Notre Dame de la Délivrance

tuesday

19

OUR LADY OF THE MIRACLE
Lima, Peru (1630)

An image of the Immaculate Conception was placed by the Franciscan friars in their first church in Lima during the Conquest. The image became known as the "La Misionera" when it accompanied the Friars on missionary journeys. In 1536 during the rebellion in Cusco, the Inca capital, the natives trapped many Spaniards in a hut and set fire to the roof. When La Misionera was seen to appeared in the sky with Santiago, all were saved with the fire coming to an end. In honor of this event, a church was built on site. When on November 27, 1630, an earthquake struck the city but the image of Our Lady was said to turn to the Blessed Sacrament and the earthquake stopped. On June 19, 1953, the miraculous statue was crowned by the papal nuncio. The feast is November 27th.

JULY 2016

s	m	t	w	t	f	s
					1	2
3	4	5	6	7	8	9
10	11	12	13	14	15	16
11	18	19	20	21	22	23
24	25	26	27	28	29	30
31						

16TH WEEK IN ORDINARY TIME

First Reading: *Micah 7:14-15, 18-20*
Responsorial Psalm: *Ps 85:2-4, 5-6, 7-8*
Gospel Reading: *Matthew 12:46-50*

July
wednesday
20

OUR LADY OF ZOCUECA
Spain (1808)

Source: Blogspot - Elorza Grupo - Cartel Novena a Ntra. Sra. de Zocueca

Near the Rumblar River in Zocueca, Mozarabic Christians built a simple chapel. When the area was re-conquered five years later in 1155 by Alfonso VII, people went to the shrine in gratitude to the Virgin. Pleading with the Virgin to save them during the cholera epidemic of 1681, the people vowed to hold an annual fiesta, in her honor preceded by a day of fasting. On every August 5th the promise has been fulfilled. During the Battle of Bailén in 1808, the people again successfully turned to the Virgin of Zocueca in a victory over Napoleon. They commemorate the battle every year with a week of civil, patriotic, and religious celebrations from July 17-22. The greatest display is on the 20th, when the Patroness, the Virgin of Zocueca, is processed through the streets of Zocueca.

JULY 2016

s	m	t	w	t	f	s
					1	2
3	4	5	6	7	8	9
10	11	12	13	14	15	16
11	18	19	20	21	22	23
24	25	26	27	28	29	30
31						

16TH WEEK IN ORDINARY TIME

First Reading: *Jeremiah 1:1, 4-10*
Responsorial Psalm: *Ps 71:1-2, 3-4A, 5-6AB, 15 AND 17*
Gospel Reading: *Matthew 13:1-9*

Source: Bulgar Souvenir – Our Lady of Kazan

OUR LADY OF KAZAN
Russia (1579)

In the year1579 on July 21 (July 8 old calendar), the Mother of God appeared three times to Matrena (10), inviting her to look under the rubble of a destroyed house. The girl was not believed, not by the archbishop, the clergy, nor the authorities, so alone with her mother, she began to dig in the earth in the place indicated until the icon was found, wrapped in old rags, and absolutely intact. The news soon spread in the city and the archbishop himself went to the place of discovery. On the day of the "discovery" two blind men, Joseph and Nikita regained their sight. The holy icon was given the highest stature within the Russian Orthodox Church, representing the Virgin as protector and patroness of the city of Kazan and was considered a palladium of Russia until its theft and likely destruction in 1904.

JULY 2016

s	m	t	w	t	f	s
					1	2
3	4	5	6	7	8	9
10	11	12	13	14	15	16
11	18	19	20	21	22	23
24	25	26	27	28	29	30
31						

16TH WEEK IN ORDINARY TIME

First Reading: *Jeremiah 2:1-3, 7-8, 12-13*
Responsorial Psalm: *Ps 36:6-7AB, 8-9, 10-11*
Gospel Reading: *Matthew 13:10-17*

July
friday

22

ICON OF THE MOTHER OF GOD OF KOLOCH
Russia (1143)

The Koloch Icon of the Mother of God manifested itself in the year 1413 during the reign of Basil I, near Koloch. A peasant of this village by the name of Luke found the holy icon and took it to his home. A paralyzed member of his household put his forehead to the icon with faith and received complete healing. This cure became known, and many of the suffering began to flock to the wonderworking icon for healing. Luke afterwards took the icon to Mozhaisk, and from there to Moscow. At the capital, the icon was carried through the streets and many of the sick were healed. Later the icon returned to Mozhaisk. At the place where the icon appeared, a church in honor of the Mother of God was built to house it. The feast day is celebrated on July 22.

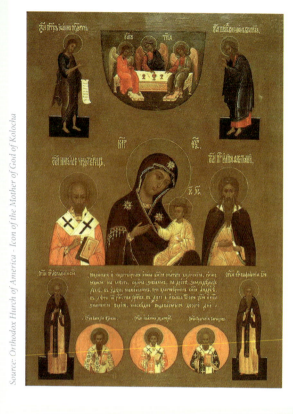

Source: Orthodox Hurch of America - Icon of the Mother of God of Kolocha

JULY 2016

s	m	t	w	t	f	s
					1	2
3	4	5	6	7	8	9
10	11	12	13	14	15	16
11	18	19	20	21	22	23
24	25	26	27	28	29	30
31						

16TH WEEK IN ORDINARY TIME
Memorial of Saint Mary Magdalene

First Reading: *Jeremiah 3:14-17*
Responsorial Psalm: *Jeremiah 31:10, 11-12ABCD, 13*
Gospel Reading: *John 20:1-2, 11-18*

Source: Parrochia di Vall'Alta - Santuario di Altino

OUR LADY OF ALTINO
Albino, Italy (1496)

A charcoal maker Quinto Foglia and his two young sons were walking from their home on July 23, 1496 in the forest of Vall'Alta near Monte Altino. It was during a heat wave and drought so stricken with thirst and afraid for his children, Quinto prayed to the Madonna. In a vision he was instructed to strike a rock with his waking stick. As a result, a spring gushed out. On the very next day, people began construction of a chapel, completed on Sept. 5, 1496. In 1865 the apparition was commemorated with a group of statues. The Madonna's statue was solemnly crowned on July 23, 1919 in gratitude for protection during World War I. The annual festa begins with an evening procession and a solemn mass on July 23, anniversary of the apparition and crowning.

JULY 2016

s	m	t	w	t	f	s
					1	2
3	4	5	6	7	8	9
10	11	12	13	14	15	16
11	18	19	20	21	22	23
24	25	26	27	28	29	30
31						

16TH WEEK IN ORDINARY TIME

First Reading: *Jeremiah 7:1-11*
Responsorial Psalm: *Ps 84:3, 4, 5-6A AND 8A, 11*
Gospel Reading: *Matthew 13:24-30*

July
sunday

24

MOTHER OF GOD OF RZEVSK
Russia (1539)

Stephen the monk was at a crossroads near Rzev in northwest Russia on Pentecost Sunday, May 26, 1539 when he discovered in the trees two sacred objects: a large iron cross and an old icon of the Virgin and Child with St. Nicholas of Myra. When a light began to illuminate the trees, many miraculous healings followed. Stephen went to Moscow to give the account to Metropolitan Joasaph, head of the Russian Church. He constructed two new churches, one in honor of the Cross of Rzev and the other for the Virgin Mary and St. Nicholas. In January 1541, the holy objects were moved to Moscow at the time of the dedication of the new churches. The feast of the Rzevsk Mother of God commemorates the return to Rzev on July 24th.

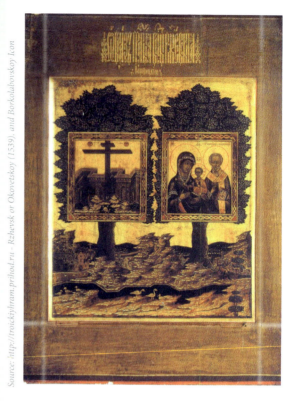

Source: http://troickiyhram.prihod.ru – Rzhevsk or Okovetskoy (1539), and Borkolabovskoy Icon

JULY 2016

s	m	t	w	t	f	s
					1	2
3	4	5	6	7	8	9
10	11	12	13	14	15	16
11	18	19	20	21	22	23
24	25	26	27	28	29	30
31						

17TH SUNDAY IN ORDINARY TIME

First Reading: *Genesis 18:20-32*
Responsorial Psalm: *Ps 138:1-2, 2-3, 7-8*
Second Reading: *Colossians 2:12-14*
Gospel Reading: *Luke 11:1-8*

July
monday

25

Source: Orthodox Church in America. Icon of the Mother of God of "the Three Hands"

MOTHER OF GOD OF THREE HANDS
Mt Athos, Greece (6th c.)

When the Byzantine Emperor Leo issued his first iconoclastic edict in 726, St. John of Damascus was head chancellor to Caliph Hisham and was a great defender of the use of beautiful art as a part of Christian worship. In 730 the Caliph felt betrayed when he received a letter in John's handwriting, addressed to Emperor Leo, offering to assist and overthrowing the Caliph. Hisham, who had lead frequent attacks against the Byzantine Empire, announced that the writer of that letter would lose his hand - and so John did. But the saint's hand was restored after he prayed before an icon to which he added a third hand of silver. The miracle proved to the Caliph that the letter was in fact a forgery from the Byzantines. The feast is celebrated on July 25 (July 12 - Julian).

JULY 2016

s	m	t	w	t	f	s
					1	2
3	4	5	6	7	8	9
10	11	12	13	14	15	16
11	18	19	20	21	22	23
24	25	26	27	28	29	30
31						

17TH WEEK IN ORDINARY TIME
Feast of Saint James, Apostle

First Reading: *2 Corinthians 4: 7-15*
Responsorial Psalm: *Ps 126: 1-2ab.2cd-3.4-5.6*
Gospel Reading: *Matthew 20: 20-28*

July
tuesday
26

OUR LADY OF THE BEECH TREE
Castelluccio, Italy
(July 26)

Near Castelluccio, a young shepherd received a vision of the Virgin Mary in 1672 who told him that she wished to be venerated at a certain place in the beech woods. The boy came across a terracotta image of the Madonna attached to a tree there. With this discovery, the 7" Madonna of the Beech was moved to a chapel, and then later to its own sanctuary in the mountains in 1722. On Ascension Day since 1756, an annual pilgrimage processed the image to the town and back again, and on St. Anne's day, July 26, the image is brought in ceremony to the site of the beech tree. Sadly in 1975 the holy image was stolen and replaced with a replica.

Source: Source: Where We Walked – Madonna del Faggio. Castelluccio, Bologna

JULY 2016

s	m	t	w	t	f	s
					1	2
3	4	5	6	7	8	9
10	11	12	13	14	15	16
11	18	19	20	21	22	23
24	25	26	27	28	29	30
31						

17TH WEEK IN ORDINARY TIME
Memorial of Saints Joachim and Anne, Parents of Mary

First Reading: *Jeremiah 14:17-22*
Responsorial Psalm: *Ps 79:8, 9, 11 AND 13*
Gospel Reading: *Matthew 13:36-43*

Source: abruzzando.com - Festa della Madonna del Carmine a Palmoli il 27 Luglio 2013

OUR LADY OF MT CARMEL
Palmoli, Italy
(13th c.)

The original ancient statue similar to the classic images of Our Lady of Mt Carmel, was replaced by the current, Neapolitan work in April 1854 when the statue was carried from Naples to Palmoli by 20 men. On July 16th in the morning, in a centuries-old tradition, the pastor of Palmoli processes with the faithful from the Sanctuary, bringing the statue of the Virgin Mary to the parish church where Mass was celebrated. On July 27 in the morning, a "parade of granòppoli and pacchianelle" marches through the streets of Palmoli where the faithful, in traditional costume, bring donations to Our Lady followed by a Mass and procession with the statue of the Virgin Mary. In the afternoon, the great procession takes Madonna back to her sanctuary.

JULY 2016

s	m	t	w	t	f	s
					1	2
3	4	5	6	7	8	9
10	11	12	13	14	15	16
11	18	19	20	21	22	23
24	25	26	27	28	29	30
31						

17TH WEEK IN ORDINARY TIME

First Reading: *Jeremiah 15:10, 16-21*
Responsorial Psalm: *Ps 59:2-3, 4, 10-11, 17, 18*
Gospel Reading: *Matthew 13:44-46*

July

thursday

28

MARY, MOTHER OF GOD
Port-au-Prince, Haiti (1985)

Sister Altagrace Doresca, a nun from the Order of the Consecrated Virgins, reported that the Virgin Mary began appearing to her on July 28, 1985.

A commission was formed to study the first appearances and the "messages" of the Virgin Mary. It was composed of priests, religious, lay persons, a biblical theologian, a psychiatrist, a historian, a doctor of general medicine, a pastor of a parish and a religious catechist. On November 12, 1987, Francoise-Marie Wolff Ligonde, Archbishop of Port-au-Prince, did not declare the apparitions to be supernatural in origin but gave his approval for the publication of the messages.

Source: http://www.wherewewalked.info/feasts/02-February/02-05.htm

JULY 2016

s	m	t	w	t	f	s
					1	2
3	4	5	6	7	8	9
10	11	12	13	14	15	16
11	18	19	20	21	22	23
24	25	26	27	28	29	30
31						

17TH WEEK IN ORDINARY TIME

First Reading: *Jeremiah 18:1-6*
Responsorial Psalm: *Ps 146:1B-2, 3-4, 5-6AB*
Gospel Reading: *Matthew 13:47-53*

Source: preghiereagesuemaria.it – SANTA MARIA DEI MIRACOLI Morbio Inferiore (Chiasso)

July
friday

29

HOLY MARY OF THE MIRACLES
Morbio Inferiore, Switzerland (1594)

The Virgin appeared to the two girls from Milan, Caterina and Angela, who were poor, sick and disturbed by the devil, on a hill in Switzerland in 1594 and cured them.

The "Madonna of milk" ordered the construction of a sanctuary that became the Holy Mary of Miracles shrine on the border of Italy.

On July 29, 1927 the image was crowned by Bishop Aurelio Bacciarini. In 1990 the sanctuary was declared as Minor Basilica by Pope John Paul II. The miracle is remembered every year at the feast day of July 29 with a novena, first Mass celebrated at 3 am and celebrations until evening.

17TH WEEK IN ORDINARY TIME
Memorial of Saint Martha

First Reading: *Jeremiah 26:1-9*
Responsorial Psalm: *Ps 69:5, 8-10, 14*
Gospel Reading: *John 11:19-27*

JULY 2016

s	m	t	w	t	f	s
					1	2
3	4	5	6	7	8	9
10	11	12	13	14	15	16
11	18	19	20	21	22	23
24	25	26	27	28	29	30
31						

July

saturday

30

ICON OF THE MOTHER OF GOD OF SVIATOGORSK
Russia (1569)

In 1563, near Pskov a "Tenderness" Icon appeared to a fifteen-year-old shepherd named Timothy. This icon was placed in the Voronicha church of St. George. A voice said that after six years this hill would be blessed. In 1569 when a Hodegetria icon appeared upon a pine tree, Timothy spent forty days there in fasting and prayer. A voice commanded that people should come on the Friday following the Sunday of All Saints. When the procession reached the hill, a light suddenly shone and fragrance filled the air and everyone saw upon the pine tree the Hodegetria icon. Both holy icons, the Hodegetria and the Tenderness, were put into a newly built chapel. The Hodegetria icon is commemorated on July 30 (July 17 old calendar).

Source: IconBM.ru – Icon of the Mother of God "Sviatohorsk"

JULY 2016

s	m	t	w	t	f	s
					1	2
3	4	5	6	7	8	9
10	11	12	13	14	15	16
11	18	19	20	21	22	23
24	25	26	27	28	29	30
31						

17TH WEEK IN ORDINARY TIME

First Reading: *Jeremiah 26:11-16, 24*
Responsorial Psalm: *Ps 69:15-16, 30-31, 33-34*
Gospel Reading: *Matthew 14:1-12*

Source: Santuario de Huachana - Fiesta 2013

VIRGIN OF CONSOLATION
Huachana, Argentina (1820)

In 1820 a girl named Telésfora Veron, told her family about the Virgin appearing in the solitude of the mountain, but no one believed her. After becoming tired of being taken for insane she left never to return home. One night, the neighbors decided to meet at the place of the apparitions and waited in the cold with a fire. At dawn, Mary surprised them and gave them her image. Her brother moved the small image to his humble home, where for many years thousands of devotees came to venerate the Virgin.   Today, with celebrations by the Bishopric of Añatuya, nearly 100,000 pilgrims from all over Argentina arrive every year to honor the Virgin at the place where Mary chose to announce her love for all.

JULY 2016

s	m	t	w	t	f	s
					1	2
3	4	5	6	7	8	9
10	11	12	13	14	15	16
11	18	19	20	21	22	23
24	25	26	27	28	29	30
31						

18TH SUNDAY IN ORDINARY TIME

First Reading: *Ecclesiastes 1:2; 2:21-23*
Responsorial Psalm: *Ps 90:3-4, 5-6, 12-13, 14, 17*
Second Reading: *Colossians 3:1-5, 9-11*
Gospel Reading: *Luke 12:13-21*

August
monday

1

OUR LADY OF MERCY
Barcelona, Spain
(1218)

In an apparition on August 1st to Saint Peter, to his confessor, Raymund of Pennafort, and to King James of Aragon, the Blessed Virgin was dressed in a white long tunic, a scapular, a cloak on her shoulders and a fine lace mantilla veiling her hair. Some images have her carrying two bags of coins for use in ransoming Christians imprisoned by Moors or her arms extended with open chains, a symbol of liberation. Through these men, she established the Mercedarian religious order (derives from the Spanish word for mercy - *merced*). Its members would seek to free Christian captives and offer themselves as an exchange. A feast day was instituted and observed on September 24th. It was extended to the entire Church by Innocent XII in 1696.

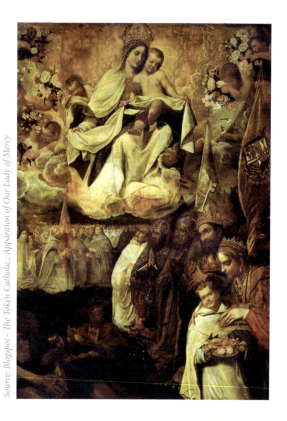

Source: Blogspot - The Token Catholic.: Apparition of Our Lady of Mercy

AUGUST 2016

s	m	t	w	t	f	s
	1	2	3	4	5	6
7	8	9	10	11	12	13
14	15	16	17	18	19	20
21	22	23	24	25	26	27
28	29	30	31			

18TH WEEK IN ORDINARY TIME
Memorial of St. Alphonsus Liguori, Bishop & Doctor of the Ch

First Reading: *Leviticus 25: 1.8-17*
Responsorial Psalm: *Ps 67: 2-3.5.7-8*
Gospel Reading: *Matthew 14: 1-12*

Source: Revista Pasos de Fe - Nuestra Señora de Los Ángeles: "Una fe, decenas de leyendas"

OUR LADY OF THE ANGELS
Cartago, Costa Rica (1635)

Juana Pereira, a mestiza, while gathering firewood found a carved black stone resembling the Virgin and Child. On August 2, 1635. She took the small 3" image to her home and put it away in a box. The next day when she was out again, she found an identical carving on the same rock. When she went to also place the new finding in the box, she found that the first was no longer there. So she locked the second one up. On the third day, it happened again: she found the same image in the same place, and found that the locked box was empty. When the parish priest placed it in the church's tabernacle, the image again returned, prompting everyone to agree to build a shrine. The feast of *La Negrita*, patron saint of Cost Rica, is celebrated August 2nd.

AUGUST 2016

s	m	t	w	t	f	s
	1	2	3	4	5	6
7	8	9	10	11	12	13
14	15	16	17	18	19	20
21	22	23	24	25	26	27
28	29	30	31			

18TH WEEK IN ORDINARY TIME

First Reading: *Jeremiah 30:1-2, 12-15, 18-22*
Responsorial Psalm: *Ps 102:16-18, 19-21, 29 AND 22-23*
Gospel Reading: *Matthew 14:22-36*

August
wednesday

3

HOLY MARY, LADDER TO PARADISE
Noto, Sicily, Italy (1498)

On August 3, 1498, a wall of rock was discovered in the countryside that bore an image of the Madonna done in fresco by angels according to pious legend. The Diocese of Noto proposes that in the late 16th century an unknown artist created the fresco of their patron saint, Madonna, Ladder to Paradise. In 1693, an earthquake destroyed the chapel there with lamps and an oratory surrounded the image. Although everything around it was destroyed, the image of the Madonna della Scala was unharmed. The image was later moved in 1708, when a group of Carmelite hermits constructed another church. The hermitage became a place of pilgrimage with the image's growing fame for miraculous healings.

Source: Diocesi di Noto - Una preghiera poetica del Vescovo su Maria Scala del Paradiso

AUGUST 2016

s	m	t	w	t	f	s
	1	2	3	4	5	6
7	8	9	10	11	12	13
14	15	16	17	18	19	20
21	22	23	24	25	26	27
28	29	30	31			

18TH WEEK IN ORDINARY TIME

First Reading: *Jeremiah 31:1-7*
Responsorial Psalm: *Jeremiah 31:10, 11-12AB, 13*
Gospel Reading: *Matthew 15: 21-28*

Source: Nuova Scintilla - Tempo distato, tempo di festa

August
thursday
4

OUR LADY OF THE APPARITION
Pellestrina, Italy (1716)

On Tuesday, August 4, 1716, the feast of St. Dominic, about six o'clock in the morning a 14 year old boy named John Di Pasquale Scarpa, while on his way to the parish church to bring communion to three sick people, saw a strange woman wearing a long blue dress embroidered red stars and a white veil.

She encouraged him to pray for the souls in Purgatory and have masses said for them. She touched his left wrist, reassuring him for a moment.

The parish priest was impressed by the boy's detailed account and welcomed the donations he collected for masses to be said for the deceased.

18TH WEEK IN ORDINARY TIME

First Reading: *Jeremiah 31:31-34*
Responsorial Psalm: *Ps 51:12-13, 14-15, 18-19*
Gospel Reading: *Matthew 16:13-23*

AUGUST 2016

s	m	t	w	t	f	s
	1	2	3	4	5	6
7	8	9	10	11	12	13
14	15	16	17	18	19	20
21	22	23	24	25	26	27
28	29	30	31			

August

friday

5

OUR LADY OF THE SNOWS
Rome, Italy (352)

A wealthy but childless Roman couple, John and his wife decided to leave their fortune to the Church. The Virgin appeared to them on August 4th and told them that she wished a basilica to be constructed on Esquiline Hill to be outlined in snow. Pope Liberius also received the same vision. When they met on the top of the hill, they discovered the footprint of a church outlined in snow and the pope ordered the construction of St. Mary Major Basilica. Although Pope Sixtus III did not include the story when he rededicated the basilica a few centuries later and was removed in the 1969 General Roman Calendar, on the feast of Our Lady of Snows in Rome, white rose petals are dropped from the ceiling of the church to commemorate the legend of the miracle.

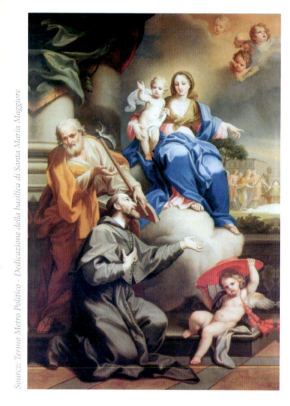

Source: Termo Metro Politico – Dedicazione della basilica di Santa Maria Maggiore

AUGUST 2016

s	m	t	w	t	f	s
	1	2	3	4	5	6
7	8	9	10	11	12	13
14	15	16	17	18	19	20
21	22	23	24	25	26	27
28	29	30	31			

18TH WEEK IN ORDINARY TIME

First Reading: *Nahum 2:1, 3; 3:1-3, 6-7*
Responsorial Psalm: *Deut. 32:35CD-36AB, 39ABCD, 41*
Gospel Reading: *Matthew 16:24-28*

Source: *Vercelli Oggi – La Madonna di Valmala*

6

OUR LADY OF VALMALA
Cuneo, Italy (1834)

On August 6 in the morning, at sunrise, four young shepherdesses pushed their herd of cows on the road that winds up the mountain. That day while they rested, they witnessed on a stone the figure of a beautiful woman of about twenty.

She did not speak but sad and lovingly looked at the four girls. They did not know who she was, maybe St. Anne, perhaps the Madonna. She disappeared as quickly as she came and the girls ran home.

On the 15th of August, the feast of the Assumption,they returned with a crowd. Nobody saw her but the girls, but all knelt, convinced that it is the Virgin Mary. The visions repeated for 50 days and a great monument was built on the site.

AUGUST 2016

s	m	t	w	t	f	s
	1	2	3	4	5	6
7	8	9	10	11	12	13
14	15	16	17	18	19	20
21	22	23	24	25	26	27
28	29	30	31			

18TH WEEK IN ORDINARY TIME
Feast of the Transfiguration of the Lord

First Reading: *Daniel 7: 9-10.13-14*
Responsorial Psalm: *Ps 97: 1-2.5-6.9*
Second Reading: *2 Peter 1: 16-19*
Gospel Reading: *Luke 9:28B-36*

August
sunday
7

OUR LADY OF THE ANGELS
Guardavalle, Italy
(13th c.)

The feast of Our Lady of the Angels is celebrated in Guardavalle first by the recitation of the Holy Rosary, followed by a solemn Mass presided over by the pastor with all the young baptized children in the community.

Later in the day a procession with the statue of Our Lady of the Angels takes place through the streets of the parish beginning and ending with Benediction. During the procession the entire Guardavalle plays. When the statue of Our Lady of the Angels arrives at the sea, a concert of Marian songs will take place in the square of the promenade. At the end of the procession, in the sports field, a huge fireworks display and musical show takes place.

Source: Francesco de Nicolo - Pirovagando.it

AUGUST 2016

s	m	t	w	t	f	s
	1	2	3	4	5	6
7	8	9	10	11	12	13
14	15	16	17	18	19	20
21	22	23	24	25	26	27
28	29	30	31			

19TH SUNDAY IN ORDINARY TIME

First Reading: *Wisdom 18:6-9*
Responsorial Psalm: *Ps 33:1, 12, 18-19, 20-22*
Gospel Reading: *Hebrews 11:1-2, 8-19*

Source: "Pieta Toscana," Lucignano Web

8

HOLY MARY OF THE OAK
Lucignano, Italy (1467)

Beneath a large oak a shrine was constructed in Lucignano with a fresco of the Pietà painted by Feliciano Batone in 1417. The title of the Madonna of the Oak became popular after the report from August 8, 1467 about a man from Siena who stopped at the shrine to pray to Mary for protection and became invisible to his enemies who were chasing him. That very year a small wooden chapel to houes the image was constructed. At the present hilltop church, consecrated in 1617, on the third Sunday of September, near the September 15 feast day of the Sorrowful Mother, Lucignano celebrates St. Mary of the Oak with religious services, food, games, and fireworks.

AUGUST 2016

s	m	t	w	t	f	s
	1	2	3	4	5	6
7	8	9	10	11	12	13
14	15	16	17	18	19	20
21	22	23	24	25	26	27
28	29	30	31			

19TH WEEK IN ORDINARY TIME
Memorial of Saint Dominic, Priest

First Reading: *Ezekiel 1:2-5, 24-28C*
Responsorial Psalm: *Ps 148:1-2, 11-12, 13, 14*
Gospel Reading: *Matthew 17:22-27*

August
tuesday
9

THE WHITE LADY
Messina, Italy
(1282)

Fighting against starvation and famine Messina with the attack of French during the Sicilian Vespers The people of the town knew that they were outmatched by their enemy, and knew their weapons would not be enough so they sought the help of the Blessed Virgin in prayer.

On August 6, 1282, heavy casualties among the French soldiers occurred when the struggled and failed to overtake the walls of the fortress of St. Saviour. The prayers of the people of Messina were answered as they were given the aid of a white lady who appeared twice in splendor using her veil to repel the arrows. Startled by the sight, the French soldiers could not look upon and began to run away in retreat.

Source: http://www.unpa.it/oadi/oadirw/?page_id=276

S MARIA DELL'ALTO
IN MESSINA

AUGUST 2016

s	m	t	w	t	f	s
	1	2	3	4	5	6
7	8	9	10	11	12	13
14	15	16	17	18	19	20
21	22	23	24	25	26	27
28	29	30	31			

19TH WEEK IN ORDINARY TIME

First Reading: *Ezekiel 2:8—3:4*
Responsorial Psalm: *Ps 119:14, 24, 72, 103, 111, 131*
Gospel Reading: *Matthew 18:1-5, 10, 12-14*

Source: Pregunta Santorial - Nuestra Señora de la Peña

August
wednesday

10

OUR LADY OF THE CRAG
Bogotà, Colombia (1685)

On August 10, 1685, Bernardino Rodríguez de León saw an unusual radiance in the peaks east of Bogotá. On drawing near, he realized the light was coming from an image of an angel, and the Holy Family outlined in the rock. News of the discovery soon spread through the capital, and after an investigation, the Archbishop authorized construction of a chapel on the mountain and public veneration of the images in 1686. Mysteriously, people claimed to see Our Lady's face change expression at times: sad, tearful, joyous. It was decided to move the images from the mountain. The images were removed from the rocks, cleaned, polished, and touched up. Now a national monument, Our Lady of the Crag is still an active church and an archdiocesan sanctuary.

AUGUST 2016

s	m	t	w	t	f	s
	1	2	3	4	5	6
7	8	9	10	11	12	13
14	15	16	17	18	19	20
21	22	23	24	25	26	27
28	29	30	31			

19TH WEEK IN ORDINARY TIME
Feast of Saint Lawrence, deacon and martyr

First Reading: *2 Corinthians 9: 6-10*
Responsorial Psalm: *Ps 112: 1-2.5-6.7-8.9*
Gospel Reading: *John 12: 24-26*

August
thursday
11

VIRGIN OF THE HEAD
Jaen, Spain (1227)

Source: Blogspot - Radio Andujar - SANTISIMA VIRGEN DE LA CABEZA

A shepherd named Juan Alonso Rivas, was tending his herds on the hills of Sierra Morena near the summit. He was a simple and fervent Christian, with a completely paralyzed left arm. The lights at night on the mountain near where he had his herd began to catch his attention along with the ringing of a bell. Finally on the night of August 11,1227, he reached the summit. Amidst the rocks, he found a small image of the Virgin, in whose presence the shepherd knelt and prayed aloud in dialogue with Our Lady who wanted to place a temple there. He went back to the city to announce the event and show everyone the recovery of his arm, thus giving credence to his words. The temple was finally built between 1287 and 1304 on the summit.

AUGUST 2016

s	m	t	w	t	f	s
	1	2	3	4	5	6
7	8	9	10	11	12	13
14	15	16	17	18	19	20
21	22	23	24	25	26	27
28	29	30	31			

19TH WEEK IN ORDINARY TIME
Memorial of Saint Clare, Virgin

First Reading: *Ezekiel 12:1-12*
Responsorial Psalm: *Ps 78:56-57, 58-59, 61-62*
Gospel Reading: *Matthew 18:21–19:1*

Source: Libero - Festa Patronale Maria SS. del Bosco

OUR LADY OF THE WOODS
Montemilone, Italy
(13th c.)

The Shrine of the Glorious Virgin was built on the slopes of a hill, about 400 meters above sea level, at the behest of the Basilian monks, who preferred to raise their convents and shrines on the banks of rivers or on the mountain ranges, with the intention to raise the spirit to heaven. The church was built starting in 1187 and finished in 1189.

The statue depicts the Virgin seated on a throne holding the Divine Child tightly to her chest. The peculiar characteristics of the statue and, particularly the crowns of the Virgin and Child, show a French influence as well as the clothing being distinctly Byzantine.

19ᵀᴴ WEEK IN ORDINARY TIME

First Reading: *Ezekiel 16:1-15, 60, 63*
Responsorial Psalm: *Isaiah 12:2-3, 4bcd, 5-6*
Gospel Reading: *Matthew 19:3-12*

AUGUST 2016

s	m	t	w	t	f	s
	1	2	3	4	5	6
7	8	9	10	11	12	13
14	15	16	17	18	19	20
21	22	23	24	25	26	27
28	29	30	31			

August
saturday
13

OUR LADY OF FORGETFULNESS, TRIUMPH AND MERCY
Guadalajara Castilla, Spain (1831)

In the afternoon of August 13, 1831 the Blessed Virgin appeared to a French nun of the Immaculate Conception, Sr. Patrocinio, known as the "Nun of the Wounds" because she bore the stigmata for 61 years.

In the afternoon of the 13th, while the nun was praying with all her sisters, Mary appeared on a throne of clouds shining, surrounded by the songs of many angels including St. Michael who placed an image of Our Lady on the altar. When the abbess called the father guardian to show the image, it disappeared. All the sisters witnessed later the reappearance of the image next to Sr. Patrocinio.

Source: Palpita La Vida – Virgen del Olvido, Triunfo y Misericordias

AUGUST 2016

s	m	t	w	t	f	s
	1	2	3	4	5	6
7	8	9	10	11	12	13
14	15	16	17	18	19	20
21	22	23	24	25	26	27
28	29	30	31			

19TH WEEK IN ORDINARY TIME

First Reading: *Ezekiel 18:1-10, 13B, 30-32*
Responsorial Psalm: *Ps 51:12-13, 14-15, 18-19*
Gospel Reading: *Matthew 19:13-15*

August
sunday

14

OUR LADY OF CONSOLATION
Ghisalba, Italy (1453)

Source: Immagini di Maria - Madonna della Consolazione

On August 14, 1453, Antoniola, a 60 year old farmer while having breakfast had a vision of Mary that the parish in that place was to erect a chapel. To prove the request she would be stabbed in the throat with a bread knife, and Mary would protect her until the sacred place had been built. When Tonolla got the commitment of the authorities for the construction, she was able to pull the knife from her throat without harm.

The chapel was built at once, and then a church was rebuilt in the seventeenth century and completely restored in 1850. The archbishop of Milan solemnly crowned the statue. On August 14, the apparition is celebrated with a novena.

20TH SUNDAY IN ORDINARY TIME

First Reading: *Jeremiah 38:4-6, 8-10*
Responsorial Psalm: *Ps 40:2, 3, 4, 18*
Second Reading: *Hebrews 12:1-4*
Gospel Reading: *Luke 12:49-53*

AUGUST 2016

s	m	t	w	t	f	s
	1	2	3	4	5	6
7	8	9	10	11	12	13
14	15	16	17	18	19	20
21	22	23	24	25	26	27
28	29	30	31			

August
monday
15

OUR LADY OF SORROWS
Florence, Italy (1233)

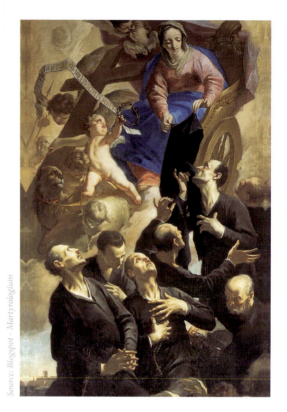

Source: Blogspot - Martyrologium

Seven men of Florentine nobility were in the brotherhood of "Laude" to venerate the Holy Virgin Mary. On the Feast of the Assumption, the Blessed Virgin appeared to urge them to make their lives even more holy and perfect so they left the business world and retired to a life of prayer. On Good Friday, in 1239 Holy Mary appeared again and showed them a black cassock that in the future they should wear, with what would motivate them to establish a new religious order. The Order would spread especially the veneration of the Sorrows that the Blessed Virgin bore with the Cross. Thus arose the Servite order, or the Friars of the Hail Mary, who found rapid and wide dissemination. "The Seven Holy Founders" of the Order were all canonized.

AUGUST 2016

s	m	t	w	t	f	s
	1	2	3	4	5	6
7	8	9	10	11	12	13
14	15	16	17	18	19	20
21	22	23	24	25	26	27
28	29	30	31			

20TH WEEk IN ORDINARY TIME
Solemnity of the Assumption of the Blessed Virgin Mary

First Reading: *Revelation 11:19A; 12:1-6A, 10AB*
Responsorial Psalm: *Ps 45: 10.11.12.16*
Second Reading: *1 Corinthians 15: 20-27*
Gospel Reading: *Luke 1: 39-56*

August

tuesday

16

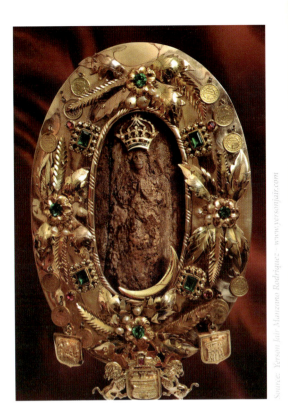

Source: Yerson Jair Manzano Rodríguez www.yersonjair.com

OUR LADY OF GRACES
Torcoroma, Colombia (1711)

Our Lady of Graces is celebrated in northeastern Colombia where the people of Ocaña commemorate the finding of a sacred image beneath the bark of a tree over 300 years ago. Cristóbal Melo, a mestizo who operated a small farm with a sugar mill with his son. On August 16, 1711 he went in search of a log to make a trough. Cristóbal removed the bark from the selected piece of wood and uncovered an image of Our Lady in the form of the Immaculate Conception carved in the sapwood. The prodigious image is venerated in an annual fiesta with masses, On August 16, 2011, Our Lady's image was pontifically crowned as part of the tricentennial celebration.

20TH WEEK IN ORDINARY TIME

First Reading: *Ezekiel 28:1-10*
Responsorial Psalm: *Dt 32:26-27AB, 27CD-28, 30, 35CD-36AB*
Gospel Reading: *Matthew 19: 23-30*

AUGUST 2016

s	m	t	w	t	f	s
	1	2	3	4	5	6
7	8	9	10	11	12	13
14	15	16	17	18	19	20
21	22	23	24	25	26	27
28	29	30	31			

August
wednesday
17

VIRGIN OF THE THREE RIVERS
Valgañón, Spain
(13th c.)

A shepherd named Agnes encountered a vision of Our Lady as he was tending his sheep by the brook. She commended him for his devotion and warned of chastisements if people in the town who did not repent. He tried to share the events and message of the apparition but no one believed him. She left the mark of her hand on his cheek as a sign and the entire town believed and began acts of penance. In the third and final apparition a statue was revealed. Upon hearing the news Fernando III of Castile, visited the village with the Bishop of Burgos, and laid the first stone of the church. On the penultimate Saturday of August, Our Lady of Tresfuentes is honored with a celebratory festival and games.

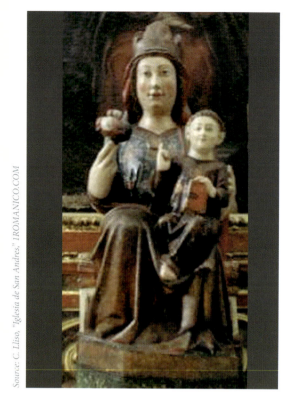

Source: C. Lliso, "Iglesia de San Andres," 1ROMANICO.COM

AUGUST 2016

s	m	t	w	t	f	s
	1	2	3	4	5	6
7	8	9	10	11	12	13
14	15	16	17	18	19	20
21	22	23	24	25	26	27
28	29	30	31			

20TH WEEK IN ORDINARY TIME

First Reading: *Ezekiel 34:1-11*
Responsorial Psalm: *Ps 23:1-3A, 3B-4, 5, 6*
Gospel Reading: *Matthew 20:1-16*

Source: Wikimedia – Val Casternone

OUR LADY OF THE LOWER
Rubiana, Italy (1713)

On the dividing ridge between the towns of Val della Torre and Rubiana, in the province of Turin, lies the shrine dedicated to Our Lady of Sorrows, Our Lady of the Lower.

On August 18, 1713 when a certain Lorenzo Nicol broke his leg in an area called the Lower. He turned to Mary and vowed to build a monument there. Immediately healed by divine intervention, Nicol returned to the country and he forgot the promise.

On August 20 of the following year, working in the same place, he was again in the same situation. He repented of his past behavior and prayed to the Virgin Mary who, once again, came to his aid. He built a monument which led to the sanctuary and placed in it a statue still venerated there.

AUGUST 2016

s	m	t	w	t	f	s
	1	2	3	4	5	6
7	8	9	10	11	12	13
14	15	16	17	18	19	20
21	22	23	24	25	26	27
28	29	30	31			

20TH WEEK IN ORDINARY TIME

First Reading: *Ezekiel 36:23-28*
Responsorial Psalm: *Ps 51:12-13, 14-15, 18-19*
Gospel Reading: *Matthew 22:1-14*

August

friday

19

OUR LADY OF VICTORY
San Marco la Catola, Italy (13th c.)

The mosaic icon of Blessed Virgin Nicopeja in the basilica of St. Mark in Venice, Italy, dates around the reign of Emperor John Comnenus. The sacred icon was carried into battle to bring good fortune. Madone Nicopeja, as she is popularly known, is the protectress of the city and the people. An enlarged replica of the original is enshrined in St.Peter's chapel of St. Mark's.

The Festival of Saint Liberatus Martyr and Our Lady of Victory is celebrated on August 19th. For the feast the statue of Our Lady of Victory is processed through the streets of San Marco La Catola. The town is adorned with lights and fireworks displays can be seen in the evening.

Source: Notizie Comuni-Italiani "Culto e festa patronale di Maria SS. della Vittoria"

AUGUST 2016

s	m	t	w	t	f	s
	1	2	3	4	5	6
7	8	9	10	11	12	13
14	15	16	17	18	19	20
21	22	23	24	25	26	27
28	29	30	31			

20TH WEEK IN ORDINARY TIME

First Reading: *Ezekiel 37:1-14*
Responsorial Psalm: *Ps 107:2-3, 4-5, 6-7, 8-9*
Gospel Reading: *Matthew 22:34-40*

Source: Legacy Icons – other of God of Valaam Icon

VALAAM ICON OF THE MOTHER OF GOD
Heinävesi, Finland (1878)

According to the inscription, the wonder-working icon of the Mother of God of Valaam was painted in 1878, "the work of the monks of Valaam."

Originally, the icon was to have been placed in the Valaam Monastery's Church of the Dormition. This never occurred and subsequently the icon was misplaced. In 1897, the icon was rediscovered and gained its miracle-working reputation after a succession of Marian visions experienced by an elderly woman Natalia Andreyevna Andreyeva who was cured from serious rheumatoid arthritis.

In 1987, an annual Orthodox feast was established on August 20 (August 7 on Julian).

AUGUST 2016

s	m	t	w	t	f	s
	1	2	3	4	5	6
7	8	9	10	11	12	13
14	15	16	17	18	19	20
21	22	23	24	25	26	27
28	29	30	31			

20TH WEEK IN ORDINARY TIME
Memorial of Saint Bernard, Abbot and Doctor of the Church

First Reading: *Ezekiel 43:1-7AB*
Responsorial Psalm: *Ps 85:9AB AND 10, 11-12, 13-14*
Gospel Reading: *Matthew 23:9B, 10B*

August
sunday

21

OUR LADY OF KNOCK
Ireland (1879)

During a pouring rain, the figures of Mary, Joseph, John the Evangelist and a lamb representing Christ on a plain altar appeared over the gable of the village chapel. When the occurrence began in the day, but witnesses could still see the figures very clearly in the dark - they appeared in a bright whitish light. The apparition did not flicker or move in any way and there were no messages associated with this vision. 15 people, between the ages of 5 and 75, were witnesses. Investigative commissions in 1879 and 1936 returned positive verdicts. In 1979 St. John Paul II visited the shrine for the 100th anniversary of the apparitions along with 450,000 pilgrims. On this occasion he presented a Golden Rose, a seldom-bestowed token of papal honor and recognition.

Source: Wikipedia - Knock Shrine

AUGUST 2016

s	m	t	w	t	f	s
	1	2	3	4	5	6
7	8	9	10	11	12	13
14	15	16	17	18	19	20
21	22	23	24	25	26	27
28	29	30	31			

21ST SUNDAY IN ORDINARY TIME

First Reading: *Isaiah 66:18-21*
Responsorial Psalm: *Ps 117:1, 2*
Second Reading: *Hebrews 12:5-7, 11-13*
Gospel Reading: *John 14:6*

Source: Flicker - Ngome "Mary Tabernacle of the Most High"

August
monday

22

TABERNACLE OF THE MOST HIGH
Ngome, South Africa (1955)

Sister Reinolda May, a Benedictine nun from Germany, claimed a vision of the Virgin Mary in white on August 22, 1955. The following March, she reported another message from Mary asking for a shrine to be built.

In December 1957, when visiting a sick person in Ngome, Sister Reinolda realized that was the place for the shrine. An artist painted the picture according to the instructions from Sr. Reinolda. On May 1, 1963, Bishop Aurelian Bilgeri allowed a tiny chapel at Ngome. The apparitions and shrine became more widely known after the seer's death in 1981.

21ST WEEK IN ORDINARY TIME
Memorial of the Queenship of the Blessed Virgin Mary

First Reading: *2 Thessaonians 1:1-5, 11-12*
Responsorial Psalm: *Ps 96:1-2A, 2B-3, 4-5*
Gospel Reading: *Matthew 23:13-22*

AUGUST 2016

s	m	t	w	t	f	s
	1	2	3	4	5	6
7	8	9	10	11	12	13
14	15	16	17	18	19	20
21	22	23	24	25	26	27
28	29	30	31			

August

tuesday

23

MARY OF SCHIAVONEA
Italy (1648)

On the night of August 23, 1648, as he watched the sea in the vicinity of the Church of San Leonardo and the Tower of the Dark, a knight Antonio Ruffo had a vision of the Blessed Virgin. She appeared sitting on a seat on the sea, with arms outstretched, calmed the astonished man and declared herself to be the Madonna of Schiavonea.

Then she asked him to commission a painting in her likeness for devotion to her. Our Lady repeated her appearance two more times before he believed in the reality of the visions and provide what she requested. He appointed a painter Scamardella of Corigliano to paint a portrait of the Virgin Mary as she appeared.

Source: Linkiesta.it – " Sibari gli stranieri lavorano nei campi, gli italiani incassano"

AUGUST 2016

s	m	t	w	t	f	s
	1	2	3	4	5	6
7	8	9	10	11	12	13
14	15	16	17	18	19	20
21	22	23	24	25	26	27
28	29	30	31			

21ST WEEK IN ORDINARY TIME

First Reading: *2 Thessalonians 2:1-3A, 14-17*
Responsorial Psalm: *Ps 96:10, 11-12, 13*
Gospel Reading: *Matthew 22: 23-26*

Source: Ricardo Ugo · "NUESTRA SEÑORA DEL MILAGRO"

August
wednesday
24

OUR LADY OF THE MIRACLE
Tunja, Colombia (1626)

Two Conceptionist nuns were crossing the patio of their convent in Tunja, Colombia in early morning darkness on August 24, 1626. After prayers, they were surprised to see a reflection in a puddle of the Virgin Mary. A vision was appearing in the sky above them. Another bright light caused them to notice the same image of the Virgin Mary mysteriously affixed a cloth in the window. The rest of the nuns all ran over to drop down in prayer to venerate the miraculous image.

The sacred painting was moved in 1880 to the Church of Our Lady of Sorrows by the Conceptionists. Now known as the Sanctuary of Our Lady of the Miracle, the church still draws big crowds.

21ST WEEK IN ORDINARY TIME
Feast of Saint Bartholomew, Apostle

First Reading: *Revelations 21: 9b-14*
Responsorial Psalm: *Ps 145: 10-11.12-13.17-18*
Gospel Reading: *John 1: 45-51*

AUGUST 2016

s	m	t	w	t	f	s
	1	2	3	4	5	6
7	8	9	10	11	12	13
14	15	16	17	18	19	20
21	22	23	24	25	26	27
28	29	30	31			

August

thursday

25

OUR LADY OF ROSSANO
Italy (6th c.)

The cult of Our Lady Acheropita began in the town of Rossano in Calabria, Italy. In a small cave at the end of the sixth century, lived a Saint Ephrem, a hermit very devoted to the Virgin Mary.

It is said that in 580, Captain Mauricio, cleared by the winds reached Rossano. The monk Ephrem came to greet him: "It was not the winds that led you here, but Our Lady, for you will be appointed emperor once you build her a temple."

In 582, Mauricio was crowned emperor of Macedonia, which covered part of the territories that are now Greece and Italy. In 590, the emperor got Mauritius, Emperor of Constantinople, to release a cave shrine dedicated to Our Lady.

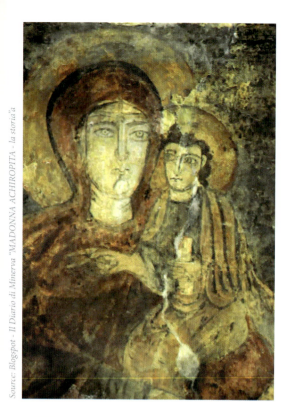

Source: Blogspot - Il Diario di Minerva "MADONNA ACHIROPITA - la storia"

AUGUST 2016

s	m	t	w	t	f	s
	1	2	3	4	5	6
7	8	9	10	11	12	13
14	15	16	17	18	19	20
21	22	23	24	25	26	27
28	29	30	31			

21ST WEEK IN ORDINARY TIME

First Reading: *1 Corinthians 1:1-9*
Responsorial Psalm: *Ps 145:2-3, 4-5, 6-7*
Gospel Reading: *Matthew 24:42-51*

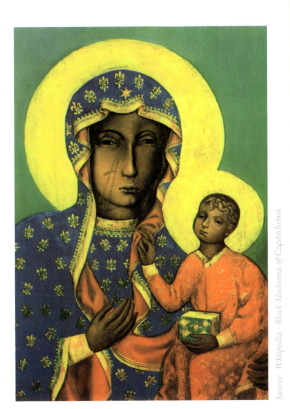

Source: Wikipedia - Black Madonna of Częstochowa

OUR LADY OF CZESTOCHOWA
Poland

Vladislaus II of Opole took possession of a castle where he hung the icon on the surrounding wall. On August 26, 1382, he had the sacred painting installed in the Church of the Assumption.

In 1430, Hussite raiders tried to make off with a wagonload of valuables, including the painting, but when their horses refused to move, they threw down the icon and slashed the face leaving the iconic scar found in all represenations of Our Lady of Czestochowa.

In 1931, Pope Pius XI established August 26 as the feast day and as pope, John Paul II visited the shrine four times.

21ST WEEK IN ORDINARY TIME

First Reading: *1 Corinthians 1:17-25*
Responsorial Psalm: *Ps 33:1-2, 4-5, 10-11*
Gospel Reading: *Matthew 25:1-13*

AUGUST 2016

s	m	t	w	t	f	s
	1	2	3	4	5	6
7	8	9	10	11	12	13
14	15	16	17	18	19	20
21	22	23	24	25	26	27
28	29	30	31			

August
saturday
27

OUR LADY OF PRASCONDÙ
Italy (1619)

In the fall of 1618, John Berardi, a lively and hard-working boy, went with his father to Pavia, to help him work and earn a bitter morsel of bread.

One cold winter evening, after a tiring day at work, the father invited John to join him in prayer. But that night, because they were tired, John refused. The father slapped him and cursed him to silence. To the father's despair, the curse worked and the boy was silent. He made a vow to pilgrimage to Loreto to implore the grace of Our Lady of the long-awaited recovery. On August 27, while grazing, John saw the Virgin Mary in a vision and agreed to build a church in her honor. The boy and his father celebrated the cure and went on pilgrimage as he had promised.

Source: Don Bosco - Apparizione della Madonna a Prascondù (Torino)

AUGUST 2016

s	m	t	w	t	f	s
	1	2	3	4	5	6
7	8	9	10	11	12	13
14	15	16	17	18	19	20
21	22	23	24	25	26	27
28	29	30	31			

21ST WEEK IN ORDINARY TIME
Memorial of Saint Monica

First Reading: *1 Corinthians 1:26-31*
Responsorial Psalm: *Ps 33:12-13, 18-19, 20-21*
Gospel Reading: *Matthew 25:14-30*

Source: Blogspot - Tierra Charra "Nuestra Señora de los Caballeros"

VIRGIN OF THE KNIGHTS
Villavieja de Yeltes, Spain (12th c.)

From time immemorial, the Virgin of Knights has been honored by the inhabitants of Villavieja with the specific date of the beginning of the devotion unknown. Popular tradition says that the Virgin appeared to a knight of Salamanca from the Knights Templar, according to documents in the Vatican archives. She was declared Patroness of Villavieja by Pope Pius XII, with Bishop of Ciudad Rodrigo D. Maximum Yurramendi making the solemn proclamation in the Plaza Mayor of Villavieja on April 18, 1948.

Townspeople celebrate festivities in honor of their patron. All dress in their finery to honor her with a Mass followed by an offertory next to City Hall where all the attendees kiss her image.

AUGUST 2016

s	m	t	w	t	f	s
	1	2	3	4	5	6
7	8	9	10	11	12	13
14	15	16	17	18	19	20
21	22	23	24	25	26	27
28	29	30	31			

22ND SUNDAY IN ORDINARY TIME

First Reading: *Sirach 3:17-18, 20, 28-29*
Responsorial Psalm: *Ps 68:4-5, 6-7, 10-11*
Second Reading: *Hebrews 12:18-19, 22-24A*
Gospel Reading: *Matthew 11:29AB*

August
monday
29

OUR LADY OF THE GUARD
Savona, Italy (1490)

According to tradition, on August 29, 1490 the Virgin Mary appeared to a peasant Benedetto Pareto and asked him to build a chapel. He replied that he was only a poor man. The Virgin Mary exhorted him "Be not afraid!" Nevertheless, Pareto went home and did not speak with anyone. A few days later he was injured falling from a tree. The Virgin Mary appeared to him again and he was miraculously healed. The event convinced him to speak about the apparition and seek help to build the chapel. The first chapel was built by Pareto himself in the site of the apparition. Due to the increasing flow of pilgrims, a shrine was built 1530. A new shrine was later built in 1890. It was raised to the title of Basilica in 1915 by Pope Benedict XV.

Source: http://digilander.libero.it/cesana/volto/04-2002.htm

AUGUST 2016

s	m	t	w	t	f	s
	1	2	3	4	5	6
7	8	9	10	11	12	13
14	15	16	17	18	19	20
21	22	23	24	25	26	27
28	29	30	31			

22ND WEEK IN ORDINARY TIME
Memorial of the Passion of Saint John the Baptist

First Reading: *1 Corinthians 2:1-5*
Responsorial Psalm: *Ps 119:97, 98, 99, 100, 101, 102*
Gospel Reading: *Mark 6:17-29*

Source: Prinvagando.it

OUR LADY OF THE WELL
Capurso, Italy (1705)

The town of Capurso (Bari), on the east coast of southern Italy, claims Our Lady of the Well as its patron under the title Madonna del Pozzo. Tradition says that it was on August 30, 1705, that the image of Our Lady sculpted in wood was found in a well. It is now preserved in the Basilica S. Maria del Pozzo, construction of which began in 1770. On May 20, 1852, the image of the Blessed Mother was solemnly crowned. Headquartered in Chicago, Illinois, USA, the Societá Maria S.S. del Pozzo, dedicated to Madonna del Pozzo and her traditions was established in 1922. The Society has its origins at Capurso.

AUGUST 2016

s	m	t	w	t	f	s
	1	2	3	4	5	6
7	8	9	10	11	12	13
14	15	16	17	18	19	20
21	22	23	24	25	26	27
28	29	30	31			

22ND WEEK IN ORDINARY TIME

First Reading: *1 Corinthians 2:10B-16*
Responsorial Psalm: *Ps 145:8-9, 10-11, 12-13AB, 13CD-14*
Gospel Reading: *Luke 4:31-37*

August
wednesday
31

OUR LADY OF THE FOUNDERS
Mt. Athos, Greece
(1st c.)

According to Sacred Tradition, three days after she fell asleep, the Blessed Virgin rose up and ascended to heaven in body at the end of her earthly life. During her ascent, she gave her belt to the Apostle Thomas. The Holy Belt, according to tradition, was made of camel leather by Mary herself. The Empress Zoe, wife of Leo VI the Wise, in gratitude for a miraculous healing, embroidered the belt with gold thread. During the XII century under Manuel A 'Komninos (1143-1180) the official feast for the Holy Belt was established on August 31. A thirteen-century legend establishes that it was brought to Prato, Italy, around 1141 by a merchant Michael whom kept it until his death in 1172, giving it to Church of San Esteban. The reconstructed church still retains the relic.

Source: Foros de la Virgen – Nuestra Señora de los fundadores

AUGUST 2016

s	m	t	w	t	f	s
	1	2	3	4	5	6
7	8	9	10	11	12	13
14	15	16	17	18	19	20
21	22	23	24	25	26	27
28	29	30	31			

22ND WEEK IN ORDINARY TIME

First Reading: *1 Corinthians 3:1-9*
Responsorial Psalm: *Ps 33:12-13, 14-15, 20-21*
Gospel Reading: *Luke 4:38-44*

Source: Flickr – Jialiu Juárez Herrera "La Aparición de la Virgen de los Remedios"

1

VIRGIN OF THE REMEDIES
Mexico (1519)

The Virgin of the Remedies is the oldest image venerated in Mexico, brought by a soldier of Hernán Cortés during the Conquest. It reached Mexican soil in 1519 with Juan Rodriguez de Villafuerte, from Basque, Spain, as guardian of his journey. It was in Veracruz where he presided over the first Mass in Mexico. Many Mexican cities have taken her as their patron. After the statue was buried in that place, in 1540 the Indian leader Juan Tovar, on Totoltepec hill, had a vision in which the bright Virgin Mary urged him to rescue her forgotten image. He told his story to the Franciscans but it wasn't until an Indian died in a factory accident that the image was found buried. Tovar reverently took the small image home where it became an object of devotion with a feast day established for September 1.

22ND WEEK IN ORDINARY TIME

First Reading: *1 Corinthians 3:18-23*
Responsorial Psalm: *Ps 24:1BC-2, 3-4AB, 5-6*
Gospel Reading: *Luke 5:1-11*

SEPTEMBER 2016

s	m	t	w	t	f	s
				1	2	3
4	5	6	7	8	9	10
11	12	13	14	15	16	17
18	19	20	21	22	23	24
25	26	27	28	29	30	

September
friday
2

OUR LADY OF THE MOUNTAIN
Polsi di San Luca, Italy (1144)

A rare unusual iron cross pulled from the ground lay in front of a young boy and his calf in 1144 at Aspromonte when the Virgin Mary appeared in a vision with the request that a devotion be started and spread. A church was built on the spot. Several centuries later, a chest with a stone statue of the Madonna inside was discovered and taken by oxen In 1560 to Aspromonte, the place of the apparition. Every year on September 2, pilgrims from Calabria and Sicily journey 24-hours to Polsi, firing celebratory gunshots at their arrival. The next day, a wooden Madonna processed through the streets. Also known as the Mother of the Good Shepherd, the Madonna of the Mountain was crowned in 1881, 1931 and on September 2, 1981.

Source: Roman Catholic Saints - Our Lady of the Mountains

SEPTEMBER 2016

s	m	t	w	t	f	s
				1	2	3
4	5	6	7	8	9	10
11	12	13	14	15	16	17
18	19	20	21	22	23	24
25	26	27	28	29	30	

22ND WEEK IN ORDINARY TIME

First Reading: *1 Corinthians 4:1-5*
Responsorial Psalm: *Ps37:3-4, 5-6, 27-28, 39-40*
Gospel Reading: *Luke 5:33-39*

Source: All Collection – "V. del Valle.Pravia, Asturias, V. de los Milagros, Ruesga-Cantabria"

VIRGIN OF THE MIRACLE
Ruesga, Spain
(14th c.)

The origin of this celebration is at the chestnut forest along the river called Vegacorredor. Towards midnight, when some soldiers were making a pilgrimage, the Virgin of the Miracle was seen along the river surrounded by tongues of fire. She approached them and they fled.

The next day, people filled with joy at the news started to come to place where the ashes were still smoldering, and found a large copper cauldron. Since then, every year on September 3rd in that field, the custom is celebrated of having a pilgrimage called the 'Milagruco', which goes throughout the neighborhoods with family groups participating.

22ND WEEK IN ORDINARY TIME
Memorial of St. Gregory the Great, Pope & Doctor of the Church

First Reading: *1 Corinthians 4:6B-15*
Responsorial Psalm: *Ps 145:17-18, 19-20, 21*
Gospel Reading: *Luke 6:1-5*

SEPTEMBER 2016

s	m	t	w	t	f	s
				1	2	3
4	5	6	7	8	9	10
11	12	13	14	15	16	17
18	19	20	21	22	23	24
25	26	27	28	29	30	

September

sunday

4

OUR LADY OF VILLAVICIOSA
Cordoba, Spain
(14th c.)

Legend places the appearance of the image in the Portuguese town of Vila Viciosa de Évora, in the second half of the fourteenth century.

At dawn, the mountain workers dedicated to rebuilding the vineyards in the area heard the sound of a hoe hitting an object underground. In the presence of the ecclesiastical and civil, authorities, they discovered an ancient lead box containing a beautiful image of the Virgin.

Convinced of a miracle, they went solemnly to the village church and then built a small shrine in that vineyard. Her fame spread everywhere and the simple Portuguese shrine was visited by various people and were blessed by many miracles.

SEPTEMBER 2016

s	m	t	w	t	f	s
				1	2	3
4	5	6	7	8	9	10
11	12	13	14	15	16	17
18	19	20	21	22	23	24
25	26	27	28	29	30	

23RD SUNDAY IN ORDINARY TIME

First Reading: *Wisdom 9:13-18B*
Responsorial Psalm: *Ps 90:3-4, 5-6, 12-13, 14-17*
Second Reading: *Philemon 9-10, 12-17*
Gospel Reading: *Luke 14:25-33*

Source: Flickr:dennisraymondm2 - N.S. del Pedancino

September
monday

5

OUR LADY OF PEDANCINO
Cismon del Grappa, Italy (700)

In Cismon del Grappa, on a cloudless spring day, a mute shepherd was with his sheep when a mysterious light unexpectedly shone over the cliff revealing a beautiful image of the Virgin and child, smiling and inviting him closer. He left his sheep behind and ran home screaming of the miracle. He went to the parish priest who heard his voice and decided to follow. On hearing the news, Bishop of Padova sent experts to examine the image and to monitor the situation. The statue was found to be of a style and composition from an unknown place. In 1748 a flood damaged the church and houses, sweeping the statue thirty miles away. The joyful announcement of the return of the statue is celebrated annually on September 5th.

23RD WEEK IN ORDINARY TIME

First Reading: *1 Corinthians 5:1-8*
Responsorial Psalm: *Ps 5:5-6, 7, 12*
Gospel Reading: *Luke 6:6-11*

SEPTEMBER 2016

s	m	t	w	t	f	s
				1	2	3
4	5	6	7	8	9	10
11	12	13	14	15	16	17
18	19	20	21	22	23	24
25	26	27	28	29	30	

September

tuesday

6

ICON OF THE MOTHER OF GOD OF ST PETER OF MOSCOW
Russia (14th c.)

The Icon of the Most Holy Theotokos "Of St Peter" was so called because it was painted by St Peter, Metropolitan of Moscow while he was igumen of the Ratsk monastery near Volhynia. During a visit to St Maximus at the Ratsk monastery, St Peter gifted him with this icon. Upon the death of St Maximus, Gerontius took this icon to Patriarch Athanasius. The journey of Gerontius was delayed, however, by a terrible storm at sea. During this storm, Our Lady appeared to him and told him the Patriarchate should pass to the painter of the icon. When he came before Patriarch Athanasius, he gave the icon to St Peter and told him that the Virgin foretold his path. St Peter took the icon to Vladimir and placed it in the cathedral.

Source: Orthodox Church in America - Icon of the Mother of God of St. Peter Moscow

SEPTEMBER 2016

s	m	t	w	t	f	s
				1	2	3
4	5	6	7	8	9	10
11	12	13	14	15	16	17
18	19	20	21	22	23	24
25	26	27	28	29	30	

23RD WEEK IN ORDINARY TIME

First Reading: *1 Corinthians 6:1-11*
Responsorial Psalm: *Ps 149:1B-2, 3-4, 5-6A AND 9B*
Gospel Reading: *Luke 6:12-19*

Source: Blogspot: Regla por El Mundo "CUBA (Nacimiento del culto)"

OUR LADY OF REGLA
Havana, Cuba
(18th c.)

The story of Our Lady of Regla is connected to Saint Augustine (354–430), who, it is said, had received heavenly instructions to carve a wooden statue of a black virgin and to place it in his chapel in Hippo. Thirteen years after his death, when Hippo was attacked and destroyed by the Vandals, the monks fled to Spain and took the statue with them. They placed it on a spot that looked out to sea, and this is where the devotion began. In time, Our Lady of Regla became the patroness of mariners. This seafaring connection lead to her adoption in 1714 as the patron saint of the small village of Regla, located on the northeastern side of Havana's Bay in a pre-Columbian Indian settlement that would later be populated by fishermen and sailors. Her feast is celebrated annually on September 7th.

SEPTEMBER 2016

s	m	t	w	t	f	s
				1	2	3
4	5	6	7	8	9	10
11	12	13	14	15	16	17
18	19	20	21	22	23	24
25	26	27	28	29	30	

23RD WEEK IN ORDINARY TIME

First Reading: *1 Corinthians 7:25-31*
Responsorial Psalm: *Ps 45:11-12, 14-15, 16-17*
Gospel Reading: *Luke 6:20-26*

September

thursday

8

OUR LADY OF GOOD HEALTH
Velankanni, India
(16th c.)

The Virgin Mary is said by tradition to have appeared to a shepherd boy named Tamil Krishnannesti Sankaranarayanam. Later she appeared to and healed a crippled boy selling buttermilk. A group of Portuguese sailors attribute being saved from a storm to her intercession. As promised, they constructed a large chapel at their landing spot.

Pope John XXIII raised the Shrine to the status of Basilica in 1962. Vatican has declared Vailankanni as a "Holy city". Innumerable are the favors obtained by all who approach her, irrespective of caste or creed inspiring the name the Mother of Good Health.

Source: Wikimapia – Basilica of Our Lady of Good Health

SEPTEMBER 2016

s	m	t	w	t	f	s
				1	2	3
4	5	6	7	8	9	10
11	12	13	14	15	16	17
18	19	20	21	22	23	24
25	26	27	28	29	30	

23RD WEEK IN ORDINARY TIME
Feast of the Nativity of the Blessed Virgin Mary

First Reading: *Micah 5: 1-4a*
Responsorial Psalm: *Ps 13: 6ab.6c*
Gospel Reading: *Matthew 1: 1-16.18-23*

Source: http://listas_20minutos.es/lista/advocaciones-de-la-virgen-maria-268793/

HOLY MARY THE ANCIENT
Panama City, Panama (16th c.)

When the founders of the town of La Guardia survived a confrontation with the natives In 1520, they fulfilled a promise to the Virgin Mary and later renamed it Santa María la Antigua. A Christian community of native converts and Spaniards developed there around the chapel of St. Mary the Ancient, once the house of Chief Cémaco. This tiny chapel of St. Mary the Ancient later became a cathedral under the Archdiocese of Seville when on September 9, 1513, Pope Leo X created the first mainland diocese with the bull "Pastoralis Officii Debitum". In 2001, September 9 was established as her feast day for the Republic of Panama when the Vatican named St. Mary the Ancient as patron.

23RD WEEK IN ORDINARY TIME
Memorial of Saint Peter Claver, Priest

First Reading: *1 Corinthians 9:16-19, 22B-27*
Responsorial Psalm: *Ps 84:3, 4, 5-6, 12*
Gospel Reading: *Luke 6:39-42*

SEPTEMBER 2016

s	m	t	w	t	f	s
				1	2	3
4	5	6	7	8	9	10
11	12	13	14	15	16	17
18	19	20	21	22	23	24
25	26	27	28	29	30	

September

saturday

10

OUR LADY OF KERIO
Noyal-Muzillac, France (1874)

Jean Pierre Le Boterff, born October 15, 1857 in Noyal-Muzillac, was a young farmer who was very diligent and committed to his work. On September 10, 1874, near the camp where he was intent on sowing, he saw a figure on the edge of the woods. This figure was surrounded by a highly luminous halo grew more distinct, until she assumed the appearance of the Mother of God: she wore a blue robe sprinkled with stars, a golden cloak and a white veil. Mary invited the industrious farmer to make a pilgrimage walk to St. Anne d'Auray. The Virgin appeared to him at other times and urged him to pray for Brittany. Some years later, Pierre entered the Frères de l'Instruction nell'Otdine Chrétienne in Brittany, in the convent of Ploermel, where he died at only 31 years.

Source: Cure Muzillac – NOYAL-MUZILLAC (et Notre Dame de KERIO)

SEPTEMBER 2016

s	m	t	w	t	f	s
				1	2	3
4	5	6	7	8	9	10
11	12	13	14	15	16	17
18	19	20	21	22	23	24
25	26	27	28	29	30	

23RD WEEK IN ORDINARY TIM

First Reading: *1 Corinthians 10:14-22*
Responsorial Psalm: *Ps 116:12-13, 17-18*
Gospel Reading: *Luke 6:43-49*

Source: *Maria di Nazareth – Apparizione di Monte Bonicca*

BLESSED VIRGIN OF MONTE BONICCA
Italy (1595)

On September 11, 1595, the Blessed Virgin appeared to the inhabitants of Campo Ligure and Masone, two villages in the Valle Stura. The two divided communities were in a bitter struggle for four centuries. Two representatives of the people of Campo went to Vico to implore peace from the Madonna del Pilone. Upon their return to Campo, during vespers some of the people fell to the ground unconscious, and a woman known to be mentally unstable was full of mystical fervor as she began to speak of great spiritual concepts. After the celebration, everyone saw on Mount Bonicca a white cloud that seemed to consist of a large army of people. This soon vanished, giving way to another equally bright cloud. The appearances were preceded by four cases of healing.

24TH SUNDAY IN ORDINARY TIME

First Reading: *Exodus 32:7-11, 13-14*
Responsorial Psalm: *Ps 51:3-4, 12-13, 17, 19*
Second Reading: *1 Timothy 1:12-17*
Gospel Reading: *Luke 15:1-32*

SEPTEMBER 2016

s	m	t	w	t	f	s
				1	2	3
4	5	6	7	8	9	10
11	12	13	14	15	16	17
18	19	20	21	22	23	24
25	26	27	28	29	30	

September

monday

12

MEDIATRIX OF ALL GRACES
Lipa, Philippines
(1948)

The Virgin Mary appeared 19 times to a Carmelite novice in Lipa City, Philippines. Teresita recounted that Our Lady stressed humility, penance, and prayers for the clergy and the Pope. Teresita reported one secret for herself, one for the Carmel convent in Lipa City, one for China, and also one for the entire world. The phenomena of rose petals with sacred images was reported at the site. Veneration of Mary was permitted under the title "Mediatrix of All Grace" but the 1951 ruling of "Established as Not Supernatural" was affirmed by the Vatican in 2010. On the feast day September 12, 2015, Archbishop Ramon C. Arguelles released an official statement declaring the phenomenon to "exhibit supernatural character and is worthy of belief".

Source: Wikipedia - Mediatrix of all graces

SEPTEMBER 2016

s	m	t	w	t	f	s
				1	2	3
4	5	6	7	8	9	10
11	12	13	14	15	16	17
18	19	20	21	22	23	24
25	26	27	28	29	30	

24TH WEEK IN ORDINARY TIME

First Reading: *1 Corinthians 11:17-26, 33*
Responsorial Psalm: *Ps 40:7-8A, 8B-9, 10, 17*
Gospel Reading: *Luke 7:1-10*

Source: Blogspot - Rendering Voices "Mother at the Mount"a

September
tuesday
13

OUR LADY OF THE MOUNT
Bandra Mumbai, India (1570)

A beautiful, wooden statue of Our Lady, depicted as the Mother of God was initially brought by the Jesuits from Portugal in 1570 when a simple mud Oratory for private devotion was built near Lands End Bandra, overlooking the Arabian Sea. In 1700, Bandra was invaded by a pirate army of the Muscat Arabs who, ransacked the chapel for treasure. Disappointed in not finding great riches, they chopped of the right forearm of the statue, thinking it was of gold. They also intended to set fire to the church, when a huge army of bees attacked them so cruelly that they were forced to leave. When the Mount Mary Chapel was rebuilt in 1761, the damaged statue was repaired. Over the centuries devotion to this statue grew as numerous favors were granted.

24TH WEEK IN ORDINARY TIME
Memorial of St. John Chrysostom, Bishop & Doctor of the Church

First Reading: *1 Corinthians 12:12-14, 27-31A*
Responsorial Psalm: *Ps 100:1B-2, 3, 4, 5*
Gospel Reading: *Luke 7:11-17*

SEPTEMBER 2016

s	m	t	w	t	f	s
				1	2	3
4	5	6	7	8	9	10
11	12	13	14	15	16	17
18	19	20	21	22	23	24
25	26	27	28	29	30	

September
wednesday
14

DOLOROUS MOTHER
Legau, Germany
(1728)

The parish church of Steinbach In 1728 acquired a set of painted wood statues of the Crucifixion, the Sorrowful Mother, and St. John. Two years later, parishioners gave accounts that the statue of Our Lady of Sorrows was moving its eyes, crying, and changing complexion. Miracles and healings also accompanied the prodigy. The bishop of the diocese established a formal investigation, that found the miracles valid in 1734. A larger baroque church was built for the increasing number of pilgrims. At the end of the 18th century, the crowds and miracles lessened but the shrine still hosts four major pilgrimages annually: the Monday after Pentecost, the feasts of the Holy Cross on May 3 and September 14, and the veterans' pilgrimage on the last Saturday of October.

Source: Pilgerziele.de – Maria Steinbach

SEPTEMBER 2016

s	m	t	w	t	f	s
				1	2	3
4	5	6	7	8	9	10
11	12	13	14	15	16	17
18	19	20	21	22	23	24
25	26	27	28	29	30	

24TH WEEK IN ORDINARY TIME
Feast of the Exaltation of the Holy Cross

First Reading: *Numbers 21: 4b-9*
Responsorial Psalm: *Ps 78: 1bc-2.34-35.36-37.38*
Second Reading: *Philippians 2: 6-11*
Gospel Reading: *John 3: 13-17*

Source: McBlog - Padre Antonio Rungi "Festa della Madonna del Colle"

September
thursday

15

OUR LADY OF THE HILL
Lenola, Italy (1602)

On the hill of Lenola in 250, a shrine had been built with an image of the Madonna and Child where Roman soldiers discovered and killed Christians in hiding. On the night of September 15, 1602 Gabriel Mattei who was selected by two troublemaker friends to carry out a murder, witnessed a radiant light appearing around the image accompanied by a heavenly voice asking him to build a shrine. When Gabriel showed his friends the image, blood began dripping from her lower lip. The bishop approved the miracle and the first stone was laid on May 7, 1607 and by 1610, the Sanctuary now called the "Madonna del Colle" was opened to the veneration of the faithful.

24TH WEEK IN ORDINARY TIME
Memorial of Our Lady of Sorrows

First Reading: *1 Corinthians 15:1-11*
Responsorial Psalm: *Ps 118:1B-2, 16AB-17, 28*
Gospel Reading: *John 19:25-27*

SEPTEMBER 2016

s	m	t	w	t	f	s
				1	2	3
4	5	6	7	8	9	10
11	12	13	14	15	16	17
18	19	20	21	22	23	24
25	26	27	28	29	30	

September

friday

16

OUR LADY OF THE FLAGSTONES
Potosí, Colombia (1754)

In 1754, Maria Mueses de Quinones, an Indian woman from the village of Potosi, Colombia and her deaf-mute daughter Rosa were caught in a storm. They sought refuge in a canyon where Rosa exclaimed with her first words "the mestiza is calling me." She did not see the figures of a woman and child that the girl described and fearfully ran back with her daughter to Ipiales and told the townspeople. On her return, the woman saw an apparition of Our Lady and Child. Some months later, Rosa died and was returned to life when her mother prayed again at the cave. The townspeople came to see at this place a miraculous image burned into the rocks. Our Lady's imprint is on a stone slab, near the bottom of a pit of the Andes.

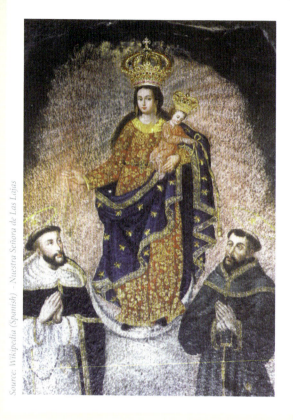

Source: Wikipedia (Spanish) – Nuestra Señora de Las Lajas

SEPTEMBER 2016

s	m	t	w	t	f	s
				1	2	3
4	5	6	7	8	9	10
11	12	13	14	15	16	17
18	19	20	21	22	23	24
25	26	27	28	29	30	

24TH WEEK IN ORDINARY TIME
Memorial of Sts Cornelius, Pope, & Cyprian, Bishop, Marty

First Reading: *1 Corinthians 15:12-20*
Responsorial Psalm: *Ps 17:1BCD, 6-7, 8B AND 15*
Gospel Reading: *Luke 8:1-3*

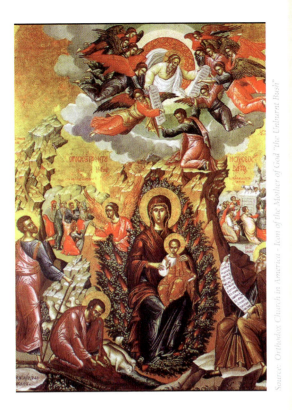

Source: Orthodox Church in America – Icon of the Mother of God "the Unburnt Bush"

ICON OF THE MOTHER OF GOD "THE UNBURNT BUSH"
Mt. Sinai, Egypt (3rd c.)

An ancient story is told about a fire which was consuming several wooden buildings. In the midst of the fire an old woman stood in front of her house holding an icon of the "Unburnt Bush." A witness happened to see her there, and marveled at her faith. The next day he returned to the spot and was astonished to see the old woman's home completely unscathed by the fire, while all the other houses around it were destroyed. This may explain why the Mother of God under this title, is regarded as the protector of homes from fire.

It is believed that the earliest icons of the Unburnt Bush originated at St. Catherine's Monastery on Mount Sinai.

SEPTEMBER 2016

s	m	t	w	t	f	s
				1	2	3
4	5	6	7	8	9	10
11	12	13	14	15	16	17
18	19	20	21	22	23	24
25	26	27	28	29	30	

24TH WEEK IN ORDINARY TIME

First Reading: *1 Corinthians 15:35-37, 42-49*
Responsorial Psalm: *Ps 56:10C-12, 13-14*
Gospel Reading: *Luke 8:4-15*

September

sunday

18

OUR LADY OF HOPE
Calasparra, Spain
(1786)

When a shepherd found an image inside the cave, authorities arranged to transfer it to one of the churches of the town. Miraculously, it became so heavy that it was thought to be a sign not to move it. The miraculous nature of the image is acknowledged to this day, with hundreds of devotees lining the walls of the chamber attached to the chapel of the Virgin. Our Lady of Hope is the official patron of Calasparra since 1840. The Canonical Coronation of the patron was held September 8, 1996. The festivities in her honor mainly focus on the celebration of a mass and pilgrimage on September 7, the feast of the Virgin. Also on September 18, another celebration is held. An annual transfer of the patron saint to Calasparra takes place on the first Sunday in May.

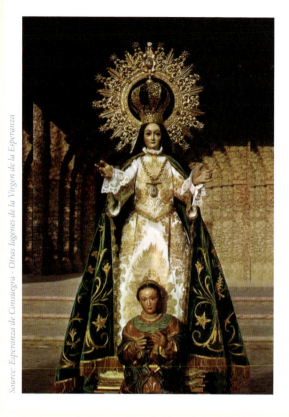

SEPTEMBER 2016

s	m	t	w	t	f	s
				1	2	3
4	5	6	7	8	9	10
11	12	13	14	15	16	17
18	19	20	21	22	23	24
25	26	27	28	29	30	

25TH SUNDAY IN ORDINARY TIME

First Reading: *Amos 8:4-7*
Responsorial Psalm: *Ps 113:1-2, 4-6, 7-8*
Second Reading: *1 Timothy 2:1-8*
Gospel Reading: *Luke 16:1-13*

Source: Wikipedia (French) - Notre-Dame de La Salette

OUR LADY OF LA SALETTE
France (1846)

Six thousand feet up in the French Alps, the Blessed Virgin Mary is believed to have come to 11 year old Maximin Giraud and 14 year old Melanie Calvat-Mathieu while they tended sheep. Her appearance in sorrow and tears called for conversion and penance for sins. During interrogations from the local authorities, the children were taken to the apparition site where a man broke off a piece of rock at the spot of the Virgin's appearance and uncovered a spring with healing powers which inspired the bishop's official inquiry. Maximin and Melanie received a controversial Secret and recorded it for Church officials who delivered their statement to the Bishop. Bishop de Bruillard published a pastoral letter in 1851 approving the apparition. In 1879, the completed basilica was consecrated.

SEPTEMBER 2016

s	m	t	w	t	f	s
				1	2	3
4	5	6	7	8	9	10
11	12	13	14	15	16	17
18	19	20	21	22	23	24
25	26	27	28	29	30	

25TH WEEK IN ORDINARY TIME

First Reading: *Proverbs 3:27-34*
Responsorial Psalm: *Ps 15:2-3A, 3BC-4AB, 5*
Gospel Reading: *Luke 8:16-18*

September

tuesday

20

OUR LADY WITH THE SILVER FOOT
Toul, France (1284)

On September 20, 1284, shortly before midnight, Helwide experienced a vision of the Virgin Mary while praying in sorrow with the death of her husband and daughter. The Virgin ordered her to go searching for Rimbert, guardian of the entrance to the city. She warned him about an enemy ready to set their homes on fire and slaughter the people there. The Virgin revealed a sign that her foot would be shown under her garment. When she relayed the news, she was mocked until the people saw the statue reveal her foot. To memorialize the event and show gratitude for the protection granted to them by the Blessed Virgin Mary, the people of Toul had a shoe of pure silver made to cover the statue's foot.

Source: Blogspot - Le Claveau Promenades "La Grande Guerre à Toul"

SEPTEMBER 2016

s	m	t	w	t	f	s
				1	2	3
4	5	6	7	8	9	10
11	12	13	14	15	16	17
18	19	20	21	22	23	24
25	26	27	28	29	30	

25TH WEEK IN ORDINARY TIME
Mem. of Sts Andrew Kim Tae-gŏn, Priest, & Paul Chŏng Ha-sa

First Reading: *Proverbs 21:1-6, 10-13*
Responsorial Psalm: *Ps 119:1, 27, 30, 34, 35, 44*
Second Reading: *1 Timothy 2:1-8*
Gospel Reading: *Luke 8:19-21*

Source: Blogspot - Cerca-Disegni "Santa Maria del Tresto (Ospedaletto Euganeo - PD)"

BLESSED VIRGIN OF TRESTO
Italy (1468)

On September 21, 1468 the Virgin appeared to Giovanni Zelo, a boatman from Padua Ponso when he was returning home. In the evening, the man had stopped to sleep in the boat under the bridge Borini. Around midnight he was awakened by a woman's voice calling him three times and he saw a beautiful woman who asked him to follow her. They walked out to the countryside in Tresto, and told Giovanni that she was the Virgin Mary, asking him not to blaspheme and to ensure that in that very place a church was built according to the design and the measures which she illustrated. She gave him a knife to pierce the ground and have it flow with blood to prove to others the vision. The church was entrusted to a Congregation of Hermits, of which Giovanni took the habit in the lay state.

25TH WEEK IN ORDINARY TIME

Feast of Saint Matthew, Apostle and evangelist

First Reading: *Ephesians 4:1-7, 11-13*
Responsorial Psalm: *Ps 19:2-3, 4-5*
Gospel Reading: *Matthew 9:9-13*

SEPTEMBER 2016

s	m	t	w	t	f	s
				1	2	3
4	5	6	7	8	9	10
11	12	13	14	15	16	17
18	19	20	21	22	23	24
25	26	27	28	29	30	

September

thursday

22

OUR LADY OF SAFE HARBOR
Lampedusa, Italy (1843)

The island of Lampedusa lies far south of Sicily, closer to Tunisia than to Italy. Since the time of the Crusades, it has been home to a rural shrine frequented by mariners both Christian and Muslim, who kept an oil lamp burning constantly before the crude stone statue of the Madonna and Child in the 1500s and 1600s. But the island was not inhabited until September 22, 1843, when two steamships of Italian colonists arrived. In Madonna Valley, they found the chapel dilapidated and the mutilated statue of the Virgin on the ground. They restored the chapel and statue, and a mass sung every year on September 22 in honor of the Madonna of Porto Salvo and the settlement of the island.

Source: Italian Notebook – "Lampedusa, Still the "Port of Safe Haven"

SEPTEMBER 2016

s	m	t	w	t	f	s
				1	2	3
4	5	6	7	8	9	10
11	12	13	14	15	16	17
18	19	20	21	22	23	24
25	26	27	28	29	30	

25TH WEEK IN ORDINARY TIME

First Reading: *Ecclesiastes 1:2-11*
Responsorial Psalm: *Ps 90:3-4, 5-6, 12-13, 14 AND 17BC*
Gospel Reading: *Luke 9:7-9*

Source: Blog Spot - Dias de fiesta en la Rioja "Peregrinaje con la Virgen de Valvanera"

OUR LADY OF VALVANERA
La Rioja, Spain
(9th c.)

The title was established at Anguiano in the community of La Rioja in north-central Spain, located near Nájera, where it is celebrated on September 23. According to tradition, one day a criminal named Nuno Onez upon hearing the pleas of his next victim, Nuno repented of his many crimes. An angel appeared to him asking him to search in Valvanera for an oak tree with a flowing fountain at its base and surrounded by swarms of bees where he would find an image of the Virgin Mary. Nuno went with a priest on the next Sunday, and found the image, just as the angel had said. In that place, he built a shrine that became known as the chapel of Santo Cristo and later resulted in the Valvanera monastery, where the Virgin is still venerated to this day.

25TH WEEK IN ORDINARY TIME
Memorial of Saint Pius of Pietrelcina, Priest

First Reading: *Ecclesiastes 3:1-11*
Responsorial Psalm: *Ps 144:1B AND 2ABC, 3-4*
Gospel Reading: *Luke 9:18-22*

SEPTEMBER 2016

s	m	t	w	t	f	s
				1	2	3
4	5	6	7	8	9	10
11	12	13	14	15	16	17
18	19	20	21	22	23	24
25	26	27	28	29	30	

September

saturday

24

OUR LADY OF WALSINGHAM
England (1061)

In 1061, Our Lady appeared to Richeldis de Faverches, a Catholic English noblewoman in the village of Walsingham in Norfolk, England. Our Lady of Walsingham presented her with the plans of the Holy House of the Holy Family in Nazareth and asked that she build the house as a shrine and place of pilgrimage.

During Pope John Paul II's 1982 visit, the Slipper Chapel Statue was taken to Wembley Stadium and was carried around the stadium prior to the Papal Mass. In 2000, he decreed that the feast of Our Lady of Walsingham, patroness of England, would be celebrated on September 24th in England. It is a solemnity for all parishes in any part of the world named for Our Lady under this title.

Source: Wikipedia - Our Lady of Walsingham

SEPTEMBER 2016

s	m	t	w	t	f	s
				1	2	3
4	5	6	7	8	9	10
11	12	13	14	15	16	17
18	19	20	21	22	23	24
25	26	27	28	29	30	

25TH WEEK IN ORDINARY TIME

First Reading: *Ecclesiastes 11:9—12:8*
Responsorial Psalm: *Ps 90:3-4, 5-6, 12-13, 14 AND 17*
Gospel Reading: *Luke 9:43B-45*

Source: infor-vallaguava.com – Virgen Maria del Rosario de San Nicolás

September
sunday
25

OUR LADY OF THE ROSARY
San Nicolás, Argentina (1983)

On September 25, 1983, Gladys Quiroga de Motta first had a vision of the Virgin Mary, while praying the rosary at home in San Nicolás, two hours north of Buenos Aires. It was the beginning of a long series of apparitions claimed by the devout housewife including over 1800 messages. A sanctuary was built in response to the devotional revival and international interest. Many miracles, including the cure of a boy's brain tumor, were recorded. In November 1983, the seer and her confessor discovered a statue in the cathedral's storage, matching the Virgin's appearance. It received a papal blessing and was sent to the sanctuary built at the Virgin's request "on the banks of the Paraná," which became a pilgrimage destination renowned for miracles.

SEPTEMBER 2016

s	m	t	w	t	f	s
				1	2	3
4	5	6	7	8	9	10
11	12	13	14	15	16	17
18	19	20	21	22	23	24
25	26	27	28	29	30	

26TH SUNDAY IN ORDINARY TIME

First Reading: *Amos 6:1A, 4-7*
Responsorial Psalm: *Ps 146:7, 8-9, 9-10*
Second Reading: *1 Timothy 6:11-16*
Gospel Reading: *Luke 16:19-31*

September
monday
26

OUR LADY OF LESNA PODLASKA
Poland (1683)

A flashing light lead two shepherd boys to find an image of Mary in a pear tree on September 14, 1683. Pilgrims in large numbers and nobility bearing gifts quickly came to see the circular stone icon, carved in low relief, became an object of pilgrimage. Catholics and Orthodox celebrate the image differently. Catholics, in Poland celebrate the feast of the Blessed Mother of Leśna on September 26 at the original site of the miracle. The Orthodox believe the original image is now at a convent in France, where it is honored on September 27. The patroness of Podlasia, is enshrined in a baroque basilica in Poland. On August 18, 1963, Stefan Cardinal Wyszyński crowned the image.

SEPTEMBER 2016

s	m	t	w	t	f	s
				1	2	3
4	5	6	7	8	9	10
11	12	13	14	15	16	17
18	19	20	21	22	23	24
25	26	27	28	29	30	

26TH WEEK IN ORDINARY TIME

First Reading: *Job 1:6-22*
Responsorial Psalm: *Ps 17:1BCD, 2-3, 6-7*
Gospel Reading: *Luke 9:46-50*

Source: Blogspot - IE N Occume Guere - SAINT JEROME EMILIEN, Confesseur, Fondateur d'Ordre

September
tuesday
27

APPARITION TO ST. JEROME EMILIANI
Treviso, Veneto, Italy (1511)

When St. Jerome Emiliani was still very young, the administrator of the fortress of Castelnuovo, he was jailed a day after an enemy attack. In the solitude of prison, he sought the help of God so He began to pray, turning to the Holy Virgin Mary, "liberation of prisoners," promising that if he returned free, he would go on pilgrimage to the shrine of Treviso. Jerome in fact obtained a release from captivity and the certain death sentence through the intercession of the Virgin, who appeared to him on September 27, 1511 and released him from his chains. The Lady then proceeded to protect him miraculously on his way to Treviso. This allowed him to cross unharmed through armies in conflict and to fulfill his vow.

SEPTEMBER 2016

s	m	t	w	t	f	s
				1	2	3
4	5	6	7	8	9	10
11	12	13	14	15	16	17
18	19	20	21	22	23	24
25	26	27	28	29	30	

26TH WEEK IN ORDINARY TIME
Memorial of Saint Vincent de Paul, Priest

First Reading: *Job 3:1-3, 11-17, 20-23*
Responsorial Psalm: *Ps 88:2-3, 4-5, 6, 7-8*
Gospel Reading: *Luke 9:51-56*

September

wednesday

28

OUR LADY OF THE ASH
Grado, Spain
(17th c.)

In centuries past, people came on pilgrimage to the sanctuary for the novenas. If all households are occupied, the visitors would spend the night in granaries, bread bins and tenadas.

In honor of the Virgen del Fresno, two festivals are held, one on September 8 and the other 28 of the same month preceded by a "St. Michael" novena that traditionally starts at four in the afternoon and took the name of "San Miguel Ninth". The novena begins on September 21 and ends on the 29th, feast of the three archangels Michael, Gabriel and Rafael, images of whom are found in the church. A booklet, "Novena of Fresno", by an anonymous author, is widespread in the area and serves as a guide for the ninth.

Source: Wikipedia – User:Urbano Suarez:gallery

SEPTEMBER 2016

s	m	t	w	t	f	s
				1	2	3
4	5	6	7	8	9	10
11	12	13	14	15	16	17
18	19	20	21	22	23	24
25	26	27	28	29	30	

26TH WEEK IN ORDINARY TIME

First Reading: *Job 9:1-12, 14-16*
Responsorial Psalm: *Ps 88:10BC-11, 12-13, 14-15*
Gospel Reading: *Luke 9:57-62*

Source: Blog.studenti.it/biscotcook – Madonna di Tirano

September
thursday
29

OUR LADY OF TIRANO
Italy (1504)

On September 29, 1504, Mario Omodei, received a vision of the Virgin Mary promising an end to the plague if a shrine in her honor would be built on the spot outside the city walls. The epidemic subsided, and the townspeople placed the first stone on March 25, 1505 of the resulting Sanctuary of the Madonna of Tirano stands on the Swiss-Italian border. Because of its crossroads location, it has always drawn pilgrims from throughout Europe. Around 1520, woodcarver G. Angelo Mayno created the silver clad Virgin statue as part of a set. The statues were desecrated when Napoleonic raiders confiscated the metal and destroyed the other statues. Pope Pius XII declared the Blessed Virgin of Tirano "special heavenly patron of all Europe" In 1946.

26TH WEEK IN ORDINARY TIME
Feast of Saints Michael, Gabriel, and Raphael, archangels

First Reading: *Daniel 7: 9-10.13-14*
Responsorial Psalm: *Ps 138: 1-2ab.2cde-3.4-5*
Gospel Reading: *John 1: 47-51*

SEPTEMBER 2016

s	m	t	w	t	f	s
				1	2	3
4	5	6	7	8	9	10
11	12	13	14	15	16	17
18	19	20	21	22	23	24
25	26	27	28	29	30	

September

friday

30

OUR LADY OF FORNO ALPI GRAIE
Italy (1629)

Peter Garino, a native of Groscavallo unearthed two ex-votos - a statue of the Madonna of Loreto and another of St. Charles Borromeo - both in poor condition. He decided to have them restored and then place them back where he found them. In 1630 he was forced to return to Groscavallo because of the plague and brought the two images, placing them in a box for safety but, at the entrance of the Valley of the Sea, going to provide food for the cattle, he suddenly found the images hanging from the branches of a tree. When he prayed in bewilderment to Our Lady, she then appeared to him, telling him to present them to the priests there, in order to "inspire more ardently the Christian life among the people."

Source: Templari Cavalieri

SEPTEMBER 2016

s	m	t	w	t	f	s
				1	2	3
4	5	6	7	8	9	10
11	12	13	14	15	16	17
18	19	20	21	22	23	24
25	26	27	28	29	30	

26TH WEEK IN ORDINARY TIME
Memorial of Saint Jerome, Priest and Doctor of the Church

First Reading: Job 38:1, 12-21; 40:3-5
Responsorial Psalm: Ps 139:1-3, 7-8, 9-10, 13-14AB
Gospel Reading: Luke 10:13-16

Source: Santuario di Valverde - Immagini - Foto del Santuario

October

saturday

1

OUR LADY OF VALVERDE
Italy (1711)

The Shrine of Our Lady of Valverde Rezzato, dates back to 1399, when Our Lady appeared to a farmer plowing his field, near the entrance of Valverde Rezzato, urging people to abandon their sinful ways, and encouraging them to live a Christian life. A small octagonal church dating from the twelfth century was built before the Rezzatesi decided to erect a larger sanctuary, completed in 1615. During the summer of 1711, the province of Brescia was hit by a severe epidemic of dying cattle. The inhabitants of Rezzato prayed to Our Lady of Valverde. On October 1, Our Lady appeared a second time to Paul Ogna, 8, and Francesco Pelizzari, 11, who went to collect chestnuts near the pond of the Sanctuary. Our Lady promised the end of the epidemic.

26TH WEEK IN ORDINARY TIME
St Thérèse of the Child Jesus, Virgin & Doctor of the Church

First Reading: *Job 42:1-3, 5-6, 12-17*
Responsorial Psalm: *Ps 119:66, 71, 75, 91, 125, 130*
Gospel Reading: *Luke 10:17-24*

OCTOBER 2016

s	m	t	w	t	f	s
						1
2	3	4	5	6	7	8
9	10	11	12	13	14	15
16	17	18	19	20	21	22
23	24	25	26	27	28	29
30	31					

October

sunday

2

MOTHER OF GOD ROZANCOWA
Krakow, Poland
(1600)

In the chapel dedicated to the Mother of God of the Rosary Dominican Basilica of the Trinity in Krakow is a copy of the ancient Roman "Salus Populi Romani" image. Brought by Cardinal Maciejowski from Rome to Krakow in 1600, the icon was crowned on October 2, 1921. In 1571, the Turks were defeated with the help of the image in Krakow. Likewise at the "Polish Lepanto" in 1621, when an allied force of Poles, Lithuanians, and Ukrainians faced a Turkish army twice its size at Khotyn, Ukraine. The whole populace joined in a rosary procession of many hours lead by the bishop of Krakow with the holy icon October 3. The Turk attack subsided and to this day in commemoration her feast is celebrated in Krakow on the first Sunday of October.

Source: Bloog.pl - monia450 - Sanktuarium Matki Boskiej Różańcowej

OCTOBER 2016

s	m	t	w	t	f	s
						1
2	3	4	5	6	7	8
9	10	11	12	13	14	15
16	17	18	19	20	21	22
23	24	25	26	27	28	29
30	31					

27TH SUNDAY IN ORDINARY TIME

First Reading: *Habakkuk 1:2-3; 2:2-4*
Responsorial Psalm: *Ps 95:1-2, 6-7, 8-9*
Second Reading: *2 Timothy 1:6-8, 13-14*
Gospel Reading: *Luke 17:5-10*

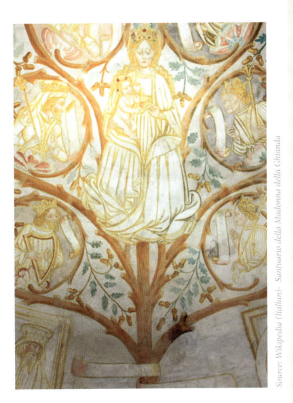

Source: Wikipedia (Italian)- Santuario della Madonna della Ghianda

October

monday

3

OUR LADY OF THE FRUIT OF THE OAK
Mezzana, Italy (13th c.)

A deaf and mute shepherd used to rest in the shade of an oak tree while watching the sheep of his father. One morning while he was waking up, the shepherd saw a great light at an oak and remained static. Through the branches he saw a lady appearing dressed in blue spoke softly: "Go back to your village, call your father". The shepherd ran to the house in tremendous shock, told his father and invited him to follow. His father and daughter with a group of people who had heard the news, went to the oak. The lady was gone but had left the witness of his miraculous presence, the deaf and mute shepherd now spoke and heard. A chapel was built to the Virgin Mary under the title Our Lady of Ghianda.

OCTOBER 2016

s	m	t	w	t	f	s
						1
2	3	4	5	6	7	8
9	10	11	12	13	14	15
16	17	18	19	20	21	22
23	24	25	26	27	28	29
30	31					

27TH WEEK IN ORDINARY TIME

First Reading: *Galatians 1:6-12*
Responsorial Psalm: *Ps 111:1B-2, 7-8, 9 AND 10C*
Gospel Reading: *Luke 10:25-37*

October

tuesday

4

OUR LADY OF MERCY
Biancavilla, Italy (1482)

According to tradition, after setting up camp, a small group of exiles hung the sacred icon on a fig tree. In the morning, when they were to resume the journey, the exiles found it inextricably tangled in the branches of the fig tree, grown overnight. The miraculous event was interpreted as the will of the Mother of God to stay in that place, where the small group could find a new home. Count Gian Tommaso Moncada, lord of the place, learning of the occurrence, gave the Greek-Albanian colony permission to stay. Several miracles including stopping a drought and a plague followed. A solemn procession is on October 4th, and the festivities honor patrons San Placido and San Zeno. After Mass, the icon is taken through the streets of the historic town center.

Source: Wikipedia (Italian) Madonna dell'Elemosina

OCTOBER 2016

s	m	t	w	t	f	s
						1
2	3	4	5	6	7	8
9	10	11	12	13	14	15
16	17	18	19	20	21	22
23	24	25	26	27	28	29
30	31					

27TH WEEK IN ORDINARY TIME
Memorial of Saint Francis of Assisi

First Reading: *Galatians 1:13-24*
Responsorial Psalm: *Ps 139:1B-3, 13-14AB, 14C-15*
Gospel Reading: *Luke 10:38-42*

Source: Basilica de la Virgen del Camino - Historia de la devoción a la Virgen del Camino

October

wednesday

5

OUR LADY OF THE WAY
Leon, Spain (1505)

Tradition has it that a captain, very devoted to the Virgen del Camino, was a native of Villamañán which was seized by the Moors. The Moor who had locked him up in chains every night in an ark, shackled him with chains and kept forcing him to deny his faith. One night, the villagers, hearing the bells and not knowing what was happening, were terrified. All went to church, preceded by the priest and found the Moor and Christian sitting in the ark, a miracle worked by the Virgin. The Moor converted to Christianity and the ark and the chain were kept inside the old sanctuary, which were venerated by the faithful. Today they can be seen in the new sanctuary in the room to the left of the image. The festivities are celebrated on September 15 and October 5, attracting a large number of pilgrims.

OCTOBER 2016

s	m	t	w	t	f	s
						1
2	3	4	5	6	7	8
9	10	11	12	13	14	15
16	17	18	19	20	21	22
23	24	25	26	27	28	29
30	31					

27TH WEEK IN ORDINARY TIME

First Reading: *Galatians 2:1-2, 7-14*
Responsorial Psalm: *Ps 117:1BC, 2*
Gospel Reading: *Luke 11:1-4*

October

thursday

6

ICON OF THE MOTHER OF GOD OF SLOVENKA
Russia (1635)

The Slovenka Icon of the Mother of God manifested itself on in the year 1635 on October 6 (September 23 on the old calendar) at the village of Slovenka, Kostroma district. A certain man while moving about hunting by chance discovered a small rickety church, overgrown with moss. He went inside and saw that all the church utensils had rotted with time, except for the altar icon of the Mother of God, which was perfectly unharmed. A monastery was afterwards built at this place.

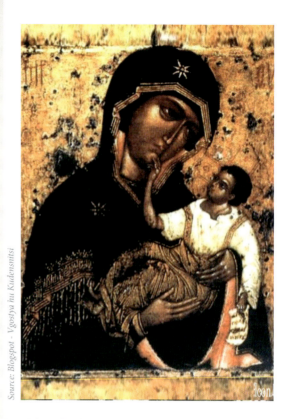

Source: Blogspot - Vgostya hu Kudensnitsi

OCTOBER 2016

s	m	t	w	t	f	s
						1
2	3	4	5	6	7	8
9	10	11	12	13	14	15
16	17	18	19	20	21	22
23	24	25	26	27	28	29
30	31					

27TH WEEK IN ORDINARY TIME

First Reading: *Galatians 3:1-5*
Responsorial Psalm: *Luke 1:69-70, 71-72, 73-75*
Gospel Reading: *Luke 11:5-13*

Source: Wikipedia Commons - Virgen de Atocha

October

friday

7

OUR LADY OF ATOCHA
Spain (8th c.)

Tradition says in 720 there was the mayor of Madrid nobleman Gracian Ramírez, who, with his wife and two daughters, was removed before the Muslim invasion. There was an ancient shrine on the outskirts of the town, in containing a venerated image of Our Lady to whom Madrid's mayor was very devoted; The town was Muslim so Gracian made furtive visits to the shrine. One time he saw that the image was gone and he went to search and began to build a new sanctuary on the spot. The Muslims attacked the construction and Gracian pre-emptively took the lives of his family. The Muslims were repelled by a great light and the family of Gracian came back to life through the intercession of the Virgin.

27TH WEEK IN ORDINARY TIME
Memorial of Our Lady of the Rosary

First Reading: *Galatians 3:7-14*
Responsorial Psalm: *Ps 111:1B-2, 3-4, 5-6*
Gospel Reading: *Luke 11:15-26*

OCTOBER 2016

s	m	t	w	t	f	s
						1
2	3	4	5	6	7	8
9	10	11	12	13	14	15
16	17	18	19	20	21	22
23	24	25	26	27	28	29
30	31					

October

saturday

8

OUR LADY OF GOOD REMEDY
Paris, France (1197)

While saying his first mass in 1197, Jean de Matha, a Sorbonne doctor of theology and newly ordained priest, saw a vision of an angel with a red and blue cross on his chest and his hands on the heads of two captives. St. Jean was inspired to found a religious order the next year dedicated to the redemption of Christians held as slaves by Moslems. Commonly called the Trinitarians, the Hospitaler Order of the Most Holy Trinity and of Captives are still marked by the founding miracle. Jean placed on their habit the cross he had seen on the angel, and as patron he gave them Notre-Dame du Bon Remède, a popular devotion from France. For three centuries they traveled from Europe into Africa to free thousands of captives with Our Lady's help. The Order celebrates her feast day on October 8.

Source: Blogspot - Com Cer Froid - La communauté des soeurs à Cerfroid

OCTOBER 2016

s	m	t	w	t	f	s
						1
2	3	4	5	6	7	8
9	10	11	12	13	14	15
16	17	18	19	20	21	22
23	24	25	26	27	28	29
30	31					

27TH WEEK IN ORDINARY TIME

First Reading: *Galatians 3:22-29*
Responsorial Psalm: *Ps 105:2-3, 4-5, 6-7*
Gospel Reading: *Luke 11:27-28*

Source: Blogspot; Caritas in Veritate – The Shrine of Our Lady of Good Help; Champion

October

sunday

9

OUR LADY OF GOOD HELP
Robinsonville, WI, USA (1859)

On October 8, 1859, the Blessed Mother showed herself to a devout 28-year-old Belgian farm woman named Adele Brise in Robinsonville, Wisconsin. The Blessed Mother desired evangelization and asked Adele to teach the children the Catechism.

On October 8, 1871 - exactly 12 years to the date since her first appearance - a raging fire that destroyed massive swaths of northeastern Wisconsin and Upper Michigan burned everywhere but the Shrine of Our Lady of Good Help where the faithful prayed for safety.

The apparition was declared worthy of belief by Bishop David L. Ricken of Green Bay on December 8, 2010.

OCTOBER 2016

s	m	t	w	t	f	s
						1
2	3	4	5	6	7	8
9	10	11	12	13	14	15
16	17	18	19	20	21	22
23	24	25	26	27	28	29
30	31					

28TH SUNDAY IN ORDINARY TIME

First Reading: *2 Kings 5:14-17*
Responsorial Psalm: *Ps 98:1, 2-3, 3-4*
Second Reading: *2 Timothy 2:8-13*
Gospel Reading: *Luke 17:11-19*

October

monday

10

OUR LADY OF MERCY
Gallivaggio, Italy (1492)

On October 10, 1492, in Gallivaggio above Chiavenna, two peasant women who were collecting chestnuts said they saw a majestic woman who turned out to be the Virgin Mary. She appeared to convert sinners, to remind the faithful to sanctify the holidays, and to pray and to do penance. On the place a chapel was built, a church followed; and many pilgrims flocked there over the centuries.

A festival is celebrated at the shrine on October 10 as a solemn reminder of the apparition.

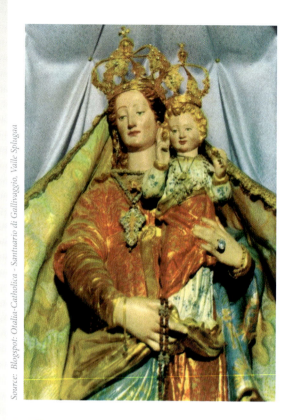

Source: Blogspot: Otalia-Catholica – Santuario di Gallivaggio, Valle Spluga

OCTOBER 2016

s	m	t	w	t	f	s
						1
2	3	4	5	6	7	8
9	10	11	12	13	14	15
16	17	18	19	20	21	22
23	24	25	26	27	28	29
30	31					

28TH WEEK IN ORDINARY TIME

First Reading: *Galatians 4:22-24, 26-27, 31–5:1*
Responsorial Psalm: *Ps 113:1B-2, 3-4, 5A AND 6-7*
Gospel Reading: *Luke 11:29-32*

Source: Having Left the Altar - Wednesday, June 1, 2011

OUR LADY OF LA LECHE
St. Augustine, FL, USA (16th c.)

When Spaniards founded the oldest city in the United States, St. Augustine, Florida in 1565, they brought with them from Madrid a statue of Nuestra Señora de la Leche (Our Lady of the Milk) in the style of the *Virgo Lactans* (The Breastfeeding Virgin). In 1765, this statue was lost at sea along with other religious articles when England took Spanish Florida as its own colony. When the Spaniards returned in 1783, the devotion to Our Lady under this title flourished. In 1938, a second copy of the original statue in Spain was created in its place.

Many miracles have been reported, especially from couples struggling with infertility who seek out Our Lady's assistance and later are blessed with children.

OCTOBER 2016

s	m	t	w	t	f	s
						1
2	3	4	5	6	7	8
9	10	11	12	13	14	15
16	17	18	19	20	21	22
23	24	25	26	27	28	29
30	31					

28TH WEEK IN ORDINARY TIME

First Reading: *Galatians 5:1-6*
Responsorial Psalm: *Ps 119:41, 43, 44, 45, 47, 48*
Gospel Reading: *Luke 11:37-41*

October

wednesday

12

OUR LADY WHO APPEARED
Aparecida, Brazil (1717)

In October 1717, three fishermen - Domingos Garcia, Joco Alves, and Felipe Pedroso - were unsuccessfully fishing for a great feast and began to pray to her for help. On their last cast, they found a statue of Our Lady of the Immaculate Conception. Next, their net became full with fish. This was the first miracle of Our Lady of Aparecida, patroness of Brazil, crowned in 1930 by Pope Pius XII. Her feast celebrated on October 12 is a national holiday. Pope John Paul II visited the Virgin "Aparecida" in her much frequented sanctuary and gave it the title of Basilica. The statue was violently broken a few days before the visit but artists put it together again and the Virgin, "Aparecida" returned to her niche in the Basilica.

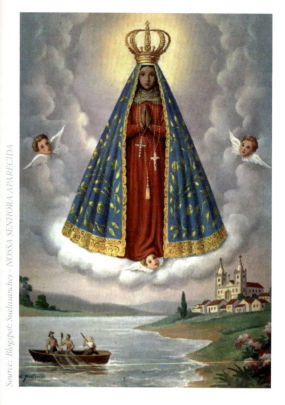

Source: Blogspot: Suelusanches - NOSSA SENHORA APARECIDA

OCTOBER 2016

s	m	t	w	t	f	s
						1
2	3	4	5	6	7	8
9	10	11	12	13	14	15
16	17	18	19	20	21	22
23	24	25	26	27	28	29
30	31					

28TH WEEK IN ORDINARY TIME

First Reading: *Galatians 5:18-25*
Responsorial Psalm: *Ps 1:1-2, 3, 4 AND 6*
Gospel Reading: *Luke 11:42-46*

Source: Wordpress ~ Island Momma "La Gomera's Five Year Fiesta"

October

thursday

13

OUR LADY OF GUADALUPE
La Gomera, Canary Islands, Spain (16th c.)

In the 1500s, a ship bound for America passed near the island of La Gomera, where the crew observed brilliant lights coming from a cave on land. Attracted, they disembarked and found in the cave a small image of the Virgin Mary holding her child. They took it aboard, but then couldn't sail no matter how they tried. After returning the image to the cave, they ship was able to proceed into port on the island, near San Sebastián. When the crew told the authorities about what had happened, everyone went to the cave on Punta Llana. The islanders named the 9" brown sculpture Our Lady of Guadalupe. The statue of the patron of La Gomera, was canonically crowned October 12, 1973.

28TH WEEK IN ORDINARY TIME

First Reading: *Ephesians 1:1-10*
Responsorial Psalm: *Ps 98:1, 2-3AB, 3CD-4, 5-6*
Gospel Reading: *Luke 11:47-54*

OCTOBER 2016

s	m	t	w	t	f	s
						1
2	3	4	5	6	7	8
9	10	11	12	13	14	15
16	17	18	19	20	21	22
23	24	25	26	27	28	29
30	31					

October

friday

14

VIRGIN OF PROTECTION
Istanbul, Turkey (911)

The church of St. Mary's in the Blachernae district of Constantinople was one of the most sacred sites in Byzantium, founded in 450 by Empress Aelia Pulcheria. A fountain of holy water, a wonderworking Virgin Mary icon, and her robe, sash, and veil were found inside. The feast of Our Lady of Protection (Russian Pokrov) is celebrated on October 14 (October 1 old calendar).

St. Andrew the Fool (d. 936), his disciple Epiphanius, and other people who were praying experienced a vision of Mary in the church during an all-night vigil. The Virgin was said to enter the church, kneel in tearful prayer, then ascend, holding her veil over the congregation as a sign of care and protection.

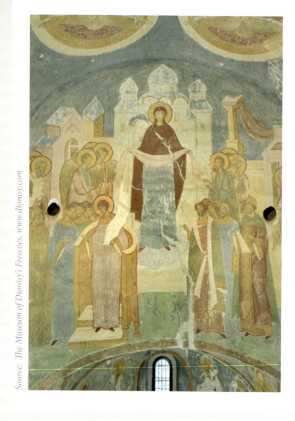

Source: The Museum of Dionisy's Frescoes, www.dionisy.com

OCTOBER 2016

s	m	t	w	t	f	s
						1
2	3	4	5	6	7	8
9	10	11	12	13	14	15
16	17	18	19	20	21	22
23	24	25	26	27	28	29
30	31					

28TH WEEK IN ORDINARY TIME

First Reading: *Ephesians 1:11-14*
Responsorial Psalm: *Ps 33:1-2, 4-5, 12-13*
Gospel Reading: *Luke 12:1-7*

Source: Wikipedia - Virgen de los desamparados

October

saturday

15

VIRGIN OF THE HELPLESS
Valencia, Spain (1407)

In the year 1414 four young men, dressed as pilgrims, came to the brotherhood. The brothers were told that in two days they could make an image of the Virgin if they were given a place and food. They were taken to the place known as La Ermita.

After four days of silence, they forced open the door and found the image of the Virgin Mary. Miracles started to occur. The incident gave rise to the legend that the angels created it.

On April 21, 1885, Pope Leo XIII issued a Papal Bull naming the Virgin of the Helpless as the patroness of Valencia.

On October 15, 1921, Pope Benedict XV granted the privilege for the coronation of the statue.

OCTOBER 2016

s	m	t	w	t	f	s
						1
2	3	4	5	6	7	8
9	10	11	12	13	14	15
16	17	18	19	20	21	22
23	24	25	26	27	28	29
30	31					

28TH WEEK IN ORDINARY TIME
Memorial of St Teresa of Jesus, Virgin & Doctor of the Church

First Reading: *Ephesians 1:15-23*
Responsorial Psalm: *Ps 8:2-3AB, 4-5, 6-7*
Gospel Reading: *Luke 12:8-12*

October

sunday

16

HOLY MARY OF THE PLAINS
Santa Rosa, Argentina (1986)

The miraculous image and title of Santa Maria de El Pueblito dates back to 1632, for this was the time when the humble priest and religious Franciscan Friar Sebastian Gallegos, skilled and inspired sculptor, who lived in the convent of San Francisco el Grande city of Queretaro, carved in his studio and with his own hands this image depicting the Blessed Virgin Mary in the mystery of her Immaculate Conception. On October 16, 1998, a replica was placed at the back of Santa Rosa Cathedral, surrounded by flags and witnessed by government officials. From that day forward, October 16 has been Santa María de la Pampa's day of commemoration.

Source: Blogspot: Cursillista LP – Cursillos de Cristiandad de La Pampa

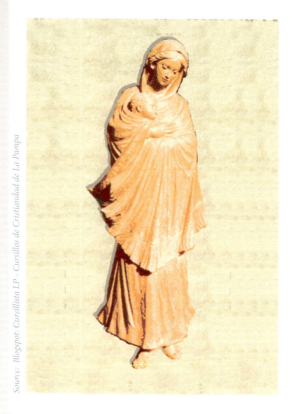

OCTOBER 2016

s	m	t	w	t	f	s
						1
2	3	4	5	6	7	8
9	10	11	12	13	14	15
16	17	18	19	20	21	22
23	24	25	26	27	28	29
30	31					

29TH SUNDAY IN ORDINARY TIME

First Reading: *Exodus 17:8-13*
Responsorial Psalm: *Ps 121:1-2, 3-4, 5-6, 7-8*
Second Reading: *2 Timothy 3:14-4:2*
Gospel Reading: *Luke 18:1-8*

Source: Flickr Fernando Sequeira Nuestra Senora Del Pueblito

October

monday

17

HOLY MARY OF EL PUEBLITO
Mexico (1632)

The miraculous image and title of Santa Maria de El Pueblito dates back to 1632, for this was the time when the humble priest and religious Franciscan Friar Sebastian Gallegos, skilled and inspired sculptor, who lived in the convent of San Francisco el Grande city of Queretaro, carved in his studio and with his own hands this image depicting the Blessed Virgin Mary in the mystery of her Immaculate Conception.

Pope Pius XII granted the coronation of the statue, delegating to Bishop Don Marciano Tinajero, who performed the solemn crowning on October 17, 1946. The people annually honor the Virgin underthis title at carnival and also commemorate the anniversary of the coronation, usually done two Sundays after October 17th.

OCTOBER 2016

s	m	t	w	t	f	s
						1
2	3	4	5	6	7	8
9	10	11	12	13	14	15
16	17	18	19	20	21	22
23	24	25	26	27	28	29
30	31					

29TH WEEK IN ORDINARY TIME
Memorial of Saint Ignatius of Antioch, Bishop and Martyr

First Reading: *Ephesians 2:1-10*
Responsorial Psalm: *Ps 100:1B-2, 3, 4AB, 4C-5*
Gospel Reading: *Luke 12:13-21*

October

tuesday
18

VIRGIN OF THE MIRACLES
Imaguer, Colobia (1619)

On October 18, 1619 a very simple woman and devotee of the Virgin found a rustic old thin tablet in the church of Almaguer, with a striking image of The Virgin Milagros. Since then almguereños devotees celebrate their patron's favors.

Another event attributed to La Milagrosa, was that the image remained intact despite the onslaught of guerrilla in March 2000 against the small village of Almaguer, where the rebels raided the Catholic Church, dynamited the altar, and destroyed the whole church, the rectory and dozens of homes in the village.

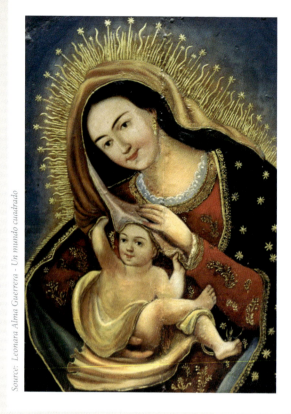

Source: Leonara Alma Guerrera - Un mundo cuadrado

OCTOBER 2016

s	m	t	w	t	f	s
						1
2	3	4	5	6	7	8
9	10	11	12	13	14	15
16	17	18	19	20	21	22
23	24	25	26	27	28	29
30	31					

29TH WEEK IN ORDINARY TIME
Feast of Saint Luke, Evangelist

First Reading: *2 Timothy 4:10-17B*
Responsorial Psalm: *Ps 145:10-11, 12-13, 17-18*
Gospel Reading: *Luke 10:1-9*

October

wednesday

19

"O ALL-HYMNED MOTHER" ICON Vladimir Oblast, Russia (19th c.)

The Icon "O All-Hymned Mother" derives its title from the thirteenth Kontakion of the Akathist to the Most Holy Theotokos: "O All-Hymned Mother who bore the Word, holiest of all the saints...."

The Mother of God wears a crown, and clasps her child to her breast with both hands. Christ is held in her left arm, and rests on her left shoulder. He is facing her, and both of His hands are placed below her neck. Instead of the usual stars on her head and shoulders, the faces of angels appear in three circles. This is similar to the Arabian Icon and the "Stone of the Mountain not cut by Hands" Icon on the iconostasis of the cathedral of the Transfiguration at Solovki.

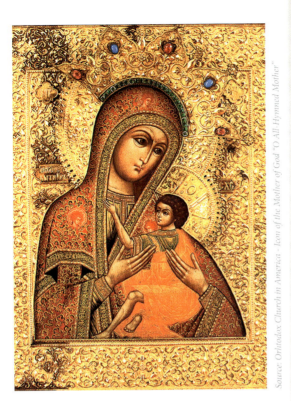

Source: Orhtodox Church in America - Icon of the Mother of God "O All-Hymned Mother"

OCTOBER 2016

s	m	t	w	t	f	s
						1
2	3	4	5	6	7	8
9	10	11	12	13	14	15
16	17	18	19	20	21	22
23	24	25	26	27	28	29
30	31					

29TH WEEK IN ORDINARY TIME
Mem. of Sts John de Brébeuf & Isaac Jogues, Priests & Martyrs

First Reading: *Ephesians 3:2-12*
Responsorial Psalm: *Isaiah 12:2-3, 4BCD, 5-6*
Gospel Reading: *Luke 12:39-48*

October

thursday

20

ICON OF THE MOTHER OF GOD "TENDERNESS" OF THE PSKOV CAVES
Russia (1521)

The "Tenderness" Icon of the Most Holy Mother of God was found in the monastery of the caves in 1521, and was transferred to the city of Pskov by the pious Christians Basil and Theodore. The Icon is particularly renowned for the deliverance of Pskov and the Pskov Caves monastery from the army of Stephen Bathory (1533-1586) in 1581.

The Tenderness Icon of the Mother of God is of the Eleousa (Umilenie) type, and is regarded as the patroness of the city of Pskov.

The October 20 (October 7 on the old calendar) commemoration was established in thanksgiving for the deliverance of Pskov from the invading army of Napoleon in 1812.

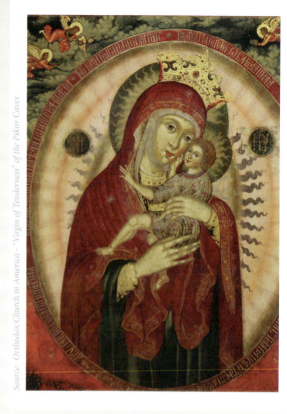

Source: Orthodox Church in America - "Virgin of Tenderness" of the Pskov Caves

OCTOBER 2016

s	m	t	w	t	f	s
						1
2	3	4	5	6	7	8
9	10	11	12	13	14	15
16	17	18	19	20	21	22
23	24	25	26	27	28	29
30	31					

29TH WEEK IN ORDINARY TIME

First Reading: *Ephesians 3:14-21*
Responsorial Psalm: *Ps 33:1-2, 4-5, 11-12, 18-19*
Gospel Reading: *Luke 12:49-53*

Source: Facebok "Noepoli - Detti e usanze"

October

friday

21

OUR LADY OF THE ROSARY
Noepoli, Italy
(17th c.)

The Church of Maria SS. del Rosario, built in 1830, is located in a farmhouse in Noepoli. It has one nave and a marble altar along with a statue of Our Lady of the Rosary from the seventeenth century and an earlier wooden crucifix. The community prepares for the celebration of the feast with a rosary novena that begins with on October 12 in the church of her namesake. On October 20, the Holy Rosary is followed by a prayer vigil in honor of Our Lady of the Rosary. The townspeople gather on October 21st for a procession of votive altars and features tarantella dance around the village. At night, a wonderful party offers food tasting with typical local dishes. The festa continues with music and dancing and finishes with spectacular fireworks.

OCTOBER 2016

s	m	t	w	t	f	s
						1
2	3	4	5	6	7	8
9	10	11	12	13	14	15
16	17	18	19	20	21	22
23	24	25	26	27	28	29
30	31					

29TH WEEK IN ORDINARY TIME

First Reading: *Ephesians 4:1-6*
Responsorial Psalm: *Ps 24:1-2, 3-4AB, 5-6*
Gospel Reading: *Luke 12:54-59*

October

saturday

22

MARY MOST HOLY
Capo d'Orlando, Italy
(1598)

On October 22, 1598, the Raffa brothers were guarding the castle on Cape Orlando when they saw a running man sounding a horn and then leaving behind a small box. Inside the box they found a statuette of the Madonna and Child. Two years later to the day, a new sanctuary on the mountain received the statue. For centuries the Virgin watched over the Cape from this place and was its intercessor against earthquakes, storms, and pirates. Unfortunately, after the theft of the original statue, a replica made from silver was put in its place.

October 22 is the date that the region celebrates with a pilgrimage to the sanctuary and procession through the streets.

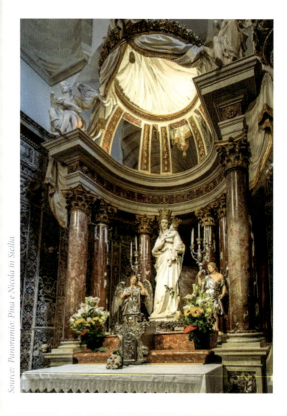

Source: Panoramio: Pina e Nicola in Sicilia

OCTOBER 2016

s	m	t	w	t	f	s
						1
2	3	4	5	6	7	8
9	10	11	12	13	14	15
16	17	18	19	20	21	22
23	24	25	26	27	28	29
30	31					

29TH WEEK IN ORDINARY TIME

First Reading: *Ephesians 4:7-16*
Responsorial Psalm: *Ps 122:1-2, 3-4AB, 4CD-5*
Gospel Reading: *Luke 13:1-9*

October

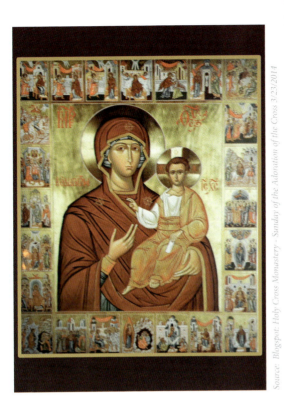

sunday

23

VIRGIN OF AKATHISTOS
Mt. Athos, Greece (1276)

Originating in Constantinople in the 6th century, the Akathistos is a long sequence of praises to the Mother of God. One day in 1276, a hermit repeated the Akathistos as was his custom before an icon of the Virgin and child at his dwelling near the Bulgarian monastery of Zografou. She answered him: "Don't be afraid, but go quickly to tell the abbot and monks that the enemy is near. The faint-hearted should escape, but those who wish a martyr's crown should stay." When he arrived at the gate, the icon was there. The abbot was given the Virgin's warning. Soon, Catalan crusaders arrived and set fire to the tower, making Orthodox martyrs of the 26 people inside on October 23 (October 10 in the old calendar).

30TH SUNDAY IN ORDINARY TIME

First Reading: *Sirach 35:12-14, 16-18*
Responsorial Psalm: *Ps 34:2-3, 17-18, 19, 23*
Second Reading: *2 Timothy 4:6-8, 16-18*
Gospel Reading: *Luke 18:9-14*

OCTOBER 2016

s	m	t	w	t	f	s
						1
2	3	4	5	6	7	8
9	10	11	12	13	14	15
16	17	18	19	20	21	22
23	24	25	26	27	28	29
30	31					

October

monday

24

OUR LADY OF MERCY
Saint Martin d'Heuille, France (1879)

On October 24, 1879, people brought a lifeless child to St. Martin's Church. They set the little corpse at the foot of the altar of Our Lady of Pity, where the Latin words *"AFFLICTIS SPES UNICA REBUS"* (only hope in all affliction) were carved below a pietà statue from the 1500s. Falling to their knees, they sang the *Salve Regina*. Suddenly the child came to life. Color returned to his face and he opened his eyes. He stayed alive long enough to receive the sacrament of baptism.

This miracle is commemorated with an annual pilgrimage on the third Sunday of September.

Source: Médiathèque de l'architecture et du patrimoine

NOTRE DAME DE PITIÉ

OCTOBER 2016

s	m	t	w	t	f	s
						1
2	3	4	5	6	7	8
9	10	11	12	13	14	15
16	17	18	19	20	21	22
23	24	25	26	27	28	29
30	31					

30TH WEEK IN ORDINARY TIME

First Reading: *Ephesians 4:32–5:8*
Responsorial Psalm: *Ps 1:1-2, 3, 4 AND 6*
Gospel Reading: *Luke 13:10-17*

October

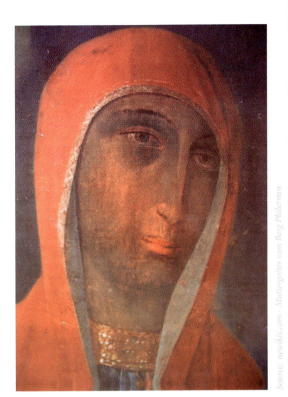

tuesday

25

MOTHER OF GOD OF PHILERMOS
Cetinje, Montenegro (1799)

The Madonna on Mount Phileremos, a Byzantine icon may have been on Rhodes before the Hospital arrived in 1306, and by 1396 it was an icon revered as wonderworking by both Latins and Greeks. A magistral bull of 1497 held that it had reached Rhodes miraculously on the waves in the time of Emperor Leo III. It was mentioned in the writings of many travelers and was taken to the city during times of danger. Considered by the Knights as their most precious possession, it was already the center of a popular cult before they conquered the island in 1306-9. The Rhodians piously venerated 'The Mother of God of Phileremos' as a painting of St. Luke and its fame as a wonder-working image was known all over the Aegean.

30TH WEEK IN ORDINARY TIME

First Reading: *Ephesians 5:21-33*
Responsorial Psalm: *Ps 128:1-2, 3, 4-5*
Gospel Reading: *Luke 13:18-21*

OCTOBER 2016

s	m	t	w	t	f	s
						1
2	3	4	5	6	7	8
9	10	11	12	13	14	15
16	17	18	19	20	21	22
23	24	25	26	27	28	29
30	31					

October

wednesday

26

ICON OF THE MOTHER OF GOD OF THE SEVEN LAKES
Kazan, Russia (1615)

The Seven Lakes Icon of the Mother of God was brought from Ustiug near Kazan on October 26, 1615 by the monk Euthymius, founder of the Seven Lakes monastery. He blessed the place with this icon. In the middle of the seventeenth century, a deadly plague raged throughout Russia, including Kazan where 48,000 people died within a short time. A monk had a vision of a man appearing to him about the establishment of a seven-day fast and the meeting of the icon of coming to them from the Seven Lakes Hermitage. The icon's procession circled the city, and after an All Night Vigil, went to each of the homes in the city. After seven days of prayer and processions, the deadly plague ended. A second deliverance from plague occurred in 1771.

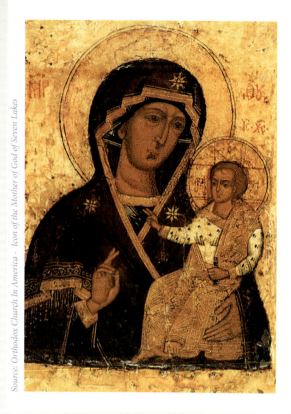

Source: Orthodox Church In America - Icon of the Mother of God of Seven Lakes

OCTOBER 2016

s	m	t	w	t	f	s
						1
2	3	4	5	6	7	8
9	10	11	12	13	14	15
16	17	18	19	20	21	22
23	24	25	26	27	28	29
30	31					

30TH WEEK IN ORDINARY TIME

First Reading: *Ephesians 6:1-9*
Responsorial Psalm: *Ps 145:10-11, 12-13AB, 13CD-14*
Gospel Reading: *Luke 13:22-30*

Source: Hostal Ejecutivo San Diego - La Virgen de la Puerta. Escudo Contra los Infieles

October

thursday

27

VIRGIN OF THE DOOR
Otuzco, Peru (1560)

The Augustinians founded the highland city of Otuzco in 1560, dedicating both town and church to the Immaculate Conception. On the church's main altar was a statue of the Virgin from Spain, carried in procession once annually on the feast of the Immaculate Conception. Gradually, the octave of the feast assumed public importance, and a second processional statue was created for use on December 15, from a workshop in Venezuela. In 1670, looters were on their way to Otuzco. Townspeople took the statue out to the road where the attackers would come, and remained there three days in prayer. The looters never came so they enshrined it above the church door. Devotion to the Virgin of the Door continued through the centuries.

OCTOBER 2016

s	m	t	w	t	f	s
						1
2	3	4	5	6	7	8
9	10	11	12	13	14	15
16	17	18	19	20	21	22
23	24	25	26	27	28	29
30	31					

30TH WEEK IN ORDINARY TIME

First Reading: *Ephesians 6:10-20*
Responsorial Psalm: *Ps 144:1B, 2, 9-10*
Gospel Reading: *Luke 13:31-35*

October

friday

28

VIRGIN OF THE ROSARY OF EL PARAUTE
Lagunillas, Venezuela (1651)

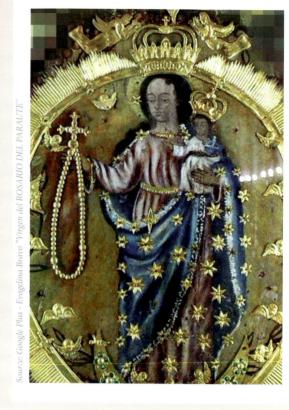

Source: Google Plus - Evagelina Bravo "Virgen del ROSARIO DEL PARAUTE"

In the northwest of Venezuela connected to the Gulf of Venezuela, Lake Maracaibo had populations that lived on it in homes built on stilts. The Paraute (now known as the Pueblo Viejo River), flows into the town of Lagunillas de Agua. An Indian sitting in a stilt house there recovered a piece of wood that kept floating in on the water on October 28, 1651. An image of the Virgin of the Rosary was present on the wood and became an object of pilgrimage when it was enshrined in the church. Despite being surrounded by water, Lagunillas has suffered many fires. The image was protected from harm and resides in the church of the Morochas district. The miraculous event is celebrated every year on October 28.

OCTOBER 2016

s	m	t	w	t	f	s
						1
2	3	4	5	6	7	8
9	10	11	12	13	14	15
16	17	18	19	20	21	22
23	24	25	26	27	28	29
30	31					

30TH WEEK IN ORDINARY TIME
Feast of Saints Simon and Jude, Apostles

First Reading: *Ephesians 2:19-22*
Responsorial Psalm: *Ps 19:2-3, 4-5*
Gospel Reading: *Luke 6:12-16*

Source: Centre for Marian Studies UK

October

saturday

29

OUR LADY OF OROPA
Piedmont, Italy
(3rd c.)

In Piedmont, there lies the Holy Mountain of Oropa, which is a complex of 19 chapels and several shelters were built in a land where Our Lady wanted to settle.

And within the complex is the ancient image of the Black Madonna of Oropa. Her veneration was introduced by San Eusebio, who in the third century brought from the Holy Land a sculpture of the Virgin that is believed sculpted by the community of St. Luke the Evangelist.

Since then the Virgin Mary has worked a number of miracles and wonders, conversions and graces to the supernatural order. The location was recognized by UNESCO as "World Heritage".

OCTOBER 2016

s	m	t	w	t	f	s
						1
2	3	4	5	6	7	8
9	10	11	12	13	14	15
16	17	18	19	20	21	22
23	24	25	26	27	28	29
30	31					

30TH WEEK IN ORDINARY TIME

First Reading: *Philippians 1:18B-26*
Responsorial Psalm: *Ps 42:2, 3, 5CDEF*
Gospel Reading: *Luke 14:1, 7-11*

October

sunday

30

OUR LADY OF MONDOVI
Italy (16th c.)

In 1592 Giulio Sargiano went hunting for game and accidentally shot a small roadside shrine containing a fresco of the Madonna and Child. Legend has it that upon seeing the damage he caused, Sargiano was filled with grief and saw blood flowing from the wounded fresco. The remorseful hunter surrendered his firearm and began to collect money to make repairs. Soon, word of the shrine spread and pilgrims began arriving in great numbers. In 1596 Carlo Emanuele I, Duke of Savoia built a grand sanctuary for the shrine to accommodate the multitude of pilgrims arriving daily. The name of the Basilica of "Madonna Santissima of Mondovi in Vico" was changed to "Regina Montis Regalis" after the coronation of the image in 1682.

Source: Photographic Gallery of Cuneo - foto.provincia.cuneo.it

OCTOBER 2016

s	m	t	w	t	f	s
						1
2	3	4	5	6	7	8
9	10	11	12	13	14	15
16	17	18	19	20	21	22
23	24	25	26	27	28	29
30	31					

31ST WEEK IN ORDINARY TIME

First Reading: *Wisdom 11:22-12:2*
Responsorial Psalm: *Ps 145:1-2, 8-9, 10-11, 13, 14*
Second Reading: *2 Thessalonians 1:11-2:2*
Gospel Reading: *Luke 19:1-10*

Source: Blogspot: Perocomi Ciudad - La Virgen del Rosario de Río Blanco y Paypaya llego a Perico

October

monday

31

OUR LADY OF THE ROSARY OF RÍO BLANCO Y PAYPAYA DE JUJUY
Argentina (17th c.)

The Lady of the Rosary has served as a watchful protectress over the city of Jujuy. Wearing her splendid pink dress, light blue cloak and wielding her scepter she intercepted invading tribes threatening the city. On several occasions the Paypaya tribe attempted to destroy it but she showed herself to them, and stopped their advance. After the Virgen del Rosario was named the Queen and protectress of that town, the Jesuits were able to evangelize the other tribes: Osas, Ojotas, Ocloyas, Toba, Mocovíes, Omaguacas, Purmamarcas until Calchaquies and other races that were attacking the people of Jujuy. They laid down their weapons and helped to spread of the Gospel.

31ST WEEK IN ORDINARY TIME

First Reading: *Philippians 2:1-4*
Responsorial Psalm: *Ps 131:1BCDE, 2, 3*
Gospel Reading: *Luke 14:12-14*

OCTOBER 2016

s	m	t	w	t	f	s
						1
2	3	4	5	6	7	8
9	10	11	12	13	14	15
16	17	18	19	20	21	22
23	24	25	26	27	28	29
30	31					

November

tuesday

1

QUEEN OF THE POOR SOULS IN PURGATORY
Heede, Germany (1937)

Mary appeared to four children on November 1, 1937 in a meadow. She was holding the Divine Child in her arms when she first appeared. Mary came to them in secret when civil authorities threatened them. Prayer, conversion, and the rosary were the themes. No formal approval to the apparitions have been given but successive bishops have encouraged the devotion. Bishop Berning authorized the faithful to place in the parish cemetery statue of "Mary Queen of the Universe" as directed by the seers.

In 2000, Bishop Joseph Franz-Hermann Bode, diocesan bishop, raised the two churches in Heede to the category of diocesan shrines.

NOVEMBER 2016

s	m	t	w	t	f	s
		1	2	3	4	5
6	7	8	9	10	11	12
13	14	15	16	17	18	19
20	21	22	23	24	25	26
27	28	29	30			

31ST WEEK IN ORDINARY TIME
Solemnity of All Saints

First Reading: *Revelation 7:2-4, 9-14*
Responsorial Psalm: *Ps 24:1BC-2, 3-4AB, 5-6*
Second Reading: *1 John 3:1-3*
Gospel Reading: *Matthew 5:1-12A*

Source: "Roma foto.te dintorni di PIAZZA NAVON" - tesoridiroma.net

November

wednesday

2

OUR LADY OF THE SOULS
Rome, Italy (1550)

Dedicated to the Virgin Mary as helper of souls in Purgatory, the church of Santa Maria dell'Anima became a place of worship for pilgrims from Germanic countries when a Dutch couple in Rome began its construction in 1350.

In celebration of the Holy Year 1500, a group of statues including that of the Madonna between two souls was placed in the central tympanum. Carved by Andrea Sansovino, the statue was designed to follow the design of the image in a previous chapel on the site.

Santa Maria dell'Anima is currently the German national church in Rome. Its wide construction features a traditional Northern European style, with four apse chapels on each side.

31ST WEEK IN ORDINARY TIME
The Commemoration of All the Faithful Departed (All Souls)

First Reading: *Wisodm 3:1-9*
Responsorial Psalm: *Ps 23:1-3A, 3B-4, 5, 6*
Second Reading: *Romans 5:5-11*
Gospel Reading: *John 6:37-40*

NOVEMBER 2016

s	m	t	w	t	f	s
		1	2	3	4	5
6	7	8	9	10	11	12
13	14	15	16	17	18	19
20	21	22	23	24	25	26
27	28	29	30			

November

thursday

3

OUR LADY OF MIRACLES AND VIRTUES
Rennes, France (14th c.)

According to popular tradition, during the War of Succession at Brittany, as Rennes was being besieged by the invading English army, the people expected the English forces to mine their way into the city.

On the night of February 8, 1357, the church bells began to ring of their own accord, and the candles were spontaneously lit. The statue of Our Lady, known as Our Lady of Miracles and Virtues, pointed out a particular slab in the church. The inhabitants of the city thus were alerted to the mine and the point of the English attack, and were able to repulse the invasion. The miracle was a popular subject for ballads. In 1634 the miracle was officially recognized by the Bishop of Rennes, Pierre Cornulier.

Source: Canal Blog: Images Saintes - "Notre Dane des Miracles et Vertus"

NOVEMBER 2016

s	m	t	w	t	f	s
		1	2	3	4	5
6	7	8	9	10	11	12
13	14	15	16	17	18	19
20	21	22	23	24	25	26
27	28	29	30			

31ST WEEK IN ORDINARY TIME

First Reading: *Philippians 3:3-8A*
Responsorial Psalm: *Ps 105:2-3, 4-5, 6-7*
Gospel Reading: *Luke 15:1-10*

Source: Wikimedia Commons – Hajdúdorog

November

friday

4

THE WEEPING VIRGIN
Máriapócs, Hungary (1696)

To celebrate his release in 1696 from his captivity as a prisoner of war by the Turks, Laszlo Csigri commissioned a wooden icon of the Virgin and Child in his hometown of Pócs in Hungary. On November 4, the icon began to lacrimate and when a priest held up a dying child to those tears he was miraculously healed. Starting starting on December 8th, the icon wept for another two weeks, Pócs became renowned as Máriapócs. At the order of Emperor Leopold II in February 1697, the miraculous image was transferred to St. Stephen's Cathedral in Vienna. To this day, the image resides in a chapel to the right of the entrance. Later, a reproduction was given as a gift by the Emperor to the church in Máriapócs, and that one wept three times, in 1715, 1750, and 1905.

31ST WEEK IN ORDINARY TIME

Memorial of Saint Charles Borromeo, Bishop

First Reading: *Philippians 3:17—4:1*
Responsorial Psalm: *Ps 122:1-2, 3-4AB, 4CD-5*
Gospel Reading: *Luke 16:1-8*

NOVEMBER 2016

s	m	t	w	t	f	s
		1	2	3	4	5
6	7	8	9	10	11	12
13	14	15	16	17	18	19
20	21	22	23	24	25	26
27	28	29	30			

November

saturday

5

OUR LADY OF THE MIRACULOUS MEDAL
Monte Sião, Brazil (1939)

In 1937 the Bishop asked the pastor of Monte Sião to withdraw the image of Nossa Senhora da Medalha Milagrosa from the altar and send it to a countryside chapel. The absence of the mother was keenly felt by the parish. Between the years 1937 and 1939 Monte Sião was plagued by a severe drought; while it rained in all the other cities of the region. The people associated the lack of rain with the absence of their Patron. On November 5, 1939, a procession was undertaken on a sunny day carrying the bier with the image of the Patron. On arriving at the entrance of the city the first drops began to fall, followed by a big rain, causing the image itself and its devotees to be drenched. From that day the rain cycle of the place returned to normal.

Source: Santuario da Medalha Milagrosa – Wallpapers

NOVEMBER 2016

s	m	t	w	t	f	s
		1	2	3	4	5
6	7	8	9	10	11	12
13	14	15	16	17	18	19
20	21	22	23	24	25	26
27	28	29	30			

31ST WEEK IN ORDINARY TIME

First Reading: *Philippians 4:10-19*
Responsorial Psalm: *Ps 112:1B-2, 5-6, 8A AND 9*
Gospel Reading: *Luke 16:9-15*

Source: Canal Blog: Crowned Places – Notre-Dame de Valfleury

November

sunday

6

OUR LADY OF VALFLEURY
France (800)

There was an ancient chapel dedicated to the Virgin near a healing spring. Our Lady of Valfleury was discovered, on Christmas Eve, shortly before the year 800. A shepherd saw blooming blossoms in the middle of a snow field. Having moved the branches, he found the statue of the Virgin seated, holding her child on her lap. The priest carried it into the church, and the next day she was found back in the bush where they erected a chapel. Benedictine monks established a priory there and called the place "valley flowers". Pilgrimages began and miracles occurred there. In 1854, Pope Pius IX granted the pilgrimage of Valfleury a plenary indulgence. Also known affectionately as La Vielle Dame d'Or (The Old Golden Lady), she is venerated annually on November 6.

32ND SUNDAY IN ORDINARY TIME

First Reading: *2 Micah 7:1-2, 9-14*
Responsorial Psalm: *Ps 17:1, 5-6, 8, 15*
Second Reading: *2 Thessalonians 2:16-3:5*
Gospel Reading: *Luke 20:27-38*

NOVEMBER 2016

s	m	t	w	t	f	s
		1	2	3	4	5
6	7	8	9	10	11	12
13	14	15	16	17	18	19
20	21	22	23	24	25	26
27	28	29	30			

November

monday

7

VIRGIN OF THE RIVER
Tarazona, Spain
(449)

Next to the old bullring in Tarazona is the Sanctuary of the Virgen del Rio (Virgin of the River), built between 1667 and 1672 in order to host the image appearing on the river of Our Lady, later known as Virgen del Rio. The Virgin of the River has since become the popular patron saint of Tarazona, celebrating her annual feast on November 7.

The Santuario de la Virgen del Río is baroque in style, made of masonry and brick, with the facade and the door at the foot of the church.

Source: Wikimedia Commons- Santuario de la Virgen del Rio, Tarazona

NOVEMBER 2016

s	m	t	w	t	f	s
		1	2	3	4	5
6	7	8	9	10	11	12
13	14	15	16	17	18	19
20	21	22	23	24	25	26
27	28	29	30			

32ND WEEK IN ORDINARY TIME

First Reading: *Timothy 1:1-9*
Responsorial Psalm: *Ps 24:1B-2, 3-4AB, 5-6*
Gospel Reading: *Luke17:1-6*

Source: *Fotos de la Virgen – Virgen de los Treinta y Tres, Uruguay*

VIRGIN OF THE THIRTY-THREE
Florida, Uruguay (1825)

Around 1779 the image of the Assumption was placed in the chapel by the Jesuits. On April 19, 1825, thirty-three Uruguayan patriots, landed on the beaches of the Agraciada to commence the liberation of their country. When they reached Florida, they went to the small church and placed the future of the new nation at the feet of the Virgin.

On August 25, 1975, on the 150th anniversary of its independence, the Uruguayan nation officially declared this church a "Historic Monument." The image was crowned canonically in 1961 by a concession of John XXIII, the next year proclaiming her "Patroness of Uruguay." The Solemnity of Our Lady of the Thirty-Three is celebrated on November 8 with a pilgrimage to this shrine from all parts of the nation.

NOVEMBER 2016

s	m	t	w	t	f	s
		1	2	3	4	5
6	7	8	9	10	11	12
13	14	15	16	17	18	19
20	21	22	23	24	25	26
27	28	29	30			

32ND WEEK IN ORDINARY TIME

First Reading: *Timothy 2:1-8, 11-14*
Responsorial Psalm: *Ps 37:3-4, 18 AND 23, 27 AND 29*
Gospel Reading: *Luke 17:7-10*

November

VIRGIN OF THE ALMUDENA
Madrid, Spain
(15th c.)

According to legend, before the Arabs attacked Madrid in 712, the townspeople sealed up an image of the Virgin in a wall to conceal it. In safer times after the reconquest of the city in the eleventh century by King Alfonso VI, the hidden image was sought. When the days long prayerful procession passed through the Cuesta de la Vega, a piece of the wall fell down, exposing the image, which not only survived in perfect condition but was surrounded by two candles that apparently had remained lit for centuries within the wall.

Another pious tradition recalls that the Castillian hero El Cid, Rodrigo Diaz de Vivar, had an apparition of the Virgin who told him to break down the wall where the figure was and bring it to the city.

Source: Wikimedia Commons - Virgen de a Almudena

NOVEMBER 2016

s	m	t	w	t	f	s
		1	2	3	4	5
6	7	8	9	10	11	12
13	14	15	16	17	18	19
20	21	22	23	24	25	26
27	28	29	30			

32ND WEEK IN ORDINARY TIME
Feast of the Dedication of the Lateran Basilica in Rome

First Reading: *Ezekiel 47:1-2, 8-9, 12*
Responsorial Psalm: *Ps 46:2-3, 5-6, 8-9*
Second Reading: *1 Corinthians 3:9C-11, 16-17*
Gospel Reading: *John 2:13-22*

Source: http://www.rottweil.de/

November

thursday

10

OUR LADY OF THE TURNING EYES
Rottweil, Germany (1643)

During the French siege in 1643, the Rottweiler population begged Mary for help. One statue in particular appeared sorrowful and people claimed to see the eyes move. Fourty-two people testified that the eyes turned twice. This was a sign that prayers were answered for many who came to venerate the statue. The Marian image became known far and wide as Muttergottes von der Augenwende (Our Lady of the Turning Eyes).

Large pilgrimages came from all over the surroundng regions, including Alsace, Lake Constance and Switzerland to Rottweil, to ask the Mother of God to comfort of their afflictions, heal their sickness, give refuge to sinners, and to provide hope to the desperate.

32ND WEEK IN ORDINARY TIME

First Reading: *Philemon 7-20*
Responsorial Psalm: *Ps 146:7, 8-9A, 9BC-10*
Gospel Reading: *Luke 17:20-25*

NOVEMBER 2016

s	m	t	w	t	f	s
		1	2	3	4	5
6	7	8	9	10	11	12
13	14	15	16	17	18	19
20	21	22	23	24	25	26
27	28	29	30			

November

friday

11

OUR LADY OF THE PORTUGUESE
Diu, India (1546)

An attack on Diu began on the eve of Easter in 1546, and the Portuguese withstood the advance of the Turks to capture the fort. The pitched battle became known as one of the greatest ever fought by the Portuguese troops in India. The fighting persisted continuously from April 20,1546 until November 7th when The Virgin Mary appeared upon the ramparts defending the fort with a lance in her hand. The enemy's camp was stricken with terror, and the attack was called off. Viceroy Juan de Castro's Portuguese fleet joined the ground forces, thus confirming Portuguese victory and their cementing their presence over the region.

NOVEMBER 2016

s	m	t	w	t	f	s
		1	2	3	4	5
6	7	8	9	10	11	12
13	14	15	16	17	18	19
20	21	22	23	24	25	26
27	28	29	30			

32ND WEEK IN ORDINARY TIME
Memorial of Saint Martin of Tours, Bishop

First Reading: *2 John 4-9*
Responsorial Psalm: *Ps 119:1, 2, 10, 11, 17, 18*
Gospel Reading: *Luke 17:26-37*

Source: "Temple of the Archangel Mihail," www.nikitnoe.mrezha.ru

November

saturday

12

ICON OF THE MOTHER OF GOD OF OZERYANKA
Ukraine (17th c.)

In the 17th century at Ozeryanka, about 15 miles outside of Kharkiv, Ukraine, an icon appeared. The image has resided in the Kuriazh Transfiguration Monastery on Cold Hill overlooking Kharkiv, being taken in procession to Ozeryanka for a two-week period. Widely considered miraculous by both Catholics and Orthodox, Ukrainians and Russians, Hryhorii Kvitka-Osnovianenko (b. 1778), was healed of blindness in his youth when the icon illuminated in the monastery. In 1896, the Ozeryanska Church was built in a hybrid style Russian-domed Roman basilica along the procession route. When the icon disappeared with its jewels in 1926, the procession stopped as well. The Orthodox feast day of the Ozeryanska icon is on November 12 (October 30 old calendar).

NOVEMBER 2016

s	m	t	w	t	f	s
		1	2	3	4	5
6	7	8	9	10	11	12
13	14	15	16	17	18	19
20	21	22	23	24	25	26
27	28	29	30			

32ND WEEK IN ORDINARY TIME
Memorial of Saint Josaphat, Bishop and Martyr

First Reading: 3 John 5-8
Responsorial Psalm: Ps 112:1-2, 3-4, 5-6
Gospel Reading: Luke 18:1-8

November

sunday

13

OUR LADY OF THE SEVEN JOYS
Sion, Switzerland (1422)

The Italian Franciscan St. James of the Marches was given a new devotion during a vision of the Virgin in 1422. The "Franciscan Crown" rosary with seven decades, representing the Joys of Mary spread rapidly through Europe with the help of the Franciscan Order. In a battle against the Saiyards in which Sion was heavily outnumbered, Bishop Walter Supersaxo lead the people in this rosary during near certain defeat and ordered "that in the future the anniversary of this triumph will be a holiday, that the feast of the seven joys of the Holy Virgin will be celebrated throughout the diocese." Until its removal from the diocesan calendar in 1915, the Diocese of Sion celebrated the feast of Our Lady of the Seven Joys on November 13.

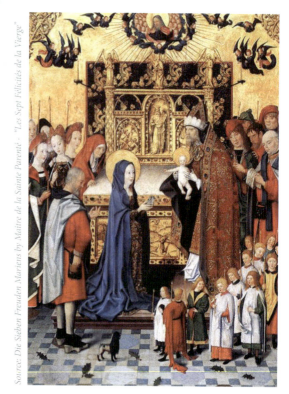

Source: Die Sieben Freuden Mariens by Maître de la Sainte Parenté - "Les Sept Félicités de la Vierge"

NOVEMBER 2016

s	m	t	w	t	f	s
		1	2	3	4	5
6	7	8	9	10	11	12
13	14	15	16	17	18	19
20	21	22	23	24	25	26
27	28	29	30			

33RD SUNDAY IN ORDINARY TIME

First Reading: *Malachi 3:19-20A*
Responsorial Psalm: *Ps 98:5-6, 7-8, 9*
Second Reading: *2 Thessalonians 3:7-12*
Gospel Reading: *Luke 21:5-19*

monday

14

OUR LADY OF THE GROTTO
Lamego, Portugal (6th c.)

Our Lady of the Grotto is very popular in Portugal, Spain, Italy and on the island of Malta. At Lamego, Portugal, during the construction of a chapel dedicated to the Blessed Mother, an image of the Blessed Virgin had been found in the hollow of a rock, and hence the name given to the statue is Nossa Senhora da Gruta (Our Lady of the Grotto).

The sanctuary is now an integral part of the panorama of the city to which it is united by a scenic stairway. Since 1984, the shrine including the staircase and park are classified as a place of public interest.

Source: Blogspot: Daedalenus - Oração à Nossa Senhora dos Remédios

33ᴿᴰ WEEK IN ORDINARY TIME

First Reading: *Revelation 1:1-4; 2:1-5*
Responsorial Psalm: *Ps 1:1-2, 3, 4 AND 6*
Gospel Reading: *Luke 18:35-43*

NOVEMBER 2016

s	m	t	w	t	f	s
		1	2	3	4	5
6	7	8	9	10	11	12
13	14	15	16	17	18	19
20	21	22	23	24	25	26
27	28	29	30			

November

tuesday

15

OUR LADY OF THE DEW
Paranaguá, Brazil
(17th c.)

Pai Berê, an African or native fisherman, discovered in his net a statue which settlers identified as Our Lady of the Dew, the beloved Virgin of Andalucia in southern Spain. This finding in the 17th century brought many miracles and healings. People asked for her intercession for help during storms at sea, the plague of 1901, and the flu of 1918. She received a shrine built in her honor at the place of the discovery of the image and in 1977 Pope Paul VI declared her the Patroness of Paraná.

On November 15th the feast of Our Lady of Rocio is celebrated with festivities at the church including a novena, outdoor Mass and procession, along with a celebration with food, the arts and fireworks.

Source: Blogspot - - nossasenhoradorocio1 "C.M.E.I Nossa Senhora do Rocio"

NOVEMBER 2016

s	m	t	w	t	f	s
		1	2	3	4	5
6	7	8	9	10	11	12
13	14	15	16	17	18	19
20	21	22	23	24	25	26
27	28	29	30			

33RD WEEK IN ORDINARY TIME

First Reading: *Revelation 3:1-6, 14-22*
Responsorial Psalm: *Ps 15:2-3A, 3BC-4AB, 5*
Gospel Reading: *Luke 19:1-10*

Source: Wikipedia - Gate of Dawn

November

wednesday

16

OUR LADY OF THE GATE OF DAWN
Vilnius, Lithuania (1363)

Trinity Monastery in Vilnius received its famous icon in 1363, when Grand Duke Algirdas of Lithuania brought back the image of the Mother of God as a present for his wife, taken from conquered Kherson (now in Ukraine). The people of the Lithuanian capital surrounded the city with a wall after the Tatar attack in 1503. On the outside of the eastern gate (*Ausros Vartai,* Gate of Dawn in Lithuanian), an icon of Jesus Christ looked out toward the enemy lands of Russia and Mongolia, and inside, the icon of the Mother of God from Kherson looked in toward the people of Vilnius.

Catholics in Lithuania and surrounding countries celebrate the Black Madonna of Vilnius on November 16 (Orthodox January 8).

NOVEMBER 2016

s	m	t	w	t	f	s
		1	2	3	4	5
6	7	8	9	10	11	12
13	14	15	16	17	18	19
20	21	22	23	24	25	26
27	28	29	30			

33RD WEEK IN ORDINARY TIME

First Reading: *Revelation 4:1-11*
Responsorial Psalm: *Ps 150:1B-2, 3-4, 5-6*
Gospel Reading: *Luke 19:11-28*

November

thursday

17

VIRGIN OF THE MIRACLE
Mazarrón, Spain
(1585)

The pilgrimage of Bolnuevo stems from an event that took place in the sixteenth century, on the coast of the Mazarrón, at that time besieged by frequent raids of Barbary pirates. According to reliable witnesses on November 17, 1585 a miracle of the Virgen del Milagro and La Purisima, saved the people of being conquered. A raid was carried out by Barbary pirates from North Africa with permission from the Ottoman Empire, who battled the Spanish Empire for control of the Mediterranean Sea. As is clear from reports and records of eyewitnesses, the Virgin drove out the Turks.

The Virgin would become the patron of the town, with a huge devotion to her and commemorating the events every November 17 with a pilgrimage.

Source: Blogspot - cristinanavarro: "cuaderno de notas: ROMERÍA DE BOLNUEVO 2009"

NOVEMBER 2016

s	m	t	w	t	f	s
		1	2	3	4	5
6	7	8	9	10	11	12
13	14	15	16	17	18	19
20	21	22	23	24	25	26
27	28	29	30			

33RD WEEK IN ORDINARY TIME
Memorial of Saint Elizabeth of Hungary, Religious

First Reading: *Revelation 5:1-10*
Responsorial Psalm: *Ps 149:1B-2, 3-4, 5-6A AND 9B*
Gospel Reading: *Luke 19:41-44*

Source: Wikipedia - Our Lady of the Rosary of Chiquinquirá

November

friday

18

OUR LADY OF THE ROSARY OF CHIQUINQUIRÁ
Maracaibo, Venezuela (1709)

On Tuesday, November 18, 1709, a poor washerwoman from Nueva Zamora de Maracaibo named Saladilla had recovered an old image of the Virgin at the shores and hung it on her wall. One day she was deep in chores, so did not pay attention to a series of knocks that were heard on the wall where the picture hung. The blows were heard again and the third time, she went and she saw the image of the Virgin of Chiquinquirá illuminated. In the street she shouted "Miracle!" and with this began a great devotion.. In this city, every year, November 18 is celebrated the "Feria de La Chinita" in honor of the Virgin. She is the patroness and queen of Colombia, the State of Zulia in Venezuela, and the city of Caraz, in Peru.

33RD WEEK IN ORDINARY TIME

First Reading: *Rev 10:8-11*
Responsorial Psalm: *Ps 119:14, 24, 72, 103, 111, 131*
Gospel Reading: *Luke 19:45-48*

NOVEMBER 2016

s	m	t	w	t	f	s
		1	2	3	4	5
6	7	8	9	10	11	12
13	14	15	16	17	18	19
20	21	22	23	24	25	26
27	28	29	30			

November

saturday

19

OUR LADY OF THE DIVINE PROVIDENCE
San Juan, Puerto Rico (1920)

Before being ordained bishop of San Juan, Puerto Rico, Gil Esteve y Tomás had served as vicar of Barcelona, Spain where ordered a statue of Our Lady of Divine Providence. The image was installed in the cathedral on January 2, 1853, and for many years Puerto Ricans celebrated the feast of the Mother of Divine Providence on this date in commemoration. The statue was canonically crowned on November 19, 1950 and proclaimed the patron of the island in 1970 by Pope Paul VI. In doing so, he moved her local feast to November 19 to coincide with Puerto Rican Discovery Day. The frequently venerated image bears only a vague resemblance to a Roman image of the same name from 1752.

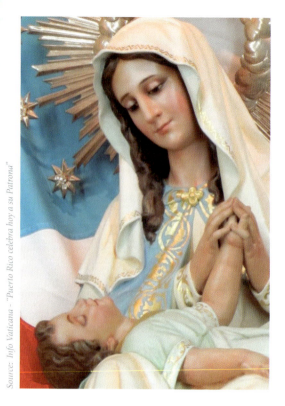

Source: Info Vaticana - "Puerto Rico celebra hoy a su Patrona"

NOVEMBER 2016

s	m	t	w	t	f	s
		1	2	3	4	5
6	7	8	9	10	11	12
13	14	15	16	17	18	19
20	21	22	23	24	25	26
27	28	29	30			

33RD WEEK IN ORDINARY TIME

First Reading: *Revelation 11:4-12*
Responsorial Psalm: *Ps 144:1, 2, 9-10*
Gospel Reading: *Luke 20:27-40*

November

sunday

20

ICON OF THE MOTHER OF GOD "THE JOYFUL" Moscow, Russia (1795)

Source: Orthodox Church in America – "Icon of the Mother of God "the Joyful"

The "Joyful" (Vzigranie) Icon of the Most Holy Theotokos appeared near Moscow on in the year 1795 on November 20 (November 7 old calendar). Nothing is known of the history of the icon, except that many miracles have taken place before it.

Icons of this name are found in the Novodevichy Monastery in Moscow, and in the Vatopedi Monastery on Mt Athos. In appearance, the "Joyful" Icon resembles the "Pelagonitissa" Icon, a variant of the Glykophylousa ("Sweet-Kissing") or Eleousa type. The Icon is sometimes called "Child Leaping for Joy."

34TH SUNDAY IN ORDINARY TIME

The Solemnity of Our Lord Jesus Christ, King of the Universe

First Reading: *2 Samuel 5:1-3*
Responsorial Psalm: *Ps 122:1-2, 3-4, 4-5*
Second Reading: *Colossians 1:12-20*
Gospel Reading: *Luke 23:35-43*

NOVEMBER 2016

s	m	t	w	t	f	s
		1	2	3	4	5
6	7	8	9	10	11	12
13	14	15	16	17	18	19
20	21	22	23	24	25	26
27	28	29	30			

November

monday

21

RECONCILER OF PEOPLE & NATIONS
Betania, Venezuela (1976)

Servant of God Maria Esperanza of Betania, Venezuela witnessed 31 apparitions of the Blessed Virgin Mary over the course of 15 years. The Virgin called herself the "Reconciler of People and Nations" and warned of impending war and suffering. Many visitors have come to the site, reporting over 500 miracles and signs, including an approved Eucharistic miracle. On March 25,1984, 108 people claimed to have witnessed a public apparition of the Virgin. On November 21, 1987, Archbishop Pio Bello Ricardo emitted the Pastoral Instruction on the apparition of Our Blessed Virgin Mary in Finca Betania, approving the apparitions. In 2010 Bishop Paul Bootkoski, Ordinary of the Diocese of Metuchen, New Jersey, opened her cause for beatification.

NOVEMBER 2016

s	m	t	w	t	f	s
		1	2	3	4	5
6	7	8	9	10	11	12
13	14	15	16	17	18	19
20	21	22	23	24	25	26
27	28	29	30			

34TH WEEK IN ORDINARY TIME
Memorial of the Presentation of the Blessed Virgin Mary

First Reading: *Revelation 14:1-3, 4B-5*
Responsorial Psalm: *Ps 24:1BC-2, 3-4AB, 5-6*
Gospel Reading: *Luke 21:1-4*

Source: PanagiaQuickToHear.com – abouta

November

tuesday

22

ICON OF THE MOTHER OF GOD "QUICK TO HEAR" Mt. Athos, Greece (1664)

Around 1110, a Docheiriou monastery wall was painted with an icon of the Mother of God as commissioned by St. Neophytos. After being hidden in obscurity for over 500 years with the monks, a voice from the image came forth in 1664. The refectory steward, Neilos, heard it say, "Stop dirtying my icon with your smoke." Thinking it a prank, he ignored the request when the voice spoke another time, she went blind. After a long repentance of several weeks, he heard the voice again: "Monk, your prayer to me has been heard; be forgiven and receive your sight as before. ... From now on let the monks fly to me for their every need, and at once I will listen to them and to all who approach me, for I am called Quick to Hear."

NOVEMBER 2016

s	m	t	w	t	f	s
		1	2	3	4	5
6	7	8	9	10	11	12
13	14	15	16	17	18	19
20	21	22	23	24	25	26
27	28	29	30			

34TH WEEK IN ORDINARY TIME
Memorial of Saint Cecilia, Virgin and Martyr
First Reading: *Revelation 14:14-19*
Responsorial Psalm: *Ps 96:10, 11-12, 13*
Gospel Reading: *Luke 21:5-11*

November

wednesday

23

OUR LADY OF THE CONCEPTION
Granada, Nicaragua (1721)

Pious tradition recounts that in 1721 women washing clothes in Lake Nicaragua saw a chest floating in, but every time it drew near, it went back out with the waves. The Franciscan friars were alerted and waded in to bring in the chest. The words, "For the city of Granada" were carved on top and Inside were two statues of the Virgin; the other was given to the city of Masaya. On November 23, 1856 a fire was set by American freebooter William Walker on his way out of Granada, after having declared himself president of Nicaragua. The city was left in ruins but the holy image of the Virgin of Conception was unharmed, now residing in Granada's cathedral. In 1862, she was honored with the title, "General of the Nicaraguan Army."

Source: Fotos de la Virgen - Nuestra Señora de Concepción de Granada, Nicaragua

NOVEMBER 2016

s	m	t	w	t	f	s
		1	2	3	4	5
6	7	8	9	10	11	12
13	14	15	16	17	18	19
20	21	22	23	24	25	26
27	28	29	30			

34TH WEEK IN ORDINARY TIME

First Reading: *Revelation 15:1-4*
Responsorial Psalm: *Ps 98:1, 2-3AB, 7-8, 9*
Gospel Reading: *Luke 21:12-19*

November

thursday

24

THE BLACK VIRGIN
Myans, France (1248)

Source: Forum Pro - L'Église de Myansa

A deadly avalanche on Mont Granier buried whole towns and killed hundreds in Savoy on November 24, 1248. The destruction carried all the way up and stopped at the small chapel of the Virgin near Myans. The Black Virgin and Child from the twelfth century would become the center of a popular devotion. Franciscans began building the church in 1452 they cared for during the next three centuries. French revolutionaries attacked the church in 1792 and desecrated the Black Virgin. The statue was later restored and reinstalled in the church crypt in 1855. Half a century later, the famous image was canonically crowned. Our Lady of Myans is celebrated locally on September 8, feast of the Nativity of the Virgin.

34TH WEEK IN ORDINARY TIME
Mem. of St Andrew Dung-Lac, Priest & Companions, Martyrs

First Reading: *Revelations 18:1-2, 21-23; 19:1-3, 9A*
Responsorial Psalm: *Ps 100:1B-2, 3, 4, 5*
Gospel Reading: *Luke 21:20-28*

NOVEMBER 2016

s	m	t	w	t	f	s
		1	2	3	4	5
6	7	8	9	10	11	12
13	14	15	16	17	18	19
20	21	22	23	24	25	26
27	28	29	30			

November
friday
25

OUR LADY OF THE ROCK
Fiesole, Italy (1446)

Source: Wikipedia (Italian) – Duomo di Fiesole

According to tradition, twin shepherdesses from Fiesole brought the sheep in and every day stopped to pray by a small cavern carved into the rock with a statue of Mary and Jesus with two angels. On the feast of the Visitation, they experienced a vision of the Virgin Mary holding the infant Jesus in her arms appeared to them in a cloud. She comforted them and asked for a church to be built in her honor, to be started by their father. They left guarding their flock and brought him to that place and the Virgin appeared to him as well and made the request again. The villagers were then able to see the vision of the Mother of God themselves. The ecclesiastical authorities approved the construction of a sanctuary dedicated to Our Lady of Roc. Her feast day is celebrated annually on November 25th.

NOVEMBER 2016

s	m	t	w	t	f	s
		1	2	3	4	5
6	7	8	9	10	11	12
13	14	15	16	17	18	19
20	21	22	23	24	25	26
27	28	29	30			

34TH WEEK IN ORDINARY TIME

First Reading: *Revelation 20:1-4, 11—21:2*
Responsorial Psalm: *Ps 84:3, 4, 5-6A AND 8A*
Gospel Reading: *Luke 21:29-33*

November

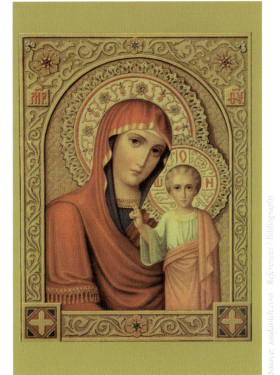

saturday

26

OUR LADY OF SOUFANIEH
Damascus, Syria (1982)

On December 15, 1982, until November 26, 1990, Myrna Nazzour of the Melkite Greek Catholic Church received apparitions of Jesus and Mary. Since 1983 she has occasionally suffered intense stigmatic wounds during ecstasy, visible to others during the day and completely gone by midnight. Many miracles have been attributed to the oil from her icon and hands. Annual anniversary celebrations begin November 26 with mass in a church, followed by evening prayers and festivities at the Nazzour home.

The apparitions were recognized in 1987 by Bishop Jacques Georges Habib Hafouri, Archbishop of Hassake-Nisibi.

34TH WEEK IN ORDINARY TIME

First Reading: *Revelation 22:1-7*
Responsorial Psalm: *Ps 95:1-2, 3-5, 6-7AB*
Gospel Reading: *Luke 21:34-36*

NOVEMBER 2016

s	m	t	w	t	f	s
		1	2	3	4	5
6	7	8	9	10	11	12
13	14	15	16	17	18	19
20	21	22	23	24	25	26
27	28	29	30			

November

sunday

27

OUR LADY OF THE MIRACULOUS MEDAL
Paris, France (1830)

Source: Wikipedia – Miraculous Medal

Catherine Laboure, a novice in the order of the Sisters of Charity, experienced two apparitions of the Blessed Virgin Mary. On July 18th, 1830, Catherine was told of the impending travails of France. Several months later she received a message detailing the designs for a medal, later known as the Miraculous Medal, now reproduced over a billion times and distributed around the world. The archbishop initiated an official canonical inquiry into the alleged visions. Catherine refused to appear, wishing her identity to be kept a secret. The tribunal, basing its opinion on the stability of her confessor and Catherine's character, decided to favor the authenticity of the visions.

NOVEMBER 2016

s	m	t	w	t	f	s
		1	2	3	4	5
6	7	8	9	10	11	12
13	14	15	16	17	18	19
20	21	22	23	24	25	26
27	28	29	30			

1ST SUNDAY OF ADVENT

First Reading: *Jeremiah 1: 4-8*
Responsorial Psalm: *Ps 122: 1-2, 3-4, 4-5, 6-7, 8-9*
Second Reading: *Romans 13:11-14*
Gospel Reading: *Matthew 24:37-44*

Source: blog.libero.it - lumonvera "IL ROSARIO DEI 7 DOLORI"

monday

28

MOTHER OF THE WORD
Kibeho, Rwanda (1981)

The apparitions began in November 1981 when six young girls and one boy claimed to have seen the Blessed Virgin Mary and Jesus. But only the visions of the first three - 17-year-old Alphonsine, 20-year-old Nathalie, and 21-year-old Marie Claire -- have received Bishop Misago's solemn approval. Because there were reservations about the other four visionaries, and the supposed visions of Jesus, Bishop Misago did not confirm the authenticity of either those visions or visionaries. The Virgin appeared to them as "Nyina wa Jambo", that is "Mother of the Word", which is synonymous to "Umubyeyl W'iamna" that is, "Mother of God", as she herself explained. Bishop Augustine Misago of Gikongoro, Rwanda, Africa, gave his approval of the apparitions.

1ST WEEK OF ADVENT

First Reading: *Isaiah 4:2-6*
Responsorial Psalm: *Ps 122:1-2, 3-4B, 4CD-5, 6-7, 8-9*
Gospel Reading: *Matthew 8:5-11*

NOVEMBER 2016

s	m	t	w	t	f	s
		1	2	3	4	5
6	7	8	9	10	11	12
13	14	15	16	17	18	19
20	21	22	23	24	25	26
27	28	29	30			

November

tuesday

29

OUR LADY OF THE GOLDEN HEART
Beauraing, Belgium (1932)

On November 29, 1932, a group of children aged 9 to 15 saw a luminous woman floating above the railroad bridge near their Catholic school. Afraid, they ran home. On the next night, they saw her there again, but she vanished, reappearing on a hawthorn bush by the school's garden gate. Glowing in white robes with blue highlights and a crown of rays, the woman did not speak until December 2, when the children asked what she wanted of them. "To be very good," she said. She later asked for a chapel, for pilgrimages and prayers, and identified herself: "Je suis la Vierge Immaculée." From December 29 until the last apparition, a golden heart showed on the Virgin's breast when she said "Adieu." The apparition was approved by the Vatican 1949.

NOVEMBER 2016

s	m	t	w	t	f	s
		1	2	3	4	5
6	7	8	9	10	11	12
13	14	15	16	17	18	19
20	21	22	23	24	25	26
27	28	29	30			

1ST WEEK OF ADVENT

First Reading: *Isaiah 11:1-10*
Responsorial Psalm: *Ps 72:1-2, 7-8, 12-13, 17*
Gospel Reading: *Luke 10:21-24*

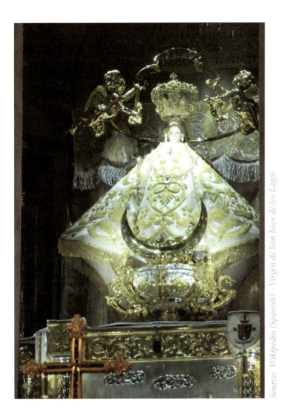

Source: Wikipedia (Spanish) - Virgen de San Juan de los Lagos

November

wednesday

30

OUR LADY OF THE CONCEPTION
San Juan de los Lagos, Mexico (1224)

In 1623, some trapeze artists brought the body of their daughter to the San Juan chapel for burial. The young acrobat had fallen during practice onto some upright blades sticking up from the ground to make the show more thrilling. The chapel caretaker, an old woman named Ana Lucia, put the Virgin's statue on the girl's breast, and the child revived. The grateful father took the fragile statue, made of cornstalks and glue, to Guadalajara for restoration. From then on the shrine's fame and miracles multiplied. Meanwhile, the town grew, changing its name to San Juan de los Lagos. A new church was built, and then another-each larger, more splendid. On November 30, 1769, the statue was installed in the third church.

1ST WEEK OF ADVENT
Feast of Saint Andrew, Apostle

First Reading: *Romans 10: 9-18*
Responsorial Psalm: *Ps 19: 1-2.3-4*
Gospel Reading: *Matthew 4: 19*

NOVEMBER 2016

s	m	t	w	t	f	s
		1	2	3	4	5
6	7	8	9	10	11	12
13	14	15	16	17	18	19
20	21	22	23	24	25	26
27	28	29	30			

December

thursday

1

MARY COMFORTER OF THE AFFLICTED
Mettenbuch, Germany (1876)

Between December 1 and 21, 1876, the Blessed Virgin Mary reportedly appeared to 4 children, NC Kraus, Francisco Javier Kraus, Teresa Sack Liebl and Matilda, ages eight to fourteen. Occasionally the Infant Jesus, Saint Joseph and angels all were reported to appear. These events were recorded in detail by the pastor and the bishop of Regensburg Ignatius Senestrey. The latter, however, distanced himself from the apparitions and decided to suspend the investigation but later a chapel was built to enshrine the image of the Virgin. The apparitions are reported during Advent and Christmas, and so while she was named "Comforter of the Afflicted," she was later was called by the people as "Mother of God of Advent."

Source: Adorare.ch "Maria – die Adventmuttergottes in der Waldschlucht von Mettenbuch"

DECEMBER 2016

s	m	t	w	t	f	s
				1	2	3
4	5	6	7	8	9	10
11	12	13	14	15	16	17
18	19	20	21	22	23	24
25	26	27	28	29	30	31

1ST WEEK OF ADVENT

First Reading: *Isaiah 26:1-6*
Responsorial Psalm: *Ps 118:1 AND 8-9, 19-21, 25-27A*
Gospel Reading: *Matthew 7:21, 24-27*

December

friday

2

OUR LADY OF DIDINIA
Turkey (363)

Legend says that it was before this shrine of Our Lady of Didinia that Saint Basil had begged the Blessed Virgin to remedy the persecution of Christianity being caused by Julian the Apostate.

After three days of prayer and fasting, Basil had a vision in which he saw Mary surrounded by celestial soldiery and heard her say: "Go call Mercury to me. He shall kill the blasphemer of my Son."

He went to the shrine of St. Mercurius whose sword was first missing and then returned covered in blood. Julian had died on campaign in Persia, from a spear that had pierced his liver and intestines, suffering a major hemorrhage from the wound which killed him.

Source: Wikipedia–Saint Mercurius Church in Coptic Cairo

1ST WEEK OF ADVENT

First Reading: *Isaiah 29:17-24*
Responsorial Psalm: *Ps 27:1, 4, 13-14*
Gospel Reading: *Matthew 9:27-31*

DECEMBER 2016

s	m	t	w	t	f	s
				1	2	3
4	5	6	7	8	9	10
11	12	13	14	15	16	17
18	19	20	21	22	23	24
25	26	27	28	29	30	31

December

saturday

3

VIRGIN OF MONTESANTO
Rome, Italy (1659)

A tiny Carmelite church on the Piazza del Popolo in Rome called St. Mary of the Holy Mountain is home to a wonderworking icon of the Madonna and Child. The painting believed to have been created by an 11-year-old girl with divine assistance was canonically crowned on December 3, 1659. Cardinal Gerolamo Gastaldi decided to build the Madonna a larger sanctuary created by three great architects. Gian Lorenzo Bernini revised Carlo Rainaldi's original plan to give the building an oval shape more in keeping with the topography, and Carlo Fontana completed it in 1679. Pius XII designated the Basilica di Santa Maria in Montesanto in 1953 the official church for artists, who still come to this day before the image of the Virgin Mary seeking help.

Source: Wikimedia Commons - Santa Maria dei Miracoli (Roma)

DECEMBER 2016

s	m	t	w	t	f	s
				1	2	3
4	5	6	7	8	9	10
11	12	13	14	15	16	17
18	19	20	21	22	23	24
25	26	27	28	29	30	31

1ST WEEK OF ADVENT
Memorial of Saint Francis Xavier, Priest

First Reading: *Isaiah 30: 19-21.23-26*
Responsorial Psalm: *Ps 147: 1-2.3-4.5-6*
Gospel Reading: *Matthew 9:35-10:1.5a.6-8*

December

sunday

4

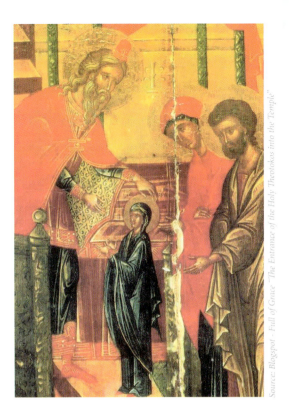

Source: Blogspot – Full of Grace "The Entrance of the Holy Theotokos into the Temple"

ICON OF "THE ENTRY OF THE MOST HOLY THEOTOKOS INTO THE TEMPLE"
Serpukhov, Russia (14th c.)

Before the Revolution of 1917, this image was in the diocesan women's convent in Serpukhov. Ven. Varlaam, who lived in the 14th century and was a disciple of St. Alexis, Metropolitan of Moscow, once was granted a vision of an icon on which was depicted the Most Holy Virgin's Entry into the Temple. Holy Hierarch St. Alexis then ordered that an icon like the one described in the vision of St. Varlaam be painted. The Icon was painted and installed in the stone church dedicated to the Entry of the Mother of God, in the Monastery of the Lord, founded in Serpukhov by St. Varlaam. Since 1377, when it was painted, it has been revered as miraculous.

2ND SUNDAY OF ADVENT

First Reading:	*Isaiah 11:1-10*
Responsorial Psalm:	*Ps 72:1-2, 7-8, 12-13, 17*
Second Reading:	*Romans 15:4-9*
Gospel Reading:	*Matthew 3:1-12*

DECEMBER 2016

s	m	t	w	t	f	s
				1	2	3
4	5	6	7	8	9	10
11	12	13	14	15	16	17
18	19	20	21	22	23	24
25	26	27	28	29	30	31

December

monday

5

VIRGIN OF THE KINGS, IMMACULATE CONCEPTION
La Antigua Guatemala, Guatemala (16th c.)

Seeking supplies for the Franciscan churches in Guatemala, Fray Antonio Tineo traveled to Spain in 1600 to ask King Felipe III's assistance. Padre Tineo brought back a new statue called the Virgin of the Kings of the Immaculate Conception from Queen Margarita's private chapel and placed it in the church of San Francisco in Guatemala City. The image was canonically crowned on December 5, 1954 in centenary celebration of the 100th anniversary of the proclamation of the dogma of the Immaculate Conception.

On December 8, an annual rezado or prayer procession with the statue takes place in the streets.

Source: Cofrades - CUATRICENTENARIA, PONTIFICIA, CONSAGRADA Y CONDECORADA

DECEMBER 2016

s	m	t	w	t	f	s
				1	2	3
4	5	6	7	8	9	10
11	12	13	14	15	16	17
18	19	20	21	22	23	24
25	26	27	28	29	30	31

2ND WEEK OF ADVENT

First Reading: *Isaiah 35:1-10*
Responsorial Psalm: *Ps 85:9AB AND 10, 11-12, 13-14*
Gospel Reading: *Luke 5:17-26*

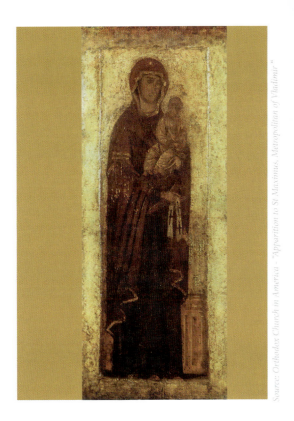

Source: Orthodox Church in America "Apparition to St Maximus, Metropolitan of Vladimir"

 *December*

tuesday

6

APPARITION TO ST MAXIMUS, METROPOLITAN OF VLADIMIR
Vladimir, Russia (1299)

The Maximov Icon of the Mother of God was painted in the year 1299 following Her appearance to St Maximus, Metropolitan of Vladimir. A description of this vision was inscribed on the left side of his crypt.

The Mother of God appeared to St Maximus when he arrived in Vladimir from Kiev. In the vision, she said, "My servant Maximus, it is good that you have come to visit my city. Shepherd the flock of my city."

The appearance of the Mother of God was a sign of approval for the transfer of the Metropolitan See from Kiev to Vladimir.

2ND WEEK OF ADVENT

First Reading: *Isaiah 40:1-11*
Responsorial Psalm: *Ps 96:1-2, 3 AND 10AC, 11-12, 13*
Gospel Reading: *Matthew 18:12-14*

DECEMBER 2016

s	m	t	w	t	f	s
				1	2	3
4	5	6	7	8	9	10
11	12	13	14	15	16	17
18	19	20	21	22	23	24
25	26	27	28	29	30	31

December

wednesday

7

OUR LADY OF SORROWS
Villatuelda, Spain (16th c.)

Villatuelda has two patrons: San Mames and Our Lady of Sorrows. The Patronal Feast of Our Lady of Sorrows occurs on December 7th, celebrated with a procession.

The image of the Virgin is usually adorned with flowers. Pastries are made by devotees usually fulfilling a promise of goodwill toward neighbors.

Source: Flickr - J.Andres 10 "Virgen de las Angustias"

DECEMBER 2016

s	m	t	w	t	f	s
				1	2	3
4	5	6	7	8	9	10
11	12	13	14	15	16	17
18	19	20	21	22	23	24
25	26	27	28	29	30	31

2ND WEEK OF ADVENT
Memorial of St Ambrose, Bishop & Doctor of the Church

First Reading: *Isaiah 40:25-31*
Responsorial Psalm: *Ps 103:1-2, 3-4, 8 AND 10*
Gospel Reading: *Matthew 11:28-30*

Source: Blogspot – Pacificaps "MASS WITH CHAMORRO COMMUNITY IN LOS ANGELES"

thursday

8

SANTA MARIAN KAMALEN
Hagåtña, Guam (1825)

Legend says that a Chamorro fisherman named Babang noticed lights in the sea, which turned out to be two crabs carrying an illuminated statue of the Virgin. Babang put the 29" ironwood statue in the garrison of the local militia.

After an earthquake, Nuestra Señora del Camarín was credited with their survival and people then would light candles on the eve in commemoration. In 1826, the image moved to the Cathedral of the Sweet Name of Mary.

On March 25, 1985, Pope John Paul II designated the church a Basilica Minor. On December 8, a national holiday, the statue comes down from its niche and processes through the capital.

2ND WEEK OF ADVENT
Solemnity of the Immaculate Conception

First Reading: *Genesis 3: 9-15.20*
Responsorial Psalm: *Ps 98: 1.2-3ab.3cd-4*
Second Reading: *Ephesians 1: 3-6.11-12*
Gospel Reading: *Luke 1: 26-38*

DECEMBER 2016

s	m	t	w	t	f	s
				1	2	3
4	5	6	7	8	9	10
11	12	13	14	15	16	17
18	19	20	21	22	23	24
25	26	27	28	29	30	31

December

friday

9

OUR LADY OF CAYSASAY
Taal, Philippines (1603)

In 1603, a small barrio in the town of Taal, a fisherman by the name of Juan Maningcad went out fishing instead of casting his net on the sea, he threw it into the nearby river. When he pulled out his net he caught a little image of the Blessed Virgin Mary. Although it was soaked in water, it had a heavenly lustre and the face twinkled like a star. Upon seeing this marvel, Juan prostrated himself before the image and began to pray. He picked it up and brought it home. The news began to spread until it reached the parish priest and the judge. Without notice they immediately went to Juan Maningcad's house and saw the beautiful image of the Mother of God. They knelt down and took the image to Taal where a fiesta was celebrated.

Source: Wikipedia - Our Lady of Caysasay

DECEMBER 2016

s	m	t	w	t	f	s
				1	2	3
4	5	6	7	8	9	10
11	12	13	14	15	16	17
18	19	20	21	22	23	24
25	26	27	28	29	30	31

2ND WEEK OF ADVENT

First Reading: *Isaiah 48:17-19*
Responsorial Psalm: *Ps 1:1-2, 3, 4 AND 6*
Gospel Reading: *Matthew 11:16-19*

Source: Orthodox Church in america - "Weeping Icon of the Mother of God 'of the Sign' at Novgorod"

December

saturday

10

ICON OF THE MOTHER OF GOD "OF THE SIGN" Novgorod, Russia (1170)

In that year the allied Russian forces, marched to the very walls of Great Novgorod. The people of Novgorod prayed for help. Bishop Elias of Novgorod heard a wondrous voice commanding that the icon of the Most Holy Theotokos be taken out of the church and carried about on the city walls. When they carried the icon, the enemy fired a volley of arrows at the procession, and one of them pierced the face of the Mother of God. Tears trickled from her eyes, and the icon turned its face towards the city. After this divine sign an inexpressible terror suddenly fell upon the enemy. They began to strike one another, and the people of Novgorod fearlessly fought and won the victory.

DECEMBER 2016

s	m	t	w	t	f	s
				1	2	3
4	5	6	7	8	9	10
11	12	13	14	15	16	17
18	19	20	21	22	23	24
25	26	27	28	29	30	31

2ND WEEK OF ADVENT

First Reading: *Sirach 48:1-4, 9-11*
Responsorial Psalm: *Ps 80:2AC AND 3B, 15-16, 18-19*
Gospel Reading: *Matthew 17:9A, 10-13*

December

sunday

11

OUR LADY OF WARRAQ EL-HADAR
Egypt (2009)

Warraq el-Hadar is a small island and a poor district in greater Cairo's Nile river (Giza governorate, part of Greater Cairo).More than 200,000 (Christians and Muslims) initially witnessed the December 2009 apparitions on the domes of Virgin Mary and Archangel Michael Coptic Orthodox Church in El-Warraq. Apparition lights in the night sky could also be seen several kilometers away from the church. People used their mobile phones to make videos of the apparitions.

The full silhouette of the Blessed Holy Virgin Mary dressed in light blue gown could be clearly seen over the domes of the church between the church crosses. The apparitions also received wide media coverage in Egyptian newspapers and Arabic TV channels.

Source: Wikipedia - Our Lady of Warraq

DECEMBER 2016

s	m	t	w	t	f	s
				1	2	3
4	5	6	7	8	9	10
11	12	13	14	15	16	17
18	19	20	21	22	23	24
25	26	27	28	29	30	31

3RD SUNDAY OF ADVENT

First Reading: *Isaiah 35:1-6A, 10*
Responsorial Psalm: *Ps 146:6-7, 8-9, 9-10*
Second Reading: *James 5:7-10*
Gospel Reading: *Matthew 11:2-11*

Source: Wikipedia – Our Lady of Guadalupe

December

monday

12

OUR LADY OF GUADALUPE
Mexico City, Mexico (1531)

Mary proclaimed herself "the Mother of the true God who gives life" and left her image permanently upon the tilma of St. Juan Diego, a man newly converted to Christianity. Her likeness was given as a sign to Bishop Zumarraga, who abided by her wishes and constructed a church on Mt. Tepeyacac, the site of the apparitions. Millions of natives were converted to Christianity during the period following her visit. Our Lady of Guadalupe has been designated as the Patron Saint of the Americas.

Juan Diego was beatified on May 6, 1990 and canonized by Pope John Paul II on July 31, 2002. During his third visit in 1999, he declared December 12th as a Liturgical Holy Day for the whole continent.

3ᴿᴰ WEEK OF ADVENT
Feast of Our Lady of Guadalupe

First Reading: *Zechariah 2:14-17*
Responsorial Psalm: *Judith 13:18BCDE, 19*
Gospel Reading: *Luke 1:26-38*

DECEMBER 2016

s	m	t	w	t	f	s
				1	2	3
4	5	6	7	8	9	10
11	12	13	14	15	16	17
18	19	20	21	22	23	24
25	26	27	28	29	30	31

December

tuesday

13

QUEEN OF THE HOLY ROSARY
Baños de Agua Santa, Ecuador (1570)

A historical account states that one night the sexton of the church of Baños saw a small statue of the Virgin hovering in the air, and down to the spring. The event was repeated several times, so the pastor and locals gathered in the chapel to beg the Blessed Virgin to clearly tell them of her intentions. The next night the Virgin appeared to the priest asking the erection of a chapel at the spring, promising healing for all who bathe with faith in those waters. When it was complete, the statue had mysteriously disappeared. Later a mule with a box was delivered to the pastor who opened it in the presence of witnesses. With great wonder they discovered the statue of the Virgin venerated today in the sanctuary of Baños.

Source: Foros de la Virgen - "Reina del Santísimo Rosario de Agua Santa, Ecuador"

DECEMBER 2016

s	m	t	w	t	f	s
				1	2	3
4	5	6	7	8	9	10
11	12	13	14	15	16	17
18	19	20	21	22	23	24
25	26	27	28	29	30	31

3RD WEEK OF ADVENT
Memorial of Saint Lucy, Virgin and Martyr

First Reading: *Zephaniah 3: 1-2.9-13*
Responsorial Psalm: *Ps 34: 2-3.6-7.17-18.19&23*
Gospel Reading: *Matthew 21: 28-32*

Source: *Where We Walked* · *"Beata Vergine del Patrocinio, Faenza, Ravenna, Emilia-Romagna, Italy"*

December

wednesday

14

BLESSED VIRGIN OF DEFENSE
Faenza, Italy (1685)

A wealthy family from Forli donated an image of the Virgin and Child to a convent church. The painting was installed in its new marble shrine on the last Sunday of September, 1650. The beginning of public veneration of the Virgin of Defense was commemorated with an annual festa on that day. In the night of November 20, 1685, a fire in the convent laundry room jumped to the parlor and then the sacristy. But the flames ceased at the point of entry to the chapel with the sacred image. Public devotion to the Blessed Virgin of Defense, later Vatican approved officially in 1721, grew following this miracle.

On December 14, 1954, the icon of the Virgin was crowned with the gold of the nuns' rings they had received at their solemn profession.

3RD WEEK OF ADVENT
Mem. of St John of the Cross, Priest & Doctor of the Church

First Reading: *Isaiah 45:6C-8, 18, 21C-25*
Responsorial Psalm: *Ps 85:9AB AND 10, 11-12, 13-14*
Gospel Reading: *Luke 7:18B-23*

DECEMBER 2016

s	m	t	w	t	f	s
				1	2	3
4	5	6	7	8	9	10
11	12	13	14	15	16	17
18	19	20	21	22	23	24
25	26	27	28	29	30	31

December

thursday

15

OUR LADY OF MONGUÍ
Boyacá, Colombia
(16th c.)

Highly venerated, the Virgin of Monguí, is the patroness of Boyacá. The story goes that when King Charles I of Spain retired from his throne, went to the monastery of Yuste to prepare for death. He went looking for painted works of the Virgin Mary to send to the New World.

In 1558, his son King Philip II sent two paintings: one of St. Martín was for the leader of Monguí, and another of the Holy Family, for Sogamoso. Although the works were marked, the destinations were reversed. The inhabitants of Sogamoso protested and asked for the exchange. But the pictures inexplicably returned to the same places and the swap could not be done. They thought it was a miracle and let the images stay in place.

Source: Flickr - Historias en construccion "Retablo de la Virgen de Monguí"

DECEMBER 2016

s	m	t	w	t	f	s
				1	2	3
4	5	6	7	8	9	10
11	12	13	14	15	16	17
18	19	20	21	22	23	24
25	26	27	28	29	30	31

3RD WEEK OF ADVENT

First Reading: *Isaiah 54:1-10*
Responsorial Psalm: *Ps 30:2 AND 4, 5-6, 11-12A AND 13B*
Gospel Reading: *Luke 7:24-30*

December

friday

16

Source: Creighton University "Our Lady of the New Advent"

OUR LADY OF THE NEW ADVENT
Denver, Colorado, USA (1991)

With Jubilee Year 2000 upon the world, Archbishop Francis Stafford of Denver, Colorado decided to hold a nine-year novena to the Virgin Mary in preparation for the new millennium. As part of the run up, he commissioned an image of Our Lady of the New Advent in 1991 which became the official icon of the Archdiocese. In 1992, the Vatican responded to Stafford's request for a liturgical feast day to honor of Our Lady of the New Advent, with the designation of December 16. At the opening of 1993 World Youth Day in Denver, John Paul II prayed in front of the "sign" style icon, "O Mary, Our Lady of the new Advent, who kept all these things, pondering them in your heart, teach these young people to be good listeners to your Son, the Word of Life."

DECEMBER 2016

s	m	t	w	t	f	s
				1	2	3
4	5	6	7	8	9	10
11	12	13	14	15	16	17
18	19	20	21	22	23	24
25	26	27	28	29	30	31

3ᴿᴰ WEEK OF ADVENT

First Reading: *Isaiah 56:1-3A, 6-8*
Responsorial Psalm: *Ps 67:2-3, 5, 7-8*
Gospel Reading: *John 5:33-36*

December

saturday

17

OUR LADY OF THE EARTHQUAKE
Paterno, Italy (1857)

In the evening of December 16, 1857 a terrible earthquake struck the population of Basilicata and neighboring regions. On the next day, the residents of Paterno decided to bring in procession the statue of the Madonna del Carmine in the streets of the country.

Legend has it that as soon as the procession reached the present district Marsh, in front of the destroyed houses and carts full of corpses, Mary turned her face, and her eyes shed tears of blood. The miraculous event is commemorated every year on December 17.

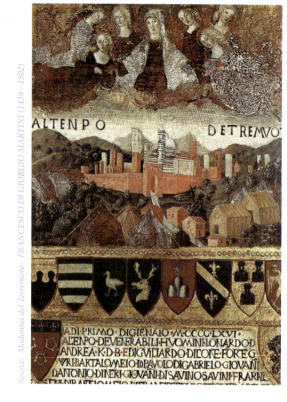

Source: Madonna del Terremoto - FRANCESCO DI GIORGIO MARTINI (1439 - 1502)

DECEMBER 2016

s	m	t	w	t	f	s
				1	2	3
4	5	6	7	8	9	10
11	12	13	14	15	16	17
18	19	20	21	22	23	24
25	26	27	28	29	30	31

3RD WEEK OF ADVENT

First Reading: *Genesis 49: 2.8-10*
Responsorial Psalm: *Ps 72: 1-2.3-4ab.7-8.17*
Gospel Reading: *Matthew 1: 1-17*

Source: Flickr – Tacho Juárez, Herrera "Altar Mayor de la Basílica de la Soledad, Cdad. de Oaxaca, Oax."

December

sunday

18

VIRGIN OF THE SOLITUDE
Oaxaca, Mexico (1620)

According to one tradition, a mule with no owner wandered from Veracruz into a pack train to Guatemala City. On December 18, 1620, when the group reached Oaxaca outside the church of St. Sebastian, the mule fell down near a chapel to the Virgin of Soledad. With the animal not going anywhere, the drivers unloaded the large box from its back and uncovered a statue of the resurrected Jesus and the head and hands for an image of the Virgin which appears complete when covered with exquisite garments. In 1670, Bishop Sariñana y Cuenca consecrated her sanctuary, later adorned with an intricate baroque facade. A focus of devotion in southern Mexico, the statue was approved by Pope Pius X to be crowned on January 18, 1909.

4TH SUNDAY OF ADVENT

First Reading: *Isaiah 7:10-14*
Responsorial Psalm: *Ps 24:1-2, 3-4, 5-6*
Second Reading: *Romans 1:1-7*
Gospel Reading: *Matthew 1:18-24*

DECEMBER 2016

s	m	t	w	t	f	s
				1	2	3
4	5	6	7	8	9	10
11	12	13	14	15	16	17
18	19	20	21	22	23	24
25	26	27	28	29	30	31

December

monday

19

OUR LADY OF HOPE
Candolim, India
(1822)

Our Lady of Good Hope is the majestic Mannerist Neo-Roman church of Candolim situated at the foot of the hills of Candolim and facing the Nerul river. After Verem, the Franciscans are believed to have built this beautiful church. Although it was repaired in 1661, the Franciscans were not satisfied with the result. The Provincial, Antonio de Assumpcaô then ordered the old church to be demolished and Fr. Jeronymo de Natividade, revised the original plans and reduced the cost. The feast of the patroness was celebrated in ancient times on the 16th of December, later the date of the feast was shifted to the 27th of December but from 1997 onwards the feast is celebrated on the 19th of December. The main altar of the church is dedicated to Our Lady of Hope.

Source: Wordpress - Goa the unique "Feast of Our Lady of Good Hope in Candolim – December 19"

DECEMBER 2016

s	m	t	w	t	f	s
				1	2	3
4	5	6	7	8	9	10
11	12	13	14	15	16	17
18	19	20	21	22	23	24
25	26	27	28	29	30	31

4TH WEEK OF ADVENT

First Reading: *Judges 13: 2-7.24-25a*
Responsorial Psalm: *Ps 71: 3-4a.5-6ab.16-17*
Gospel Reading: *Luke 1: 5-25*

Source: Cravegna.it "LE MEMORIE PERDUTE DELLA MADONNA DI CRAVEGNA"

December

tuesday

20

OUR LADY OF CRAVEGNA
Italy (1492)

In 1486, some pious women of Cravegna, collected alms to create a *virgo lactans* image on the wall of the church. On December 20, 1493, the sacristan of the church of San Giulio, Lorenzo di Francesco di Giovan, noticed that during the hour of vespers lasting 16 hours, the image of the Madonna started to emit tears from both eyes and the face was flooded. The same occurred on the right eye of the Child.

The entire face and other exposed parts of the figure of the Madonna and Child appeared then as blankets of fresh sweat. The event lasted the next two days. Even though everything else was frozen in the cold weather, and tears flowing out of the sacred image did not freeze.

4TH WEEK OF ADVENT

First Reading: *Isaiah 7:10-14*
Responsorial Psalm: *Ps 24:1-2, 3-4AB, 5-6*
Gospel Reading: *Luke 1:26-38*

DECEMBER 2016

s	m	t	w	t	f	s
				1	2	3
4	5	6	7	8	9	10
11	12	13	14	15	16	17
18	19	20	21	22	23	24
25	26	27	28	29	30	31

December

wednesday

21

GREAT MOTHER OF AUSTRIA
Mariazell, Austria (1157)

There are three legends about the "Magna Mater Austria", a 48 cm tall statuette made of linden. On December 21, 1157, a monk named Magnus was sent into town as a minister. When his way was blocked by a rock, he set down the statue and the rock broke apart clearing the way. On a nearby bank, he built a chapel and living quarters.

The second legend relates how Henry Margrave of Moravia and his wife, having been healed through the help of Our Lady of Mariazell made a pilgrimage to that place around 1200. They built the first stone church on the site of the wooden chapel.

The third legend recounts Hungarian King Ludwig I victory over the Turkish army. Out of gratitude he built the Gothic church.

Source: Wikipedia - Mariazell Basilica

DECEMBER 2016

s	m	t	w	t	f	s
				1	2	3
4	5	6	7	8	9	10
11	12	13	14	15	16	17
18	19	20	21	22	23	24
25	26	27	28	29	30	31

4TH WEEK OF ADVENT

First Reading: *Song of Solomon 2: 8-14*
Responsorial Psalm: *Ps 33: 2-3.11-12.20-21*
Gospel Reading: *Luke 1: 39-45*

Source: Basilica di Maria Ss. Delle Grzie "La 'Madonna delle Grazie'"

22

HOLY MARY OF GRACE
San Giovanni Valdarno, Italy
(1478)

Monna Tancia, 75, was left to care for a 3-month-old grandson whose parents both died in the plague of 1478 in San Giovanni Valdarno. She was desperately in search of a wet nurse but found no one willing to oblige. On December 22, at a fresco of the Madonna on the old gate of the city, she implored the Virgin Mary for help. Returning to the house, she herself was able to nurse the baby for several months. When the report of this miracle became known and the townspeople built a shrine, which later became a basilica. The image is also called the Madonna del Latte (Our Lady of Milk), although it depicts the child Jesus admiring a bird, not nursing. On her feast day, September 8, 1704, there was a coronation of the Madonna of Graces.

DECEMBER 2016

s	m	t	w	t	f	s
				1	2	3
4	5	6	7	8	9	10
11	12	13	14	15	16	17
18	19	20	21	22	23	24
25	26	27	28	29	30	31

4TH WEEK OF ADVENT

First Reading: *1 Samuel 1: 24-28*
Responsorial Psalm: *1 Samuel 2: 1.4-5.6-7.8abcd*
Gospel Reading: *Luke 1: 46-56*

December

friday

23

OUR LADY OF THE GOOD NEWS
Rennes, France (1720)

Making good on a promise made during the battle of Auray in 1364, Jean de Montfort, the victorious Duke of Brittany, founded the Dominican convent in Rennes of Our Lady of Good News. A panel painting in the convent's cloister became known as a miraculous icon and a separate chapel was built for it. When the plague of 1632 missed Rennes, the people there in gratitude gave Our Lady of Good News a solid silver replica of the city. This gift was celebrated every year on September 8 following 1634. A miracle also occurred during the great fire of December 23, 1720, when the wooden homes ignited, the townspeople of Rennes witnessed a vision of Our Lady of Good News look down in compassion from the sky and stopping the flames.

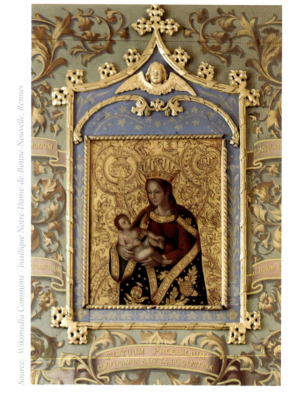

Source: Wikimedia Commons - basilique Notre-Dame-de-Bonne-Nouvelle, Rennes

DECEMBER 2016

s	m	t	w	t	f	s
				1	2	3
4	5	6	7	8	9	10
11	12	13	14	15	16	17
18	19	20	21	22	23	24
25	26	27	28	29	30	31

4TH WEEK OF ADVENT

First Reading: *Malachi 3: 1-4.23-24*
Responsorial Psalm: *Ps 25: 4-5ab.8-9.10&14*
Gospel Reading: *Luke 1: 57-66*

Source: Blogspot – Chile Virgen María "VIRGEN DEL ROSARIO"

saturday

24

OUR LADY OF THE ROSARY
Andacollo, Chile (1676)

Andacollo receives its name from a miracle of the Virgin. An Indian who was mining perceived a strange light in the copper mine where he worked. The vision said "There are many steps ahead - look among the highest cliffs that are in the plain that stretches over your head. Collo Anda".

And there he found a small wooden statue of the Virgin of dark complexion, which then proved to be miraculous.

The dedication has two feasts, the Great Feast that is between 24 and 26 December, and the feast celebrated on the first weekend of October. The image of the Virgin of Andacollo was solemnly crowned on December 26, 1901. The decree was signed by Pope Leo XIII.

4TH WEEK OF ADVENT

First Reading: *2 Samuel 7: 1-5.8b-12.14a.16*
Responsorial Psalm: *Ps 89: 2-3.4-5.27&29*
Gospel Reading: *Luke 1: 67-79*

DECEMBER 2016

s	m	t	w	t	f	s
				1	2	3
4	5	6	7	8	9	10
11	12	13	14	15	16	17
18	19	20	21	22	23	24
25	26	27	28	29	30	31

December

sunday

25

COMFORTER OF THE AFFLICTED
Kevelaer, Germany
(1641)

Kevelaer is the most popular Marian shrine in all of Germany. The tradition goes back to Christmas of 1641 when Hendrik Busman von Geldern was absorbed in prayer before a cross on the moors. Suddenly he heard the voice of Madonna: "In this place I need you to dedicate a chapel." Mary repeated twice more this desire to Hendrik and his wife saw a chapel illuminated in a dream. The couple convinced the pastor, James Schink, to build the chapel from the dream. When this was built, a small image of the Madonna, a copy of the "Comforter of the Afflicted", was used. This small chapel soon became a point of attraction for the devotees.

Source: Angelfire - El Mision de Nuestra Senora de Kevelaer

DECEMBER 2016

s	m	t	w	t	f	s
				1	2	3
4	5	6	7	8	9	10
11	12	13	14	15	16	17
18	19	20	21	22	23	24
25	26	27	28	29	30	31

CHRISTMAS WEEK
The Nativity of the Lord (Christmas)

First Reading: *Isaiah 52: 7-10*
Responsorial Psalm: *Ps 98: 1.2-3ab.3cd-4.5-6*
Second Reading: *Hebrews 1: 1-6*
Gospel Reading: *John 1: 1-18*

26

VIRGIN OF THE ROSARY
Chiquinquirá, Colombia (1562)

Source: Wikipedia - Virgin of Chiquinquirá (by Baltasar Vargas de Figuero)

On December 26, 1586, as María Ramos was leaving the room after prayers, the painting fell. A native woman named Isabel exclaimed, "Look!" The picture stood upright, glowing, its colors deep and its torn fabric restored. More miracles, a church investigation, and a series of church buildings followed. Although the picture faded with time, devotion increased.

The Colombian patronal feast of the Virgin of Chiquinquirá commemorates the canonical crowning of the painting on July 9, 1919. The Basilica celebrates both that day and December 26 with a novena, vigil fireworks, street procession, and mass in Plaza Libertad.

CHRISTMAS WEEK
Feast of Saint Stephen, first martyr

First Reading: *Acts 6:8-10; 7:54-59*
Responsorial Psalm: *Ps 31:3CD-4, 6 AND 8AB, 16BC AND 17t*
Gospel Reading: *Matthew 10: 17-22*

DECEMBER 2016

s	m	t	w	t	f	s
				1	2	3
4	5	6	7	8	9	10
11	12	13	14	15	16	17
18	19	20	21	22	23	24
25	26	27	28	29	30	31

December

tuesday
27

OUR LADY OF THE ROSARY
Atibaia, Brazil (1817)

Slaves who couldn't attend St. John the Baptist's church in Atibaia, started construction of their own church in 1763 later known as Nossa Senhora do Rosário dos Pretos (Our Lady of the Rosary of the Blacks). It was completed in 1817. The region's oldest and most active *congada* tradition in the region is found here in Atibaia with five congada groups combine African and Portuguese religious practices, in devotion to St. Benedict and Our Lady of the Rosary. As they have for over two centuries, the congadas gather outside Our Lady's church at dawn, dressed in brilliant uniforms of scarlet, green, blue, pink, or white, and carrying swords, banners, and musical instrument. The December 27 celebrations begin with a serenade and ends with fireworks.

Source: Fotos de la Virgen – Nuestra Señora del Rosario de Atibaia, Brazil

DECEMBER 2016

s	m	t	w	t	f	s
				1	2	3
4	5	6	7	8	9	10
11	12	13	14	15	16	17
18	19	20	21	22	23	24
25	26	27	28	29	30	31

CHRISTMAS WEEK
Feast of Saint John, Apostle and evangelist

First Reading: *1 John 1:1-4*
Responsorial Psalm: *Ps 97:1-2, 5-6, 11-12*
Gospel Reading: *John 20:1A AND 2-8*

Source: Elche.me - Antonio de Villanueva, "Virgen de la Asunción" (hacia 1747)

wednesday

28

VIRGIN OF THE ASSUMPTION
Elche, Spain (1370)

According to pious tradition, a lookout named Francesco Cantó watching the coast off Elche, spotted a chest floating in the sea on December 28, 1370. When he rode his horse back to tell the Council, the Virgin went with him. She waited at the Garden of the Red Gates until the Council's official proclamation. The committee found there a chest was a statue of the Virgin of the Assumption and the libretto of a mystery play to re-enact her dormition and assumption to heaven.

The *Misterio de Elche*, the name for this play, is performed annually at the Feast of the Assumption in August. La Venida de la Virgen (the Coming of the Virgin), is remembered yearly on December 28 with a recreation of the events.

CHRISTMAS WEEK
Feast of the Holy Innocents, martyrs

First Reading: *1 John 1:5-2:2*
Responsorial Psalm: *Ps 124: 2-3.4-5.7cd-8*
Gospel Reading: *Matthew 2: 13-18*

DECEMBER 2016

s	m	t	w	t	f	s
				1	2	3
4	5	6	7	8	9	10
11	12	13	14	15	16	17
18	19	20	21	22	23	24
25	26	27	28	29	30	31

December

thursday

29

OUR LADY OF THE FLOWERS
Bra, Italy (1336)

On the evening of December 29, 1336, in the small town of Bra, a young expecting mother was passing by a votive column consecrated to the Blessed Virgin Mary. Two rough soldiers, from a band of mercenaries, were lying in wait. Egidia Mathis, seeing that she was going to be raped despite her condition, clung on desperately to the image of the Madonna, calling for her help. Without warning, a beam of light flashed from the image, blinding the two mercenaries who fled in a panic. Then, the Madonna herself appeared to Egidia comforted her for several minutes and assured her that the danger over. Then Our Lady vanished. Due to such feelings of fear and emotion, Egidia gave birth at the foot of the column. Flowers still bloom at the site of the apparition.

Source: Panoramio - Giancarlo Ticozzi - Santuario Madonna dei Fiori, Bra (CN)

DECEMBER 2016

s	m	t	w	t	f	s
				1	2	3
4	5	6	7	8	9	10
11	12	13	14	15	16	17
18	19	20	21	22	23	24
25	26	27	28	29	30	31

CHRISTMAS WEEK

First Reading: *1 John 2: 3-11*
Responsorial Psalm: *Ps 96: 1-2a.2b-3.5b-6*
Gospel Reading: *Luke 2: 22-35*

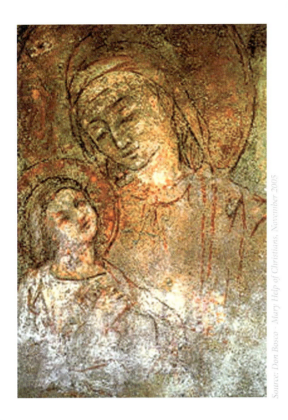

Source: Don Bosco - Mary Help of Christians, November 2005

December

friday

30

OUR LADY OF THE MIRACLE
Milano, Italy (1485)

n the morning of December 30, 1485, Don Giovanni Pietro Porro was celebrating Mass before the holy image, when the veil covering the picture was lifted and the Madonna, in a flash of light raised the baby to the faithful. The miraculous appearance, which was confirmed by the rigorous investigation of the ecclesiastical canon, was a sign of special favor from the Madonna, in what was a very sad year due to the spread of plague. By the will of the city authorities and the entire people of a shrine was erected worthy of the protectress of Milan, called by the people, "Our Lady of Miracles." The Sanctuary of San Celso become the center of devotion to Our Lady of the Milanese. In 1576 the plague struck Milan again, and after a solemn procession the terrible scourge ended.

CHRISTMAS WEEK
The Holy Family of Jesus, Mary and Joseph

First Reading: *Sirach 3:2-6, 12-14*
Responsorial Psalm: *Ps 128:1-2, 3, 4-5*
Second Reading: *Colossians 3:12-21*
Gospel Reading: *Matthew 2:13-15, 19-23*

DECEMBER 2016

s	m	t	w	t	f	s
				1	2	3
4	5	6	7	8	9	10
11	12	13	14	15	16	17
18	19	20	21	22	23	24
25	26	27	28	29	30	31

December

saturday

31

HOLY MARY THE ROYAL
Uxue, Spain
(8th cent.)

Legend has it that a pigeon was in and out of a hole in the rock and a young shepherd, moved by curiosity, approached the rock with an intent to frighten the bird.

When taking a look at the dove while it continued its insistent flutter; he approached and found a beautiful Romanesque image that seemed to have come from Basque country.

The town of Uxue was formed, according to legend, around the site of the discovery of the image of Our Lady of Uxue (Uxue, in Castilian means dove.) The settlement took the form of a castle-fortress built in the late eighth or early ninth century as an outpost of his kingdom against Islam stretching across the West Bank.

Source: Flickr - Maria J. Leza "Nuestra Señora de Ujué"

DECEMBER 2016

s	m	t	w	t	f	s
				1	2	3
4	5	6	7	8	9	10
11	12	13	14	15	16	17
18	19	20	21	22	23	24
25	26	27	28	29	30	31

CHRISTMAS WEEK

First Reading: *1 John 2: 18-21*
Responsorial Psalm: *Ps 96: 1-2.11-12.13*
Gospel Reading: *John 1: 1-18*

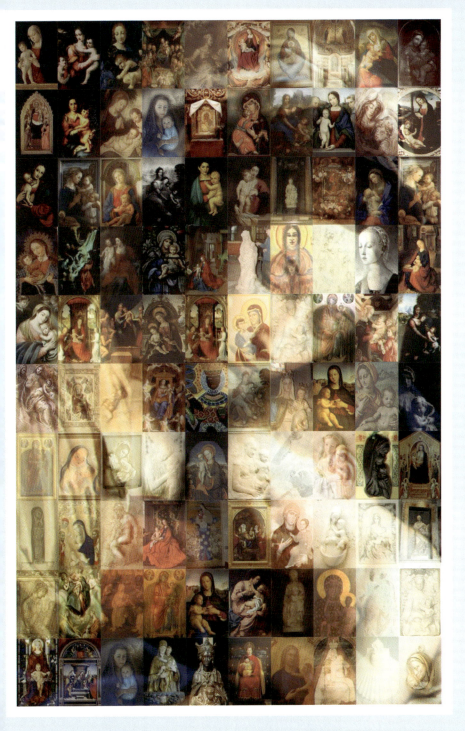

"Devotion to the Mother of the Lord, when it is genuine, is always an impetus to a life guided by the spirit and values of the Gospel" - Pope John Paul II

Mary, Undoer of Knots,
Pray for us.

Prayer to Mary, Undoer of Knots

Virgin Mary, Mother of fair love,
Mother who never refuses to come to the aid of a child in need,
Mother whose hands never cease to serve your beloved children
because they are moved by the divine love
and immense mercy that exists in your heart,
cast your compassionate eyes upon me
and see the snarl of knots that exist in my life.

You know very well how desperate I am,
my pain and how I am bound by these knots.

Mary, Mother to whom God entrusted
the undoing of the knots in the lives of his children,
I entrust into your hands the ribbon of my life.
No one can take it away from your precious care.
In your hands there is no knot that cannot be undone.

Powerful Mother, by your grace and intercessory power
with Your Son and My Liberator, Jesus,
take into your hands today this knot...
I beg you to undo it for the glory of God, once for all,
You are my hope.

O my Lady, you are the only consolation God gives me,
the fortification of my feeble strength,
the enrichment of my destitution
and with Christ the freedom from my chains.

Hear my plea. Keep me, guide me, protect me, o safe refuge!
Mary, Undoer of Knots, pray for me.

Novena to Mary, Undoer of Knots

1. Make the sign of the cross.

2. Make an Act of Contrition. Ask pardon for your sins and make a firm promise not to commit them again.

3. Say the first 3 decades of the Rosary.

4. Make the meditation of the day. (See next section)

5. Say the last 2 decades of the Rosary.

6. Finish with the Prayer to Our Lady the Undoer of Knots.

Meditation of the Day

Day 1: Dearest Holy Mother, Most Holy Mary, you undo the knots that suffocate your children, extend your merciful hands to me. I entrust to You today this knot....and all the negative consequences that it provokes in my life. I give you this knot that torments me and makes me unhappy and so impedes me from uniting myself to You and Your Son Jesus, my Savior.

I run to You, Mary, Undoer of Knots because I trust you and I know that you never despise a sinning child who comes to ask you for help. I believe that you can undo this knot because Jesus grants you everything. I believe that you want to undo this knot because you are my Mother. I believe that You will do this because you love me with eternal love. Thank you, Dear Mother. Mary, Undoer of Knots, pray for me.

Day 2: Mary, Beloved Mother, channel of all grace, I return to You today my heart, recognizing that I am a sinner in need of your help. Many times I lose the graces you grant me because of my sins of egoism, pride, rancor and my lack of generosity and humility. I turn to You today, Mary, Undoer of knots, for You to ask your Son Jesus to grant me a pure, divested, humble and trusting heart. I will live today practicing these virtues and offering you this as a sign of my love for You. I entrust into Your hands this knot (...describe) which keeps me from reflecting the glory of God. Mary, Undoer of Knots, pray for me.

Day 3: Meditating Mother, Queen of heaven, in whose hands the treasures of the King are found, turn your merciful eyes upon me today. I entrust into your holy hands this knot in my life...and all the rancor and resentment it has caused in me. I ask Your forgiveness, God the Father, for my sin. Help me now to forgive all the persons who consciously or unconsciously provoked this knot. Give me, also, the grace to forgive me for having provoked this knot. Only in this way can You undo it. Before You, dearest Mother, and in the name of Your Son Jesus, my Savior, who has suffered so many offenses, having been granted forgiveness, I now forgive these persons...and myself, forever. Thank you, Mary, Undoer of Knots for undoing the knot of rancor in my heart and the knot which I now present to you. Amen. Mary, Undoer of Knots, pray for me.

Day 4: Dearest Holy Mother, you are generous with all who seek you, have mercy on me. I entrust into your hands this knot which robs the peace of my heart, paralyzes my soul and keeps me from going to my Lord and serving Him with my life.

Undo this knot in my love...., O mother, and ask Jesus to heal my paralytic faith which gets down hearted with the stones on the road. Along with you, dearest Mother, may I see these stones as friends. Not murmuring against them anymore but giving endless thanks for them, may I smile trustingly in your power. Mary, Undoer of Knots, pray for me.

Day 5: Mother, Undoer of Knots, generous and compassionate, I come to You today to once again entrust this knot...in my life to you and to ask the divine wisdom to undo, under the light of the Holy Spirit, this snarl of problems. No one ever saw you angry; to the contrary, your words were so charged with sweetness that the Holy Spirit was manifested on your lips. Take away from me the bitterness, anger and hatred which this knot has caused me. Give me, o dearest Mother, some of the sweetness and wisdom that is all silently reflected in your heart. And just as you were present at Pentecost, ask Jesus to send me a new presence of the Holy Spirit at this moment in my life. Holy Spirit, come upon me! Mary, Undoer of Knots, pray for me.

Day 6: Queen of Mercy, I entrust to you this knot in my life...and I ask you to give me a heart that is patient until you undo it. Teach me to persevere in the living word of Jesus, in the Eucharist, the Sacrament of Confession; stay with me and prepare my heart to celebrate with the angels the grace that will be granted to me. Amen! Alleluia! Mary, Undoer of Knots, pray for me.

Day 7: Mother Most Pure, I come to You today to beg you to undo this knot in my life... and free me from the snares of Evil. I renounce all of them today, every connection I have had with them and I proclaim Jesus as my one and only Lord and Savior. Mary, Undoer of Knots, destroy the traps set for me by this knot. Thank you, dearest Mother. Most Precious Blood of Jesus, free me! Mary, Undoer of Knots, pray for me.

Day 8: Virgin Mother of God, overflowing with mercy, have mercy on your child and undo this knot...in my life. I need your visit to my life, like you visited Elizabeth. Bring me Jesus, bring me the Holy Spirit. Teach me to practice the virtues of courage, joyfulness, humility and faith, and, like Elizabeth, to be filled with the Holy Spirit. Make me joyfully rest on your bosom, Mary. I consecrate you as my mother, Queen and friend. I give you my heart and everything I have (my home and family, my material and spiritual goods.) I am yours forever. Put your heart in me so that I can do everything that Jesus tells me. Mary, Undoer of Knots, pray for me.

Day 9: Most Holy Mary, our Advocate, Undoer of Knots, I come today to thank you for undoing this knot in my life...You know very well the suffering it has caused me. Thank you for coming, Mother, with your long fingers of mercy to dry the tears in my eyes; you receive me in your arms and make it possible for me to receive once again the divine grace.

Mary, Undoer of Knots, dearest Mother, I thank you for undoing the knots in my life. Wrap me in your mantle of love, keep me under your protection, enlighten me with your peace! Amen. Mary, Undoer of Knots, pray for me.

(The Novena has the Cardinal ecclesiastical approval, receiving the "NIHIL OBSTAT and IMPRIMATUR" Imprimatur Paris Archdiocese.)

History of devotion to Mary, Undoer of Knots

A German nobleman, Wolfgang Langenmantel (1568-1637) was distraught when his wife Sophia was planning to divorce him. To save the marriage, Wolfgang sought counsel from Fr.Jakob Rem, a Jesuit priest, respected for his wisdom and piety, at the University of Ingolstadt. On his fourth visit there on 28 September 1615, Wolfgang brought his 'wedding ribbon' to Fr.Rem. In the marriage ceremony of that time and place, the maid-of-honour joined together the arms of the bride and groom with a ribbon to symbolise their union for life. Fr.Rem, in a solemn ritual act, raised the ribbon before the image of 'Our Lady of the Snows', while at the same time untying its knots one by one. As he smoothed out the ribbon, it became dazzling white. This was taken as confirmation that their prayers were heard. Consequently, the divorce was averted, and Wolfgang remained happily married!

To commemorate the turn of the century in the year 1700, Wolfgang's grandson, Fr.Hieronymus Langenmantel, Canon of St.Peter am Perlach, installed a family altar in the church, as was customary then. He commissioned Johann Schmidtner to provide a painting to be placed over the altar. Schmidtner was inspired by the story of Wolfgang and Fr.Rem, and so based his painting on that event. The image came to be venerated as Mary Undoer of Knots. The original Baroque painting is found in the church of St.Peter am Perlach, in Augsburg, Bavaria, Germany. The painting has survived wars, revolutions and secular opposition, and continues to draw people to it.

In the 18th century the devotion to Mary Undoer of Knots was localised to Germany. The devotion was augmented during the Chernobyl Nuclear Power Plant disaster (1986), when victims sought help through the intercession of Mary Undoer of Knots.

Devotion of Pope Francis to Mary, Undoer of Knots

In the 1980s, while doing his doctoral studies in theology in Freiburg, Germany, as a Jesuit priest, Jorge Bergoglio saw a painting in a church in Augsburg entitled 'Mary Untier of Knots'. He was so impressed by its stark symbolism that he took postcards of the image back with him to his home province of Argentina. He used to enclose copies in every letter he sent out. An Argentinian artist-friend of his made an oil-on-canvas miniature painting of the picture, which was hung in the chapel of Colegio del Salvador in Buenos Aires where Bergoglio was posted. The college staff was so attracted by it that they persuaded the local pastor to get a larger copy made. This was displayed in the parish church of San José del Talar, in 1996. Eventually, devotion to Mary under the title 'Untier of Knots' spread across Latin America.

Shortly after Cardinal Joseph Ratzinger was elected pope, as Benedict XVI, the then-Cardinal Bergoglio presented the German-born pope with a silver chalice engraved with the image of Mary Undoer of Knots along with that of Our Lady of Luján, a popular Marian devotion in Argentina.

On September 20, 2014, when the Argentine President Cristina Fernandez de Kirchner met Pope Francis at the Vatican and discussed Argentina's economy which is suffering a recession, she presented him with a copy of the German painting "Mary, Undoer of Knots," his favorite depiction of Mary.